Merry
Christmas,
Dear Old Dad!
~1980~

love, Pat

My Own Brand

My Own Brand

JACK HORNER

Hurtig Publishers Ltd.
Edmonton

Hurtig Publishers Ltd.
10560 – 105 Street
Edmonton, Alberta

Canadian Cataloguing in Publication Data

Horner, Jack
   My own brand

   ISBN: 0-88830-189-8

   1. Horner, Jack, 1927-   2. Politicians—
Canada—Biography.   I. Title.

FC626.H67A3   324.271'00924   C80-091066-4
F1034.3.H67A3

Printed and bound in Canada
by John Deyell Company

Contents

Foreword

My association with the Hon. Jack Horner grew out of my association with the Rt. Hon. John G. Diefenbaker and my role as principal writer-historian for the Diefenbaker memoirs, *One Canada*. Mr. Diefenbaker, interestingly enough, was most concerned lest my collaboration with Jack suggest this book carry the Diefenbaker imprimatur. Of course it does not. Jack Horner, as the reader will discover, is his own man.

Jack Horner/My Own Brand — the book, like the man, is a surprise. I am not certain exactly what I expected this book to be. I suspect that my expectations were largely shaped by Jack's press image: rough, tough, straight from the shoulder, partisan, extreme, the ultimate Diefenbaker cowboy. This was a combination to guarantee commercial success. Well, in fact, this book is rough and tough and straight from the shoulder. It is partisan. But it is not extreme. And if Jack Horner is the ultimate Diefenbaker cowboy, then I for one really didn't know what this was, until now. Jack Horner is a man of intellectual and moral substance, a journeyman parliamentarian, a Westerner passionately concerned for his country. His record is what representative democracy is supposed to be about. All this and more shaped the pages that follow. Further, working with Jack Horner has been one of the high points of my life.

An editor's tasks are many and varied. He cannot perform them without support. I am indebted to the ladies, in particular to Helen Aikenhead, but also to Pat St. Louis, who typed the transcripts of the sixty-odd hours of interviews that formed the basis of this text, who xeroxed the thousands of pages of Hansard which constituted the basic documentation for this manuscript, and who typed and retyped the successive chapters of this book until I, at least, was satisfied they captured the sound and character of their subject. To those of my family who undertook assignments, driving portions of this manuscript hundreds of miles across the prairies (thank you Michael), and particularly to Joan, I have much to repay. Finally, to Carlotta Lemieux, Hurtig Publishers' highly competent and charming editor, must go great credit for the volume's final structure.

John A. Munro, Editor
University of Saskatchewan
August 1980

1

1/The West

A reporter asked me following the 1979 election, "Well, Jack, aren't you happy having a Westerner as prime minister?" I have never known my reaction to be stronger. It just welled up: "Clark, a Westerner? For heaven's sake, he can't even ride a horse!"

Like so many remarks I've made in public life, it went full across the nation: Joe Clark can't ride a horse. Bruce Hutchison, the noted West Coast journalist, went so far as to write an entire column on Clark's inability to ride. Now, I know that many Westerners hardly ever see a horse, let alone ride one. What I meant was that, in my concept, the new prime minister was not in the slightest sense a Westerner — that he was absolutely alien to things western.

What makes a Westerner? I don't think the critical question is where anyone was born and raised. Doug Roche, MP for Edmonton-Strathcona, was born, raised, and educated in Montreal. Joe Clark, on the other hand, was born and raised in High River, Alberta, the epitome of a western horse town. Our country is made up of people who have migrated from one region to another or immigrated from other lands. The significant consideration is whether a person can embody the spirit that made the settlement of the Canadian West a success.

In the spirit of the West, once a friend, always a friend. A friendship is true, something one stands by. It is the most valuable of a man's possessions. It is not thrown over for personal gain. This was one of the reasons why I found Joe Clark so difficult to accept as party leader. In 1964, Clark, then president of the Conservative Student Federation, made a great defence of Diefenbaker; in 1966, he worked against him. Why? Because it suited Clark's well-defined future interests. Clark had a singleness of purpose that allowed him to think only of his own ambition to be prime minister. Clark isn't a true Westerner, for all his High River childhood.

A Westerner tends to relate to the image of the big-hearted, hard-working pioneer who believed in the growth of his area and the greatness of his country. He relates to the history of men and women who believed one should be rewarded for efforts made and risks taken, to people who believed they were strong enough to reach out and give the less fortunate a helping hand, and to those big enough to accept a world made up of all kinds of people. The West was settled by every type, be they hucksters or cattle rustlers or any of the variety of people who came to take advantage of a new sort of life. A true Westerner understands all this; it's a feeling, a sense of true values, that seeps into him without his even knowing it.

My own childhood was spent in the small prairie town of Blaine Lake, Saskatchewan, which lies about fifty miles north of Saskatoon and eighty miles west of Prince Albert. Born in 1927, I was the fifth in a family of nine. (During my years in Ottawa, I often remarked that being the middle child, with four ahead of me and four behind, suited me well to be a diplomat. For some reason, the concept of Jack Horner, diplomat, always engendered laughter.) Mother was the diplomat, the peacemaker. With six boys and three girls, and lots of fights over who hadn't done their chores, someone had to keep us from tearing out one another's hair. My mother was a tremendous person, a pillar of the United Church, on the Blaine Lake School Board for many, many years, active in community endeavours, and very interested in politics as well. With nine children, how she found the time is amazing. Hers must have been a fair task without the conveniences we take for granted today. She was quite often alone; Dad would be away on some deal, shipping carloads of horses somewhere, or else he would be in Ottawa.

Dad was appointed to the Senate when I was seven. Twice, in 1917 and 1929, he had run unsuccessfully as a provincial Conservative candidate. In 1931, R. B. Bennett appointed him a director of the CNR. This was followed, two years later, by the appointment to the Senate. But despite Dad's position, he never made any attempt to live above the people. From our earliest childhood, he instilled in us the importance of being part of the people — that we should always think of others and try and understand their problems, that we were duty bound to try and help our fellow men. We children never quite understood why all this was so important, but when I entered the world of politics I quickly learned to treasure my upbringing. I think this is why so many of our family have been interested in politics. It wasn't so much Dad telling us to get into politics as it was a process of osmosis: we learned by his example.

In our family we were always expected to have something useful to do, something to pursue with purpose. The biggest sin was to be lazy. When I was a boy, if anyone accused me of laziness he immediately had a fight on his hands. Dad was a great believer in the work ethic, and all his children learned the value of honest labour early in life. As we grew older we were thankful that he had instilled in us these values, though I don't know how exactly he did it. He never laid a hand on any of us. But he could be pretty vicious with his tongue. I had to be particularly careful, because I argued and stood up to him more than the others did. When he caught me off base, I was fair game for a verbal blistering. In a big family, one learns to take the knocks early in life; but those were good times.

Looking back, the worst part was that we worked mighty hard amongst it all. I remember one summer putting up hay. We never quit until the sun went down. This was pitching hay; there was no machine, you used a fork. Dad came home: "What have you kids been doing? Haven't been doing a thing!" He would arrive from Ottawa, grab a pitchfork (he was a big strong man) and out-pitch anybody in the country. But he only did it for a couple of days, and then he would be off somewhere again. When Dad was away, the oldest one on the job was boss and ran the show. It was good training to be in charge for a week or a month until Dad came home and criticized how much you had or hadn't done. We all got our turn. It made us accept responsibility at a pretty early age. Young people today don't mature as quickly as they did years ago. A young man used to mature at sixteen because he had to get out and earn a living, he had to fend for himself. Dad was inclined to be a little bit of the old school, so we matured early in the sense of responsibility and getting the job done. For instance, when I left home at eighteen, I left to run a ranch. And Dad himself had been only twenty-one when he came to Saskatchewan to homestead.

Dad had been raised in the East. The Horners had come from Ireland originally, settling in the Sherbrooke area of Quebec's Eastern Townships early in the nineteenth century. Sometime later, they moved up to Shawville in the Pontiac region of western Quebec along the Ottawa River. Certainly, the 1840 census records them as landowners there. My grandfather, William Horner, had a family of ten, and the Shawville area, not surprisingly, continues to have its share of Horners. I spent the first winter of my life in Shawville.

I think Grandfather resented my father moving to western Canada. He and Dad didn't get along well. By all accounts, Grandpa Horner was a devoutly religious Methodist, never shaved, didn't allow card playing, and wasn't interested in politics. Grandmother, however, was very interested in politics. She was an Argue, a big woman, nearly six feet tall, a head taller than Grandfather. We, of course, knew about Dad's brothers. Asa Horner was a classmate of Lester Pearson's at the University of Toronto; played football and baseball with him. Asa graduated in law, joined the army, and was killed at Vimy Ridge. My namesake Henry Horner (I was christened John Henry) came out to western Canada sometime after Dad to settle in southern Saskatchewan. Following his death in 1912, his wife took their young family back to Shawville. Another uncle, Norval, also settled in southern Saskatchewan. He was a Progressive Party member in the Saskatchewan legislature from 1929 to 1934. His son, my first cousin Harold Horner, as Saskatchewan's deputy minister of Agriculture, established a record for tenure at the provincial level in Canada. Through both CCF and Liberal governments, I think he served his province very well indeed.

Despite our Quebec roots, I doubt if any of us growing up in the West grasped the importance of the French fact in Canada. Perhaps we did more than our neighbours, but not as much as we should have. Often, Dad told us we should be learning French; it was the one thing he regretted not doing as a boy. Living in Saskatchewan, we never saw the need to learn it and didn't grasp its significance. I do think Dad tried to implant in us the importance of seeing the entire nation, including the province of Quebec, and not just focusing our view on the problems of the prairies.

My mother, May Victoria Macarthur, was born and raised in the prairies. She was teaching at Leask when she married Dad. Her father had been the second mayor of Prince Albert and in the early days had started a bank there. Her people had come from Scotland directly to western Canada, to the Red River, and in 1869 her uncle, Peter Macarthur, was jailed with Thomas Scott by Louis Riel. He escaped, was recaptured and given twenty-four hours to get out of the settlement. He trekked from Fort Garry clean down to St. Paul, Minnesota, in the dead of winter. A fair hike! The following spring, Sir John A. Macdonald invited him to Ottawa to testify before a parliamentary committee. Subsequently, Sir John saw that he was rewarded for his defence of the Queen and his loyalty to the Government of Canada: he received a grant of land in Manitoba with timber on it. This enabled him to start a shipyard, where he built some of the early paddle-wheelers which plied the rivers of the West. Thus, the family on both sides goes back in Canada a long way.

By comparison, most of our neighbours in Blaine Lake were relative newcomers to Canada. The land round there had become open for homesteading with the break-up of the Doukhobor communes and the migration of the original settlers to British Columbia. Although many individual Doukhobors stayed on in the area, there was now room for other settlers, including many of Ukrainian as well as Polish descent. The first generation of these immigrants had come to Canada at the turn of the century. Their sons, by and large, continued on the land. It was the grandchildren, beginning with those my age, who strove so hard to succeed in other areas of endeavour. You can find people from Blaine Lake, Saskatchewan, all over Canada, in every profession. I think this is because their grandparents stressed that Canada was a land of great opportunity where young people could succeed, could get an education and make a contribution to their country. This resulted in a good deal of competition in school, at the ball diamond, and in the hockey rink. Being of British descent offered no advantages that I ever saw. In the game of politics, I have been accused many times of being a bigot and everything else, but I can't remember ever not having time for people because of their origins or accents. Blaine Lake was a good place to grow up in.

Jean was the eldest of our family. Something of a perfectionist, she found her career in the army and the air force. Bill was next in line. He was the quiet one and Mother's favourite. He had the great knack of being able to read a book in the midst of a family row, oblivious of all about him. But when he spoke, it always seemed to be the final word. He became an engineer and runs a manufacturing plant in Winnipeg. He was such a fine athlete that I was never able to beat him at anything. I recall a family reunion in 1962 when I devised a stratagem to win at something: we would have a horseshoe tournament. Well, I practised and practised, but Bill beat me nevertheless.

Ruth, I thought, was the smartest in our family. She was the valedictorian of her class, never had any trouble in school. A great cook, she could feed a troop of people quicker than anyone I know. She became a teacher, earned her Master's in education, and married another educator — a nice guy, Frank Flanigan. Hugh was more like myself, a jack-of-all-trades. He joined the navy during the Second World War after two years of pre-Med at the University of Saskatchewan in Saskatoon. We always felt that Hugh didn't really want to go into medicine, that it was more Dad's idea than his. After the war, he finished his medical studies at the University of Western Ontario, interned in Calgary, and became a pretty successful doctor as well as a pretty successful politician. He's a great worker, a great dreamer, always thinking of something different, something to make money at. He has been a lumberman, potato grower, cattle breeder. . . . I think he even built houses at one time. Only two years older than me, Hugh and I have been very close.

Byron came after me. He was the laziest of the children and Dad often told him so, but this didn't seem to bother him. Byron had the happy faculty of being able to laugh at Dad. The madder Dad got, the more Byron laughed, and Dad learned to like it really. Dad could quote the Bible or the oddest piece of poetry at the oddest time, and Byron could do the same. He went on to become a lawyer, and I think a pretty good one. He was the Official Guardian of Saskatchewan under Ross Thatcher. Under Allan Blakeney, he accepted the job as the chairman of the Securities Commission. More recently, he accepted a position with the National Energy Board in Ottawa.

Norval is next in line. Norval ran in Battleford-Kindersley, was elected, and served in the House of Commons from 1972 to 1974. A quiet, slow-moving guy, he has a great sense of humour. But just as Byron liked and understood Dad, Norval probably had the most trouble with him, mainly because he stayed at home and worked with Dad longer than any of us. In due course, he took a degree in agricultural engineering and then one in education. He is now principal of a high school in Namao, north of Edmonton.

Kathleen, the second youngest, went into education and is a librarian at a high school in Saskatoon. Very interested in politics, she ran once as a Conservative in the provincial election and did fairly well against the Finance minister in Blakeney's government. Quite outspoken, she knows her goals, knows what she considers right and wrong in the game of politics. Likeable and capable, maybe someday she will continue in public life.

Bennett, the youngest, is without doubt the darling of the family. He is a doctor, a specialist in internal medicine. His wife is a doctor as well. Because he interned in Washington, D.C., and spent a further two years at Rochester, he had plenty of opportunities to stay in the United States, but he wanted to live in Canada. He is just a delightful person who must have a tremendous way with his patients; at the 1976 Conservative leadership convention, he stole the hearts of everyone who worked for me. With his appealing personality, his energy and youth, if he wanted to go into politics, he could succeed. At the last Horner family reunion in 1978, we got to making speeches. Speeches seem to run in the family, perhaps an inheritance from Dad. Of course, everyone expects this from Hugh and me as politicians, from Norval as well. Byron is a lawyer, and it's said that a lawyer could talk in hell. But it was Bennett who stole the show with his reflections on what goes into the making of a family. Certainly, we Horners remain a family, in the traditional sense of the word.

We grew up in the age of the *Saturday Evening Post* and the "Hockey Night in Canada" radio broadcasts. There was always a lot of conniving, scrambling, and fighting over who would get the *Saturday Evening Post* after Dad was finished. The Tugboat Annie and Luke Shortt stories, the cartoons and the Rockwell drawings were part of our North American heritage. But it was the Saturday night hockey games that were the big thing. You just didn't miss them, you had to be there! Each of us boys had his team. Mine was the New York Rangers, although this was largely because the older boys had first choice: Bill had Toronto, and Hugh had taken Boston. It was a privilege to stay up late to hear the broadcast. First, you had your Saturday night bath. Then you sat silently, listening to the play by play, intent on every word. After the game you were whisked away to bed without complaint. It amuses me now to hear the commentaries on the increasing violence in hockey. Fiddle! There has always been violence in hockey. Eddie Shore and Red Horner weren't exactly gentlemen hockey players. I don't believe that young people are affected by hockey violence on television. I don't believe this at all. I remember those games, sitting listening to the radio in our parlour. Foster Hewitt was always the homer for Toronto of course, but he described vividly all the action and every rough play.

We seemed to grow up on skates. I can't remember exactly, but I must have been four or five when I joined my brothers shovelling the snow off the rink to skate and play hockey, like the rest, imagining myself some big-league star or other. By the time Hugh was seventeen he had shown enough promise, according to Pete Dick our hockey coach, to make the NHL. Instead, he went to university, and with all his studies he forgot about hockey. Even during the time we were in Ottawa together, when a game came up between the MPs and the press, I could never get Hugh out on the ice. The winter I was sixteen I had a ruptured appendix and couldn't play. But the next winter I came into my own and played some pretty fair hockey for the Blaine Lake High School team. Three of us — Hugh Coflin, Alex Atamanenko, and I — were good enough to be included as a kid line on the local senior team for tournaments. A number of the town's businessmen told Dad I was worth helping towards a hockey career. Dad, however, was not particularly keen on his sons playing professional hockey. And at the time, as much as I loved the game, I wanted more than anything to be a farmer or a rancher. I wanted Dad to buy a ranch in Alberta. I told him I would run it if he bought it.

I had not been a particularly good student. I was good in math and good in history (I could remember the dates and the battles, 1066 and all that), but I hated English and I couldn't spell and I couldn't write well enough to please any teacher. I never thought I was smart. Although, looking back, in grades ten and eleven I missed the first month of school each fall. We were farm kids, we were harvesting, and when we finished up at home we went out and worked for the neighbour — anything to avoid going back to school. I had to work to catch up, but I caught up. My parents, of course, followed our educational progress with quite a bit of interest. Byron, Norval, and I all wanted to quit school early to run the farm, but this was just unheard of. We could mutter about it around the house, but no one paid any attention. We were going back to school next year, and that was it! Our parents ran the show; we might not like it sometimes, but still we listened and did what they wanted to quite a large extent.

Certainly we got our interest in politics from them. Politics surrounded our home. I have often said that I was born into the Conservative party. Although Mother came from a Liberal family, she had changed to Conservative on marrying Dad. He was always very active in his support of the party: Diefenbaker's name was familiar to us long before it was known in the rest of the nation. Dad supported Dief, collected money for him, and drove him to meetings during the bleak period of the Chief's long political career. Diefenbaker, in his later years, liked to describe how he had met me when I was a little boy. I had difficulty remembering the occasion, though of course Mother recalls Diefenbaker coming to our place a number of times with his first wife Edna. Because we had a family of nine and the Diefenbakers had none, Edna half-jokingly used to suggest she take one of us home.

The most vivid political impression of my early life is of the farmers in our area who came to see Dad during the Depression in the hope that he could do something to prevent the banks foreclosing on their land. Many of them were of Russian descent, speaking broken English. In their minds, the Conservative party and the financial community of eastern Canada were one and the same. As Dad was a member of the Conservative party and a member of the Senate, it followed — or so they thought — that he should be able to do something about the way the banks were tightening up on them. Dad would take them into the living room and close the doors. We really never knew what went on, but it became clear that he could do very little for them. During the 1930s in Saskatchewan it wasn't the easiest thing in the world to be a Conservative. Privately, I was ashamed of the party's ineffectiveness, and it was only out of family loyalty that I defended it at school. I think it was then I resolved that if I ever joined the Conservative party, I would have a long look at the people who led it and ran it. I wanted my own sons to be proud of any party I belonged to.

Despite the mood in Saskatchewan, I think Dad himself was highly respected. By and large, people understood that he tried but couldn't do much for them, except on a personal level. Years later, driving through the countryside, he would point to this place or that, telling me he had given the farmer there a load of seed wheat or a load of seed oats. "I should stop in and collect," he would say. But he had no intention of stopping. As their friend, he had helped them out in his own way, in as many ways as he could, even though it was not enough.

I remember my first political discussion. I must have been seven, coming on eight years old. Social Credit was on the march in Alberta. I was walking down to the pasture on a hot summer's day along with a couple of friends. We had bare feet and the road was terribly hot. The trick was to walk on the edge of the road and kick up the loose dust which wasn't nearly as hot. I remember telling my friends that Social Credit would never work; if the government ever started to print money like that, it would be very inflationary. Obviously, I must have heard this at home. But I guess we knew what we were talking about to some degree. At least we had quite an argument about whether the government could give everybody twenty-five dollars a month, whether it was earned or not.

My first political meeting came ten years later, in the election of 1945. Blaine Lake was in Prince Albert constituency at this time. John Diefenbaker wasn't running there; he was running in Lake Centre. It was the prime minister, W. L. Mackenzie King, who was running in Prince Albert. I went to a CCF meeting — not the sort of thing I particularly wanted to tell Dad about, but I thought I would find out what their candidate, E. L. Bowman, had to offer. He had nothing but a standard socialist line. I was shocked on election day when he beat Mackenzie King. I remember coming home and asking Dad, "How *could* that guy? He didn't look like he had any brains at all! How could he beat the prime minister of the country? What were the people thinking about, voting for socialism and voting for that guy?" Dad explained that it was difficult to know what people had voted for, but apparently the people had bought Bowman's line. This was democracy.

I was nearly eighteen at the time, my birthday virtually coinciding with the end of the Second World War. The war had seemed a long way away to us in Blaine Lake, even though we had immediate family, friends, and acquaintances in the forces. Hugh had quit university to join the navy (which annoyed Dad considerably), Jean was in the army, and Bill was thinking of joining up. Every night we heard how many people had been killed in action. I dreaded the horribleness of war, though I knew we were on the side of right and that we had to win. But I found it appalling that the world leaders couldn't settle their problems any other way. Of course, when I later had the opportunity to see how governments operate and how untrusting they are of one another, it wasn't difficult to understand how war could become an almost inevitable instrument of national policy.

Some people in our community were accused of being German sympathizers and some were accused of being Communists. The latter were — they didn't make any bones about it. A couple were arrested and sent to work camps for the duration. Then there was the problem of the Doukhobors who were conscientious objectors. Those drafted refused to serve, and they too were rounded up and sent to work camps in the north somewhere. Naturally, we listened to Dad's words on the subject. Being in the Senate, of course he followed the course of the war pretty closely. Dad was not a strong advocate of conscription, but he went along with the Conservative position on it. Although, when our hired man was called up, Dad got him off for farm work.

In the spring of 1945, Dad took an option on a ranch near Calgary. He put down $2,500. He had to close the deal by October, and as the deadline approached he had second thoughts and decided to forfeit the money, to allow his option to expire. I convinced him this was really crazy. So he went ahead with it. Of course, he then had to have someone to manage it. I said I wasn't going back to school anyway, that I'd do it. We had quite an argument. Finally, because I gave my word to go back to school the following year, he agreed. So at the age of eighteen, I was the first of the Horners to move to Alberta.

Dad was shipping horses to northern Ontario for bush work at the time. He began the next spring to ship the best ones to the ranch for me to work over the summer. In those days, Dad had up to one hundred teams in the bush. He was paid about thirty-five dollars a month per team, which wasn't a bad income. If they weren't broken, my job was to break them. Come winter, I shipped them to the bush, sometimes as late as December, depending on snow conditions and when the companies needed them. Dad wanted to get them to work as quickly as he could. If they were still a bit wild, it didn't matter, they were all insured for twice their purchase price. If the pulp company injured or lost a horse, payment was forthcoming. I remember Dad once buying close to thirty head of horses at the Calgary horse sale. They were the meanest, toughest, unbroken nags you ever saw. Two of those horses stand out in my mind. They were full brothers. The older was a nice-looking horse, not too big and really a fine animal if a bit on the wild side. The younger one, a four year old, was bigger than his brother and totally wild. I would work that horse all day on the land. Come night, I'd go to unharness him and he would jump and roar and snort so much that you'd swear to god he had never been worked at all. I shipped him to the bush that winter. First chance he got, he ran away.

In the spring of 1947 Dad sold the Calgary operation. He had been offered a big price, and he used the profit to start me out at Pollockville. The land was cheap here, but I didn't want Dad to buy this place. The whole countryside was so desolate, so far away from everything. I remember Dad saying, "If you want to ranch, son, you've got to realize you can't do it on Main Street. You've got to get out in the country."

In Alberta, the spring of 1948 was a long time coming. I was at university in Edmonton but my mind was on what was happening at the ranch. In April, it snowed every day so that by the month's end it was impossible for the hired men to get feed to the livestock. Dad had shipped back a bunch of horses. In addition, there were my saddle horses and fifty, sixty head of cattle. The bush horses were pretty thin. After working all winter, they just weren't equipped to handle rugged conditions. The carload of oats Dad shipped out sat untouched. When I came home in early May, I found a pretty tough scene. There were dead cattle and nine dead work horses, but it was my saddle horses that really hurt, two dead mares and two dead colts. I thought to myself, "I'm going to need a pretty good reason to go back to university if this is what is going to happen in my absence." Consequently, of our whole family of nine, I was the only one not to graduate from university. A rare distinction!

Early the following year, Dad wrote to me suggesting I come to Ottawa to see Parliament and some of eastern Canada. I sent him a long letter back saying I had no money and that when I did have any money I was going to buy farm equipment. I certainly wasn't wasting it on travel. It was an early spring in '49, and we were going to start to farm by the end of March. Dad replied by sending me the ticket and a long letter which in essence said, "Never mind the money, you are only young once. I will cover your expenses. You get down here and take a look." Thus, much against my will, I went to Ottawa, sat up in the galleries, listened to George Drew speak (he was a great speaker) and listened to Dad in the Senate. I visited Shawville and met the Shawville Horners, and I went down to Galt, Ontario, where my older brother Bill was working as an engineer. We went in to see a Maple Leaf hockey game in Toronto. By this time, I was anxious to get back home. I didn't like looking at the buildings and the crowded city. The only thing I really liked about Toronto was the lake, because off across the water I could see into the distance, just as I can out here. It was then I knew that this part of Canada had started to grow on me.

When I think back over thirty years, we've put a lot of improvements on the Pollockville ranch. It was terribly run down when we bought it. No one had lived in the house for years. My sister Ruth, who came out to cook for me my first summer here, and I both agreed that the best thing would be to burn it to the ground, but we never did. In this entire part of Alberta, east-central Alberta, only one house could boast a coat of paint in 1947. During the Depression, people had left by the thousand. Indeed, the government provided free freight out for all a family's possessions, including cattle and machinery. If a man had any money at all, he got out to settle up in the Peace River country or in some other part of Alberta. In my first couple of elections, I met many people who had moved from this area and were thankful they had. Invariably, they seemed impressed that I'd made such a success of the ranch: "Anybody who can make a living in that country must be one heck of a person!" they'd say. Actually, what happened was that so many people moved out that the ones left behind had room to prosper. The people living in this area were to become as well off and credit-worthy as those in any other part of Alberta, although this did not even begin to happen until after the war.

This part of the province had begun as ranching country. Then, in 1909, settlers from the United States began homesteading here, thinking it would be easy land to break and farm because there were no trees. There were some good crops in the early years, but by the twenties people started to move out. In the thirties they departed in droves. A large portion of the land became what is called "tax recovery land". When the farmer quit paying taxes (either because he moved out or didn't have the money) the municipality took over his land. In turn, the municipalities went broke. So in 1938 the provincial government enacted a Special Areas Act, whereby it took over the bankrupt municipalities in this area and set up a Special Areas Board to provide local government. The tax recovery land is administered by this board. It leases its land back to local ranchers on a twenty-year term, but only for grazing, except for a small portion — 10 per cent — held under cultivation leases.

This was a good policy at first because in 1938 a substantial portion of the farmland taken over was a mess. It was going back to grass. There were just a few people left, and most didn't have the machinery to farm; a farmer might have an outfit of horses, but that was about all. Hardly anyone in Canada realizes that in east-central Alberta, an area comprising nearly one-tenth the total land designated agricultural in the province is tax recovery land. Better than anything else, this shows the extent of the Depression here.

I doubt, however, the present necessity of retaining government ownership or insisting that most of the tax recovery land be used for grazing rather than agriculture. I think it's about time we started making some adjustments. What bothered me about the set-up from the very beginning was that I didn't own my land. I leased it. Of my 15,000 acres, I only actually owned 3,000. This had very practical ramifications. When I was making my start here, the Farm Credit Corporation wouldn't lend money in this area. Nor would the provincial Farm Loan Board. The farmers and ranchers were financially solvent (largely because of the economic benefits of this leasing arrangement) but they were handicapped because they couldn't borrow money on the strength of their assets. In fact, the lease was an asset, but no lending institution recognized it as such. This was one of the first problems I tackled in Ottawa after I was elected to the House of Commons in 1958.

When we came in 1947, there was another restriction, a regulation unique in Canada. For a newcomer to buy land, the price agreed with the vendor had to be advertised in the local paper for a month, and if any established resident was prepared to meet this price, he got the land and the newcomer didn't. It was a good policy because it allowed those already ranching to become large enough to succeed. I'm not so sure it shouldn't have been kept on. But it was difficult for a newcomer. In the Pollockville locality, we were the first new owners since the late twenties.

I well remember thinking, "I will spend ten years here, and that's it." It was such a dispiriting experience: the dusty roads; the land as dry as could be; the crops, just terrible. I didn't know at the time, but the neighbours were pretty nearly taking bets on how long I'd last. Of course, they didn't know me. Once I had a stake, I had to stay. I had to prove to the world, as a young guy, that I could hack it.

For the first few years, I never quit until the sun went down. On the farming side of the operation, I had a steel-wheeled John Deere tractor, but mainly I used horses. I bought my first rubber-wheeled tractor in 1950 from a dealer in Hanna for about $1,800. It was a good deal. Mind you, compared to today's tractors, it was very small. Also, it was strictly gas, not diesel. This was a DC Case — no cab, no heater, no air-conditioning, no radio. Recently we bought a new Case, a 2290. Besides having far more horsepower, it has the cab, the air-conditioning, the radio, the lights, the mirrors. But it has a price tag of close to $37,000!

With a six-foot cultivator or six-foot disker, it used to take a long time to do ninety acres. The new outfit will pull thirty-six feet of diskers: it's six times faster. In the old days, dressed in my big sheepskin coat, I would spend all night on the tractor in the spring. I would come in for breakfast in the morning hardly able to move. Nowadays, no one would do it. My boys are pretty good workers, but they wouldn't ride a tractor all night without a cab. But if you wanted to get in the crop, you had to spend the hours in the field. Everybody did it. It is of tremendous advantage to get your crop planted early when the moisture is there. Using horses, it used to take me two weeks to plough my big field, and the moisture was all gone long before I was finished. With a big cultivator, the same field can now be ploughed in half a day. That's why it is completely wrong to treat this land as if it were still 1938. This area is not being given a chance to develop and grow.

The Alberta government, as yet, hasn't decided to change the tax recovery land system. The idea, however, that only 10 per cent of some 94.5 square miles should be open to cultivation has long since ceased to make economic sense. Further, the cultivation lease itself (where the land rental is paid to the provincial government in the form of one-sixth of one's crop) is no different from the old feudal system. This is the landlord riding around on his big white horse demanding his share. I don't like this system, I never have. Nothing could be less in keeping with the spirit of

15

the West. Sure, the old-time farmers and ranchers, those who lived through the Depression, love the security of the provincial government owning the land. No finance company or bank can take it from them. But more and more people are coming round to my way of thinking — that the lessee should own all his land so that he can develop it any way he wants. He should be able to break up and farm those choice pieces he thinks would fit his farm or ranching unit better than if he grazed them. They may be just the other side of the barn, they may be just the other side of the house, they may be adjacent to a piece he is already farming. To me, it only makes good economic sense to do this.

To quell the fear that the lessee would somehow lose the land he now ranches or farms, the government could easily pass a regulation to ensure that only the lessee would have the opportunity to buy his lease from a special fund to be created for this purpose. Our area produces an immense amount of gas, oil, coal, and gravel — all nonrenewable resources on which the government receives a high royalty. So we have a right, in a way, to claim part of the Heritage Fund as a special account to help this part of Alberta go ahead. The lessee could borrow from this fund at a nominal rate of interest to buy his land. I haven't yet been able to convince the Alberta government to do this. They are so busy looking after Calgary and Edmonton and the development of the North that they have forgotten east-central Alberta.

When I came here in 1947 I thought this country would grow. I thought that while we were the first in, there would be more to come. However, this area has gone down in population, a great disappointment to me. Farms and ranches have grown bigger; modern machinery, of course, allowed them to. The oil industry has brought in some people, but it too can largely be automated. The only thing that will increase the population is some kind of irrigation project. No one can stop progress and water is the key. This area could produce not only three times its present yield in cereal grains, but its cattle-carrying capacity could be tripled as well if we had water. I have written to Premier Lougheed, I have written to his ministers of Agriculture and the Environment in an attempt to generate some interest. I have yet to receive a satisfactory reply.*
Lougheed's political strength is based in northern Alberta and that is where his interest lies. His oil and gas battles with Ottawa reflect this. He really hasn't paid much attention to the area in which I live, despite our oil and gas. To give it credit, the government is to develop the coal mine at Sheerness. And the roads in this area are getting slightly better, certainly better than they were thirty years ago, although still behind what they are

*See Appendix 1.

16

in other parts of Alberta. The logic is that because there aren't very many people down here, no one needs a good road.

As I mentioned earlier, there were even fewer people here when I first came to Pollockville. Of course, we all knew one another. In winter we used to play hockey, though only when it was cold enough to freeze the sloughs. Often the winters were so mild that there wasn't any good ice. When there was, I had no trouble outskating anyone around: this wasn't northern Saskatchewan where you learned to skate as soon as you could walk. When, in 1952, Hanna built a new arena, I went up there one Saturday night to watch the Hanna team play the army. The next week, while in town picking up some tractor parts, I told one of the players, a fellow by the name of Danny Smith, that he didn't have much of a team. He asked if I played.

"Yes, sure. Haven't played very much in the last three or four years, though."

"Come out to our practice."

"When?"

"Five o'clock."

I played five years with the Hanna Hornets. It was a lot of fun. We travelled all over southern Alberta, playing teams like the Okotoks Oilers and the Medicine Hat Tigers. In sport, one meets a lot of people, and I guess the only notice I received around here before getting into politics was as a hockey player. Everyone in Hanna knew me as the big guy on defence: "He's rather quiet. Can he talk?" It's a period I look back on with fondness.

Later, when I went to Ottawa, I became involved in the occasional charity game — the MPs versus the press. One game I particularly recall was scheduled the same night I was to curl in the Ottawa bonspiel. I determined to do both. At the bonspiel, we had lost before the eighth end. So I told my third, "You skip. Do what you like with my rocks. I'm going over to Hull to that hockey game." When I finally found the Hull Arena, the second period was just underway; it was 2–0 for the press. I had my skates, nothing else. I said to Gerry Regan, who was coming off the ice, "Give me your gloves and stick." The final score: 9–2 for the MPs.

Regan (later to become premier of Nova Scotia and recently Labour minister in the federal government) has never forgotten that game. The next year the press wouldn't take us on at all. The year after that it was "Look, Horner, get your team together." I thought something was up, and I was right. Bill Johnson, who now writes for the *Globe and Mail*, had come to town to cover the Hill for the Toronto *Telegram*. He was a pretty good hockey player. Consequently, the press thought they had a team. In the game, Johnson was assigned to get me, but he wasn't very big and I was pretty solid on my skates. After the game, I went into the press dressing-room to apologize for hitting him so often.

On another occasion, they used Bob McKeown as their ringer. Bob, who is now with CBC radio in Ottawa, was attending Princeton University on an athletic scholarship and was home for the vacation. At the end of the first or second period, he knocked me flat. His dad, who was in the press gallery, a very quiet guy and really a fine fellow, couldn't help but rub it in just a little. Well, in the third period, just as McKeown was coming down our end of the ice, I stepped into him just as fair and square as ever a man stepped into another, and down he went. It was a great deal of fun. In all the time I was an MP we never lost a ball game or a hockey game to the press. Actually, we did lose one ball game — but I wasn't playing.

The ball games and the hockey games provide a pleasant break in the parliamentary regime, a little bit of an outing. They also develop something of a rapport between the press and the MPs, and between individual MPs as well. Long before I joined the Liberal party, Bud Cullen was my second baseman. Lorne Nystrom pitched and I caught, quite a combination in itself! Talking about building a rapport between people, Jack Davis, a man who, in my estimation, had difficulty in communicating with people, used to play first base. Didn't do a bad job either. Roch LaSalle could play almost any position, but he did a great job at shortstop, really could throw that ball around, had the hustle a good shortstop needs. John Reid, from Kenora–Rainy River, was another of our pitchers.

One afternoon, just as we were about to begin the game on Parliament Hill, Trudeau's limousine stopped and out he stepped. I asked him if he wanted to play. He did.

"What position?"

"Pitcher."

"Okay, you pitch the first inning."

He had a slow spinner, didn't do too badly. Yet his performance resulted in a terrible story in *Time*. Even I said it wasn't fair. It was written by Dan Turner. "Boy, were you hard on Trudeau!" I told Turner when I saw him a few days later. He agreed, "I wanted to get him." One of the few times I talked to Trudeau during my years in the Conservative party, I took the opportunity to tell him I thought Turner's story completely unjustified: "You are not a bad ball player at all; you even look like you might have pitched ball a little." He replied, "Well, thank you, Jack, but that's the press, you know."

About three weeks later, we had another ball game scheduled. I went to Stanfield and asked him if he wanted his picture in the paper. I said the ball game would guarantee it. Oh, he didn't think so. But, lo and behold, he showed up at the game. He wasn't as good as Trudeau, but the next day, covering half the front page of the *Montreal Star* there was a picture of Bob Stanfield looking really good, pitching that soft ball. Stanfield was delighted. He came up to me in the House to thank me. I hadn't done a thing.

It was the mood of the press. One guy wanted to rub Trudeau, the next wanted to build Stanfield. There were probably dozens of pictures taken to obtain the one conveying the desired message. This is the power of the press. Television only multiplies it in a hundred ways. Live television is generally safe, they can't very well edit it. The worst they can do is shoot you from an unflattering angle. But with a taped program or shots of a particular scene or meeting, or even of Stanfield fumbling the football in the '74 election, they can do whatever they please. Stanfield probably caught the football five times before he dropped it. This is the sort of thing everyone in politics has to live with.

Involvement in politics was the farthest thing from my mind during those first ten years at the ranch. Of course, under Drew, I saw nothing to get me interested in the Conservative party at all. When I left home, it was to carve my niche in life. So far as I was concerned, politics could only come after you had established your competence in some area of endeavour. Nowadays, it's quite common for a young person just out of high school to go into politics and get elected (or at least, pretty nearly). When I first ran in 1958, my biggest criticism of myself was that I was too young, that I hadn't proved myself sufficiently. I how could I possibly help guide the country? From 1947 to '57 my game was to work hard and keep my nose to the grindstone. But, given the effect of federal policies on the cattle industry, it was never practical to lose sight entirely of what was happening in Ottawa. For example, when I first began ranching, there was an embargo against Canadian cattle exports to the United States. When this was lifted in 1948 by Jimmy Gardiner, the Agriculture minister under Mackenzie King and St. Laurent, cattle prices doubled overnight, from about 15 cents to 30 cents a pound. Then in 1951, with the outbreak of foot and mouth disease, the border closed. At this time, cattle prices had gone up to slightly over 50 cents a pound, and suddenly they were cut in half. Those cattlemen who had borrowed recently to increase their herds — and there were many of them — were hurt very badly. Fortunately for me, there hadn't been enough money left after buying the ranch to stock it properly. I had only fifty or so cows to begin with and, what is more, I had sold my steers just before the disease struck.

Nevertheless, I became very aware of Ottawa's role in the life of a rancher or farmer, not to mention the Wheat Board's role. Certainly, I knew that if ever I were to go into politics, it would be at the federal level.

In the meantime, I was busy keeping the ranch going. This posed certain problems on the social side. I lived fifty miles from nowhere, and the ranch had no modern conveniences; everything was pretty run down, at least to begin with. A lot of young women wouldn't look twice at a man in my situation, they had their sights set on something better. Thus, I was more than pleased when I met Leola Funnell, the lady who would share my life.

Leola had been born at Oyen, Alberta, and raised in Sunnynook, fifteen miles up the line where her dad, Arthur Funnell, was a grain buyer for the Alberta Wheat Pool. Arthur was a pleasant, humorous man, and I was amazed when I first heard the story of his background. He had been born in England at the turn of the century and orphaned as a newborn baby. His grandfather and his older sisters (the eldest of whom was only about six years older than he was) had looked after him until he was eight. Then, one day, a welfare group had come round and found his grandfather giving little Artie a pipe to smoke. They concluded that Grandfather wasn't fit to raise him, so they took little Artie away and shipped him over to Canada. At the time, there were a number of so-called philanthropic homes in England for orphans and neglected children which specialized in shipping their wards off to the far reaches of the Empire. From 1867 to 1912, some sixty thousand juveniles and children were shipped to Canada, largely to work with farming families. Arthur Funnell was one of these children.

In later life, the only thing he could remember about the trip across the Atlantic was two weeks of bawling on the boat. He was sent to help a pioneer family in Alberta. Then, in the First War, he joined the army and was about to be sent overseas when he broke his leg. So he didn't get home to see his family. As things turned out, it wasn't until Arthur was in his seventies that he was reunited with his one surviving sister, Gladys. It was unbelievable to me the extent to which they were alike — the same sense of humour, everything — having lived their lives an ocean apart.

Arthur's daughter Leola was teaching at Rose Lynn, about thirty miles from Pollockville, when I first met her. She had become friendly with my sister Ruth, who was also teaching nearby, and I guess it was Ruth who introduced us at one of the local dances. I wasn't much of a dancer; Leola was quite splendid. Her dad led one of the local country dance bands. Most important, she liked this country and didn't mind the idea of having a farmer or rancher for a husband.

Things worked out very well between Leola and me, and we were married on April 11, 1950. But she made me promise that I wouldn't go into politics. As I recall it, though, what I actually said was, "How could I go into politics? There aren't enough people down here to elect anybody. I'd never get well known enough to get into politics."

However, when Diefenbaker became leader of the Conservative party in 1956, I began to take a little interest. Dief had made his reputation supporting the underdog, not eastern financial interests. Dad was very suspicious of him. Diefenbaker had too much evangelical fervour and not enough reason or logic to suit Dad. I think Dad had supported Donald Fleming for the leadership. But he wasn't upset when Dief won, not in the sense of the eastern establishment, which wept and cried. Dad was prepared to suspend judgement until he saw what Dief could do.

Interestingly, when I came to Pollockville in 1947 there wasn't a Conservative to be found in this entire area. In the general election of 1953 the party couldn't find a candidate to field, and in 1957 they had to bring one in from outside the constituency — a chap by the name of Kent, who filed his nomination papers and promptly disappeared from sight. Today, people here will tell you they have been Conservatives all their lives, which is pretty nonsensical. Social Credit was their party from 1935 until the switch in 1958, after which it was the Diefenbaker party, not the Conservatives *per se*.

During the 1957 campaign I had attended the Diefenbaker rally at Drumheller in the adjoining Palliser riding. Knowing that the party didn't have a candidate in our Acadia riding, Dief asked me if I'd like to run there. But I was president of the Rural Electrification Association in my area, and we were on the verge of success; it was up to me as president to push as hard as I could. (By 1958 the scene had changed; we had got electric power.) So I told Cam Kirby, who was with Diefenbaker, that there was no way I could run. Cam was provincial leader at the time, a lawyer out of Red Deer and a nice fellow (Dief later made him a judge). I said that maybe next time I'd consider it.

Acadia riding took its name from east-central Alberta's Acadia Valley, and the sitting member in 1957 was a Social Crediter by the name of Victor Quelch. Dad knew Quelch in Ottawa and found him a likeable and agreeable person. Quelch was not one of the crackpots that Alberta regularly returned, like Blackmore and Hansell. In 1957, Quelch was re-elected. But then, in 1958, he decided to retire. If I was going to get into the game, this was an opportune time. Better to run when the slate was clean. In any case, Social Credit loyalties were weakening. In '58, it was "Give Dief a majority," and the sweep was on! So when the president and the secretary of the local Conservative party (Dunc Gardner and Doc

Wright) visited me one day in early 1958 to see if anyone around here was interested in politics, I told them I was "kind of half interested".

"Would you put your hat in the ring?" they asked.

"I might, if I could get the nomination meeting held in Hanna" (where I had a chance of winning it).

When I said I'd throw my hat in the ring *maybe*, my hat was in the ring according to them. Leola was fairly annoyed, and quite rightly so. She swore up and down that she was going to vote against me, but she didn't. She has gone along with all my antics in politics, even though she's a very sensitive person and easily hurt when I am the subject of attack by the media. If I bring home a newspaper article about myself, she refuses to read it for fear it says the wrong thing. It's the same with radio or television; she would rather turn it off at the mention of my name lest it's something critical. On the other hand, Leola is a good barometer: she has a good sense of what the average person will buy politically. I remember one time sitting with her watching Stanfield on TV. Afterwards, Leola said, "I found myself just begging him to say something quickly, but he didn't. He'll never sell." She was so right.

I often accuse Leola of being the better politician of the two of us. When you live in a polling district like Pollockville, with fifty-five voters or whatever, and you're away quite a bit of the time, and you win forty-nine of the fifty votes cast, these are votes for the family. Leola can move around this community in the various organizations to which she belongs, being a leader without anyone realizing it. This makes a pretty good politician. She has never cost me a vote and has made me plenty, although she has never campaigned for me. I've never asked her to. (We once had a provincial member whose wife was a great campaigner. It got to where a lot of people said, "Well, if his wife were running, I'd sure rather vote for her than him.") Nevertheless, I've put Leola through an awful lot in this game of politics, and she's stood the test pretty well. She doesn't feel at home with people until she knows them. I'm completely different. I can talk to anybody. If they don't like it, they can lump it.

When I let it be known that I might run, almost everyone I knew told me I was absolutely crazy: "You've got a good ranch. Don't get into politics." The only person who encouraged me was the local bank manager, an old fellow by the name of Tom Horn, a very fine man. Some people get into politics because they want to be at the seat of power. This wasn't the motivating force for me. It was the desire to do things. In this area, I could see so much potential, and I still can. I felt that this was the forgotten part of Alberta and that agriculture was the forgotten part of Canada. I thought I had something important to say. This is why I got into the game of politics.

2/New Member from Acadia

I wasn't the only one interested in the Conservative nomination for Acadia in 1958. There were five of us. Although it had proved impossible to find a local Conservative candidate in the elections of 1953 and 1957, in 1958 there was a Diefenbaker sweep and people everywhere were going Conservative.

One of my opponents was Philip Rock, not a bad guy at all, the son of old P. J. Rock, a well-known Alberta Liberal. Philip Rock had appeared before the Commons Agricultural Committee to defend a $100,000 payment under the St. Laurent government to compensate for the destruction of the Rock sheep herd by scrapies disease. I guess he took a liking to what he saw in Ottawa, knew that Diefenbaker was going to win, and wanted the Conservative nomination. He worked very hard for it. Ossie Parry was another of my opponents. He was an implement dealer in Morrin, a fine man and a good curler. Rock and Parry lived within fourteen or fifteen miles of one another, which is practically next door in a constituency as large as this. Parry really didn't want to get into politics, but, as I found out later, a number of their neighbours didn't want Rock to get the nomination, so they convinced Parry to cut him off at the pass. The other two candidates proved not to have much support. The local Conservative executive placed their good offices behind my nomination, although I didn't know this until after the convention. I didn't campaign. As Leola was against my entering politics, I'd promised her I wouldn't do anything to win. I mentioned to the implement dealers and businessmen I knew that my hat was in the ring — "If you have some time, come on over to the meeting" sort of thing — but nothing else.

That convention seems like yesterday. Jimmy Dove (who started Jimmy's Service Station in Hanna) and I had to go downstairs to carry up more benches. The place was filled with strangers. Some five hundred people showed up in Hanna from all over the riding, and I didn't know ten per cent of them. Fortunately, most came with relatively open minds. I suspect this was because joining the Conservative party was a new experience for them and they were looking for a candidate they could easily support. They were in the main of Social Credit stripe; maybe some Liberals too, I don't know.

Dr. Argue from Hanna was to nominate me. Nominators were allowed to speak for three minutes. The nominee was allowed five minutes. Old Doc Wright, the dentist from Stettler who was secretary of the constituency association, asked me what I was going to say. I replied that I hadn't a clue.

He asked, "Do you know Diefenbaker?"

"I know Diefenbaker well."

"Then just get up there and say his name as many times as you can. The people here all came to hear about Diefenbaker, they didn't come to hear about you or anyone else. You'll win this nomination, Jack, if you just tell them how much you think of Diefenbaker and how well you know him." This was easy. In my five minutes, I think I mentioned Diefenbaker's name sixteen times.

As we came down to the wire on the balloting, there were three of us left. Ossie Parry was first and I was second, three votes ahead of Philip Rock. Rock dropped out. I knew that Parry and Rock came from the same part of the riding, and as I knew nothing of their personal rivalry, I naturally thought Rock's votes would go to Parry. I was sitting on the platform, telling myself, "Don't get alarmed, be cool, take it easy." While the final ballot was being counted, I began to talk curling with Ossie; there was no use talking politics. We were having a fairly animated discussion about the bonspiel in which Ossie had just played when they announced the result. To my surprise, I won. The Rock supporters had decided to fix Ossie by voting for me.

The next day at the bonspiel in Pollockville, one of my favourite neighbourhood antagonists asked me how it had gone. I told him. He was amazed, but not encouraging.

"You may have won that, but you sure can't win the constituency."

I stated, "I've won the constituency. This whole country is going Conservative. All I've got to do is look good and keep my foot out of my mouth."

This was my first campaign, and I worked hard, drove a lot of miles, met a lot of people. Interestingly, the electoral boundaries of Acadia in 1958 were very much the same as those of Crowfoot in 1979 and 1980. As my campaign manager, I had a young guy, a former radio announcer who was farming around here and is now a lawyer in Edmonton. He knew how to spend money, booking advertising on radio and so on. I had been told to make certain the party gave me a reasonable amount of money. I was being short-changed initially because I didn't know any better and because they thought I couldn't get elected. The bagman for the Conservative party in Alberta was a crusty old fellow by the name of Ross Henderson who had made his fortune in sand and gravel. I suspect I was the cheapest candidate they had, but I could see I was spending more money than the fifteen hundred dollars they had allocated me. Consequently, about two weeks before the election, I phoned Henderson from Stettler.

"Look, you haven't given me enough money. We're doing the best we can, but we're going away over. I know we're going to be two thousand dollars over on election day."

Henderson asked, "Are you going to win?"

"Certainly."

"You win, Horner, and we'll cover you. You won't have any trouble."

I won all right and the money came through.

Ross Henderson came up with double that amount for me on a later occasion. I think he felt a kinship with me because he knew a little bit about how tough this area was. He had taught school at Cessford in the early 1920s when the kids didn't have a thing. There was hardly a ball glove in that part of Alberta (Ross had himself bought the first bat and ball for the Cessford kids). That's the way he was. He was a good soldier on behalf of the Conservative party, no question. In the old days, he would underwrite everything personally and then collect his money. This was the way the old bagmen operated; and if they couldn't collect enough, they were out of pocket. When Ross gave up the job in the sixties, the party had one heck of a time replacing him.

In 1958, the mood in Acadia, as in so many other places in Canada, was "Give Diefenbaker a chance. He is a great man, he's having trouble with Parliament, and he needs a majority." There was no general excitement about Dief's Northern Vision or any other specific in the Conservative platform. Perhaps this was because in this constituency only fifteen per cent of the people read a daily paper. They all listened to radio, and they read their weekly papers and their weekly magazine; but because they weren't subscribers to a daily paper, somehow the media-engendered mass excitement of the cities was missing. Also, not having had a serious Conservative contender before had its effect. A person living in one part of the riding didn't know what people in the other part were thinking. In my travels around, I discovered they were all thinking the same thing: Give Dief a majority. When a person knows he's on the right track it kindles an excitement and enthusiasm, but there was no way in 1958 that the average person in Acadia could be certain he was on the right track, given the absence of a common medium of communication.

Awaiting the results at home on election night, I was satisfied I'd given the campaign the best shot I could. Now, we had to sit back and see what happened. When I won the majority of polls, I was very pleased; but apprehensive. I knew it was going to change our lives. Leola would have her hands full. We had three sons by this time, and they were all very young, the youngest only one and a half years. The 1958 election was on March 31; the House was to sit on May 12. I had a lot of work to do to get the ranch in order so that we could leave it, and the crop to plant as well. I would have to employ a second hired man. There were so many things on my mind unrelated to politics and Parliament. I suppose, in this sense, I was unlike most other new members.

In Jasper-Edson my brother Hugh, who had been practising medicine in Barrhead, had also been elected for the first time. He suggested that we go to Ottawa together by train. I liked the idea; it had been a long time since Doc and I had spent much time together. Accompanied by our wives, Hugh and I and Terry Nugent (Edmonton-Strathcona) and Bill Skoreyko (Edmonton East) travelled east on the same train. When we arrived in Ottawa, the whip of the Conservative party had arbitrarily arranged our office accommodation. Because I represented a western rural riding, I was to share offices and a secretary with an eastern rural MP. I didn't like this idea.

"I don't know this guy you're putting me in with at all," I said to Clyde Lyons, secretary to the whip. "Why don't you put Skoreyko and me together?"

"Oh, he isn't a farmer."

"I don't care. I'll be with Skoreyko."

This might not have been the best thing for the party, but it was a good thing for me because Skoreyko and I became fast friends right off the bat. From what we saw of the guys they'd intended to put us with, we were doubly glad we'd insisted on having our own way.

On the domestic front, Leola and I rented a fully furnished house. The two things I remember about it were that it had a pet turtle which our boys played with and somehow or other kept alive, and that its library had but two books, both volumes of *Lady Chatterley's Lover* (thus, when the subject came up in Parliament, I was quite knowledgeable). We only stayed in that house for the first session. After that I bought one.

Of course, we went home to Pollockville when Parliament wasn't sitting; and I was able to go home every weekend after 1964 when an Air Canada voucher system was introduced whereby, without personally having to absorb the cost, an MP could fly once a week to the airport closest to his constituency. It was one of the best things Pearson ever did, because it more or less put Ottawa an equal distance from every MP's constituency, so every MP could have a continuing rapport with his constituents, to say nothing of his family. Many a weekend ball tournament I've played at Pollockville as an MP.

Young guys would say to me, "Aren't you the MP?"

"Yeah."

"What are you doing home?"

"I'm playing ball right now."

"When are you going back?"

"Oh, I'll go back on Monday."

Certainly, the Air Canada vouchers had their effect on attendance in the House of Commons on Mondays and Fridays. Before 1964 the western MPs ran the House on Fridays because they couldn't go home. All the Ontario and Quebec members could and did. In fairness, Pearson only gave the western MPs the opportunity to enjoy what those from Ontario and Quebec had long since come to take for granted. The Hill, in consequence, has become a very poor show Monday morning and Friday afternoon, but I don't see any road around it. Had we had three daughters, I might have sold the ranch. But I had three sons. I wanted them to grow up on the ranch and learn first-hand the conditions and problems of ranching. Pearson helped me keep my family at home.

If you have to live in a city, however, Ottawa is a pretty nice place to live. Beautiful in the summer time, with the Driveway, the Rideau Canal, and Dow's Lake. Gorgeous in the fall. My oldest son, Blaine, started school in Ottawa as did our second boy, Craig. The boys were too young to have much of an opinion, but Leola didn't like Ottawa much. The problem was that an MP's hours, if he attended to his job, were rather long. I would help Leola get the kids off to school in the morning. Then I would be gone for the rest of the day and half the night; the House didn't shut down until ten at night, which put me back home about eleven. The kids would be in bed. Leola would be tired and, no doubt, pretty bored. I am embarrassed to admit it, but I was so busy with Parliament that I didn't have enough time to do the necessary to get my eldest son into little league baseball. To complicate things further, we were only in Ottawa half the year, from January until some time in July. It was only after 1962, when the family returned to Pollockville permanently, that I could really do justice to the kids in organized sports.

The boys have taken to politics pretty well. Blaine and Craig roll with a lot of the punches. Brent, who is the youngest, feels that he has been hurt most by my life in politics. He's probably the toughest and the most sensitive of the three. He doesn't speak too much unless he gets aroused. But when he takes a stand, you don't change his mind, you don't detour him. Of the three, Craig has the widest knowledge of politics, mainly because he attended university and was exposed to other points of view a bit more than his brothers. When Craig was a delegate to the leadership convention in 1976, Paul Hellyer sent him a copy of his book *Agenda*. My comment was, "It's stupid for Hellyer to send that book to delegates, it's a colossal failure of a book. It doesn't make economic sense. If his ideas were implemented, they would tie up the country in all kinds of controls and regulations." I wasn't worried that Craig might vote for Hellyer, but I wanted him to grasp the facts of life pretty quickly. His reaction was that he was going to make up his own mind. About two weeks later, he told me, "I took a look at it, Dad. I didn't read it all but I browsed it thoroughly. You were right. If the government ever implemented the changes Hellyer advocates, it would bring in a great number of controls." I was pleased that he'd taken the time and pleased with his conclusion as well.

Coming back to my entry into politics in 1958, my brother Hugh and I were both young red-blooded Westerners who had gone to Ottawa to advocate a number of causes. Dad, with his nearly twenty-five years' experience in the Senate, took us aside. "Just remember that it's far more important to create a public understanding of the issues than it is to legislate." You know, this rather simple statement is so true.

Fortunately, I never thought I was going to change the world overnight. I knew enough about Parliament to understand that change comes slowly and that the trick is to sit and learn. In any case, the cabinet ministers and their deputies put me in my place in a hurry.

"Who are you?"

"Well, I'm Jack Horner. I'm the newly elected member from Acadia."

"Oh, you got in on Diefenbaker's coattails."

You had to establish your credibility around Ottawa before anyone would listen. Everyone had to know that what you said could be substantiated. This came home pretty quickly. Right off the bat, I saw that if you hadn't done your homework, the ministers, deputies, and assistant deputy ministers of whatever department would shoot you full of holes. So I set about quietly and determinedly to establish my reputation as someone who fought hard, worked hard, and knew what he was talking about.

In my early years in the House, there was some importance attached to private members' hours, later to the private members' day. The principle was that the individual MP could bring up matters that were near and dear to him, to voice a strong plea for something which may have been affecting his constituency or the rights of a particular group. The importance of private members' initiatives in the past twenty years has gradually diminished with the strengthening of the party system, which I think is a sad thing. In those days, the government acknowledged the right of MPs (perhaps even their duty) to bring private bills to the floor of the House. Invariably, these legislative initiatives were simply talked out; they were not part of the government program.

To me, the private members' hours presented an opportunity to learn my new trade as a parliamentarian. I went to see the party whip, told him I wanted to learn to speak on any subject, and asked him to give me a call if I could help in any debate. In one of these debates, I remember speaking in defence of trading stamps. A private member's bill had been introduced to outlaw trading stamps. I was killing time, talking it out. My line of reasoning was that one received trading stamps in direct relation to the amount of goods and services purchased, and that the trading stamp was worth such-and-such. Was there any difference, I asked, between this practice and that of a co-op with its dividends — apart from the five-dollar membership number? Loblaws gave me trading stamps, the Co-op gave me dividends. There was no difference at all, other than that I didn't swear allegiance to Loblaws. So, if one practice was acceptable, why shouldn't the other be?

Harry Jones, the member from Saskatoon, who's long since gone, was responsible for seeing that this particular bill died on the floor. He came over to me after the debate: "Jack, that's an interesting theory, I hadn't thought of it that way."

"Well, to tell you the truth, Harry, I hadn't thought of it that way myself until I started this speech."

You know, ever since, I've been unable to see anything wrong with trading stamps. More important, it's a good example of what a member must do purely for the sake of becoming familiar with the House of Commons. I wanted to feel at ease. The Commons is the most difficult place in the world to make a speech when the desks are empty. If you're the first speaker up after Question Period and you see everyone leaving, you feel like exclaiming, "Hey, you! Come on! Sit down and listen!"

When I was first in Ottawa, I was considered an angry young man in a hurry. I know I have mellowed a lot since then, but I hope not completely. As I mentioned, I arrived in Ottawa with a number of causes. The most important thing I did in my first parliament was to get the Farm Credit Corporation to come to the Pollockville area to make loans on lease land — the tax recovery land that comprised such a large proportion of the ranches and farms in east-central Alberta. It was the 1960 session, and the Agriculture minister, Alvin Hamilton, was guiding his estimates through the House. As he walked by my desk on his way to his seat, he saw my pile of books and notes. He stopped.

"You're not going to make a speech?"

"Yes, I am."

"Well, don't! For heaven's sakes, don't. You'll stir it all up again. My estimates are going through this afternoon."

"Not until I make my speech."

"You don't have to. Come and talk to me afterwards."

Alvin was a great guy. You could always talk to him — though you invariably ended up listening. I had discovered this already, so I refused his offer and made my speech, spelling out the difficulties my district was having with its credit rating. Alvin did listen for once and saw the necessity for changes. This resulted in the Farm Credit Corporation officials coming to Hanna to discuss how loans could be made on lease land.

I invited three old-established ranchers from the area to the meeting: Ferg James, Jim Cameron, and Ed Bell who is the only one of the three still alive. We met in the Hanna Hotel and went over what would be an economic unit — how many cows, how much deeded land, and how much lease land there should be before the corporation would loan money. We had a very good meeting. The result was the opening of a Farm Credit Corporation office in Hanna. I wouldn't know how much money they have loaned in this area since, but a considerable amount. And not a single default. After the Farm Credit Corporation began loaning money in the area, the Provincial Farm Loan Board became very active too.

Of course, I knew the subject well. To a large degree, my mind was still at the ranch during that first parliament — what we should seed in this field, what we should seed in that, what cows we should sell. I was a young rancher a long way from home and it was often a conscious effort to concentrate on legislation. But, as the years went by, slowly but surely I found myself preoccupied more and more with legislative problems, occasionally saying to myself, "Well, by jove, I should take time to look at what's happening on the ranch." The whole thing reversed itself. It was an interesting experience to watch oneself change so much. Of course, I never dreamed I would one day run for the leadership of the party. I never dreamed I would ever be half as effective as I became. At the time, being an MP was accomplishment in itself, and I didn't think I was particularly suited to go higher, didn't think so until part way through the fights over Dief in 1966. Therefore, I didn't have any great goals. Perhaps if I had, I would have attained them, I don't know.

To begin with, however, there was a great deal for a young MP to learn. I served on every House of Commons committee I could: Transportation, Finance, Agriculture, and Broadcasting. In those days, committees had sixty members. It was simply a matter of telling the whip, "I want on Agriculture." The whip would then announce in the House: "Mr. Speaker, under Standing Order so-and-so". . . and my name would be placed on Agriculture and someone else's removed. Later, when this was changed to where the whip only had to sign a form, one could be on a committee in half an hour. The rules, however, were also changed to reduce the numbers on committees. This made them difficult to get on and in the process gave the party even more power over the ordinary MP. The only troublesome committee in my early days was the sessional committee on the CNR and Trans Canada Airlines. This was limited to twenty-four members and was eagerly sought after because it was a grabber. It was here, as opposed to Transportation, that Donald Gordon came before Parliament. Here, the inner workings of the CNR and TCA were examined. I tried for years to get on this committee. Finally, I worked out a deal with Art Smith, the Conservative member for Calgary South. Art wasn't interested in the CNR; he was interested in TCA. Our deal was that I would serve for the railway part and he'd look after the airline. When Art was no longer in Parliament, I worked the same arrangement with Terry Nugent.

The two Conservative MPs I found most interesting to watch in committee were Art Smith and Ged Baldwin. A quiet, skilled lawyer, Baldwin always seemed to lead off with the simplest question in the world, building towards a climax by the third or fourth question. At this point, he normally had the witness cornered. Smith, on the other hand, never seemed to work very hard, but he always captured the headlines. I wondered how he did it. He didn't proceed in an orderly manner like Ged. He would come to committee with one pertinent, well-phrased question. Whether or not he'd done some work with the press beforehand I don't know, but he appeared to possess the knack of knowing exactly what would interest them. I never acquired Art Smith's flair, but I think I reasonably mastered Ged Baldwin's technique. I was meaner than Ged in many respects, but I took his concept of proceeding slowly from the easy first question to where the guy was ready to step off the cliff. As I say, however, I was never able to emulate Smith's ability for knowing exactly what would interest the press.

In fairness, Art Smith was rated one of the better speakers in the House of Commons. He knew the oil and gas industry well, and when he spoke in the House he was fully prepared. In those days, I was observing everybody very carefully to learn what I could. Art was great with his horn-rimmed glasses. He used them with considerable effect when he was speaking. At first, I didn't understand what he was doing: he seemed to take them off to read, put them back on to talk. Finally, I realized they were a theatrical prop! Meanwhile, I worked hard in committees and made a lot of speeches in the House. I considered this was what I'd been sent to Ottawa for. I also did most of my own research. I would guess that today half of the research done for Liberal and Conservative members in the House is wasted. It's either inappropriate or superfluous. Only the individual MP knows what he is trying to prove, so he alone is the best researcher if he can find the time. Over the years, many newly elected young fellows have asked me for advice and help. I remember Don Mazankowski coming to me with a collection of reports and research papers.

"Horner, does being an MP mean you have to read all this stuff? Do I have to know all this? It's like going back to school, and I quit school a long time ago."

"To start with," I replied, "get interested in something that affects your part of Canada. You'll find yourself wanting to search out and read if you really get interested." Maz turned out, as I've often said, to be my best student. He did a lot of reading and a lot of work — a good member of Parliament.

To survive in Ottawa, one has to avoid certain pitfalls. Boredom is the danger. For example, an MP has a problem presented to him by a constituent. He takes it to the appropriate minister, executive assistant, or deputy minister. Someone says, "Okay, we'll deal with it." Weeks go by. If his committee work is limited and he has few chances to speak in the House, what does he do in the meantime? Ever-present are the bunch who want to play a little poker, sometimes for pretty steep stakes; ever-present is the problem of booze; and, of course, there are always available women. Three pitfalls no whip's office will ever do away with. Personal crises, sometimes tragedies, scandals major and minor, result. The history of Parliament will be ever thus. Mike Starr, an able cabinet minister and house leader, was one of the few guys who could play poker all night and sit in the House the next day without falling asleep.

I had the mistaken notion when I was first elected that anyone who wrote his MP was a crackpot. (This was mainly because we had an old neighbour, a genuine crackpot, who wrote to anyone and everyone: Mackenzie King, "Father" Manning, Victor Quelch.) I soon found I was absolutely wrong. I received some very serious letters from constituents who had run afoul of the government one way or another and wanted redress. If they were to get any satisfaction, it was up to me to prove their points. To take a relatively uncomplicated case as an example, a constituent had mailed in his income tax return and paid in the neighbourhood of five hundred dollars, which in those days was quite a little bit of money. National Revenue in Calgary hadn't received his return until May 8 and in consequence had assessed him a 10 per cent penalty. It wasn't a question of the money, according to my constituent, it was the principle. He hadn't mailed it late. Would I ask the department to take a look at this? I wrote the necessary letter. The department was unyielding. From personal experience, I knew that the taxation branch kept the envelopes on late returns. My constituent ran a local post office and common sense suggested he hadn't stamped his return later than the April 30 deadline. So I merely wrote back to the department and to Hanson Dowell, the minister's executive assistant, and said in essence, "I've been over this road before. I will believe my constituent until you produce the envelope to prove it was dated later than April 30. Please look up the envelope." I received a reply that yes, they'd found the envelope and "the matter is now closed." The fact that my constituent was CCF and that I would never get his vote didn't matter. The individual citizen, in dealing with the civil service on even the simplest of matters, occasionally needs a determined MP.

Constituency work takes on a variety of aspects. When I was at home during one Christmas recess, some people from Elnora contacted me about a dangerous railway crossing which needed site and line improvement. Would I take a look? We set a date. That December 15 was the coldest day on earth. I had lots of winter clothes and I could have worn the biggest pair of overshoes ever seen, but I wanted to look like an MP. Consequently, I had on a suit, shirt and tie, and oxfords with low rubbers. Leola looked at me in disbelief: "You're not going to Elnora?" By the time I arrived, there was quite a crowd. I could sense that everyone was looking at me with the same thought: "What have we got here? We've got us an MP. Let's prance him around in the snow for a while, see how much he can take." So they walked me up to the top of the hill to look at the cut where the train came through. We were there about five or ten minutes. Cold! My hands and feet were freezing, but I never complained; I'd learned that game a long time ago. Finally, we heard the train. The stop watches came out. We had about four seconds to get off the crossing from the time the train came into view. Pretty short notice. If someone ran into trouble, he might just find himself hit by the dayliner. I went to work and with the help of C. Rump, secretary of the Transport Commission, managed to get this site line improved. But I was amused at the paces my constituents put me through. It was all part of the job, though. And to this day I've got a good name in Elnora. Mind you, it ceased to be in my constituency after 1968.

On another occasion, when the Combines Investigation Act was being changed to allow companies in certain industries (*i.e.* fish packers) to work in co-operation for export sales, I received a letter from a local farm union group requesting that I come out to speak on the subject. I was on the committee considering these changes and I took this request very seriously. In Hanna, I picked up Spike Donaldson, who had been my campaign manager, and we drove up north of Galahad to the meeting.

On the way, Spike asked, "What did you say you were going to talk about?"

"Combines legislation."

"For heaven's sake, Horner, nobody up here knows a darn thing about combines legislation. They're interested in combines that harvest their grain, the only ones they know anything about."

I disagreed. "They asked. They're concerned. I can give them the story. I've been on the committee, I know it backwards and forwards."

We argued until we arrived at the hall. We sat through their monthly meeting and then I spoke for fifteen or twenty minutes. Basically, it went all right. But no one asked a question and a number of people looked a little puzzled. I had told Donaldson that a Mrs. Jackson was the driving force in the local farm union and that she might give me a rough time. After the meeting, at the luncheon in the back of the hall, Spike introduced me to Mrs. Jackson, insisted I try one of her brownies: "Jack, I've got the recipe, I'm taking it home to Mother. She's going to learn to make brownies like Mrs. Jackson's!" He put on the darndest show.

Driving back, he said, "Look, Horner, I know the game of politics. You go back there, they're only going to remember one person — me. They're not going to remember you. You were the guy who talked about something they didn't understand."

He was quite right. I went back into that area north of Galahad in the 1979 election, twenty years later. There were people who still remembered Spike Donaldson.

In 1958, all seventeen members from Alberta were Conservative. We would caucus every once in a while. Dief frowned on provincial caucuses, and naturally we tried to live up to his beliefs. Nevertheless, in government there are important appointments to consider and important questions to decide. For example, the Alberta caucus provided the sense of urgency necessary to begin the Pine Point Railway. Ged Baldwin was parliamentary secretary to Diefenbaker at the time and received the credit, but it wouldn't have happened if the Alberta caucus had not agreed on its route. Until then, there had been no sign of consensus on this question, and Dief and company were not making up their minds without this. The decision of the Alberta members placed the route to the west, through Ged Baldwin's Peace River constituency, rather than up the waterways on the east through Jack Bigg's Athabasca constituency.

My brother Hugh was quicker than I was in learning the political game, in watching who got what, and where. I was the youngest member from Alberta and didn't swing much weight in appointments, nor did I expect to. But I was successful, with the help of Marcel Lambert and Eldon Woolliams, in getting Dunc Gardner, president of Acadia riding, appointed district court judge. When appointments came up to various agricultural boards (the Prairie Farm Assistance Act was the big thing in those days) I held my own, but not otherwise. Doug Harkness was

Alberta's senior member, first elected in 1949 and in the cabinet (originally as Agriculture minister, subsequently in Defence). On patronage, he was the political heavyweight, but he was not my kind of guy.

I suspect the Alberta caucus fought more than other provincial caucuses. Marcel Lambert was often in the thick of it. He would sit there looking like a Chinese warlord, practically daring anyone to take a position against him. I discovered that if Marcel took one position, I could almost invariably support the opposite and be right. Everyone thought he was very smart, not because he was a Rhodes scholar, worked hard and read a lot, but because they didn't know what he was talking about. He was one of those people who have the unhappy faculty of so complicating and compounding an issue that nobody else can understand it.

Marcel loved to think he alone represented Edmonton, that Terry Nugent and Bill Skoreyko didn't have a voice. He would try to steal their thunder. I remember one occasion when Skoreyko was to announce officially, for the government, the construction of a large district post office in his constituency. Marcel jumped in and gave the story to the press a couple of days beforehand, completely ruining Bill's occasion. Bill and Terry were forever cursing him. The only way to curb Marcel was to call caucus and say, "Let's hear Terry and Bill on this." Meanwhile, these two would gang up on him whenever they got the chance. Marcel, of course, is no slouch in an argument. He would come back hard as a rock.

The Calgary members weren't much more harmonious. Art Smith and Doug Harkness represented Calgary, and at least they got along on the surface better than the three Edmonton members. But Eldon Woolliams, who represented Bow River, was terribly jealous of Art Smith. At the time, Art was everything Eldon appeared to want to be: accepted by the oil and gas industry in Calgary, respected in the House, and generally regarded as possessing the potential to be a leader politically.

Ours were stormy sessions. Lawrence Kindt (Macleod) and Ted Brunsden (Medicine Hat) were generally at the centre of it. They had gone to university together in the late thirties, to meet again as MPs. Ted had a marvellous command of the English language. He could write a report to his constituents from Parliament Hill or do a radio broadcast quicker and easier than any man I ever saw. And he wasn't that bad an MP, though he most often had the gout or some other problem, and, poor guy, he did have a drinking problem (though not nearly as bad as some others who have been in Ottawa). But he really had it in for Kindt. Kindt was so literal-minded, no sense of humour. When all was smooth and cool, Ted would provoke him and away they'd go. Ged Baldwin was the only one not to get into fights. The rest would line up on one side or the other of any argument. As for the Horner brothers, I guess some would say they caused the odd fight. (Can't imagine it!)

With 208 Conservative MPs, there was also a good deal of dissatisfaction in the government caucus. Three-quarters of us had landed in Parliament for the first time, and most of us had no idea how to do things. Nor did we understand how slowly the entire system works. Discontent would increase to just below boiling point. Then Dief would make one of his appearances in caucus. He could read our every mood. First thing you knew, you were cheering to beat the band, one great united team. Everyone was happy, everyone had his answer, every problem was going to be solved. Then we would gather back in Hugh's office to discuss caucus, and there would be five points of view as to what Diefenbaker had said. I would say, "Well he dealt with this and he said that," but someone else would say, "Oh no, Jack, you misinterpreted him, here's what he said." Time and time again, I swore to myself that I'd never be like that. When I spoke, I wanted all who heard me to have a clear understanding of what I was saying. But Dief, with his command of the English language and his ability to go so far and no farther on a subject, allowed you to race ahead of him to come to your own conclusion. He might have hinted at something, he might have said it wasn't a bad idea, but it was you who assumed he had endorsed it as a good idea. He held you so tightly by your emotions that they worked overtime, and you imagined he was going to do this or that when he wasn't. It was half in your mind and half in his. Two or three weeks after his appearance in caucus we would be dissatisfied again. And Dief would come and do it to us one more time. This was his strength and his weakness. There was no one like him.

All the same, we in the Horner family were annoyed at Dief. There was provision for sixteen parliamentary secretaries, and Dief only appointed fifteen. Waldo Monteith in Health and Welfare was the one minister who didn't have a parliamentary secretary. Hugh was ideal for the job. There he was, a medical doctor, giving up the major share of a good practice to be an MP. Dief could easily have made him parliamentary secretary to Monteith. Of course none of us, Hugh nor I nor anyone else, ever went to Dief to tell him so. We were above that sort of thing. A mistake! The only time I ever threw this up at anybody was one day when Heward Grafftey was running down Dief to me. "What have you got to complain about?" I said. "What talents have you demonstrated around here? Dief made you parliamentary secretary to George Nowlan, and what on earth did you ever do? He gave you everything you deserved, and then some. The Horners were the ones who didn't get anything." And really we were. But you learn to live with your life. We Horners either won on our merit or we didn't. Though, of course, in the game of politics you don't win anything on your merit, you have to elbow your way to the front.

I am not as harsh as most in my judgement of the Diefenbaker cabinet. Dief was handicapped by his devotion to tradition and precedent. Following the 1958 election, he should have retired half the ministers appointed in 1957. By and large, his was an eastern establishment cabinet, not much different, one might suspect, than one that George Drew might have selected. To me, its glaring weakness was that only one minister was a farmer, Paul Comtois, and he was soon to become lieutenant governor of Quebec. Doug Harkness and Alvin Hamilton were the successive Agriculture ministers. We worried about Hamilton tremendously. He was a dreamer with some very strange ideas. Also, he was a little like Marcel Lambert when it came to compounding the issues with complexities. Nobody really understood what he wanted. But, somehow or other, he did all right.

Now Davie Fulton, I thought, was a good cabinet minister because he tried to keep the members informed. He had what he called his "Justice caucus". Although I wasn't a lawyer, I was a member of his committee because I wanted to know what was going on. Fulton wouldn't tell us what was in impending legislation, which annoyed me. (Of course, one still isn't allowed to see legislation before it is tabled in the Commons.) But he would discuss the broad principles underlying his legislative plans. We spent a lot of time on subjects like the humane slaughter of animals, doing away with the old axe and hammer. This ought not to have been a big issue, but it caused all kinds of trouble. There were religious considerations (mainly Jewish) and, in addition, a lot of small killing plants couldn't afford to slaughter any other way, or so they thought.

Capital punishment was the issue we talked about the most. Fulton was a strong believer in its retention. Diefenbaker was an abolitionist. At the time, we were introducing new laws to distinguish between capital and non-capital murder — a very necessary distinction. Previously, anyone convicted of murder, whether premeditated or not, was sentenced to be hanged. During this period, there were two murder trials right in my riding. In the first, a man was convicted of killing his daughter-in-law and her young baby near New Brigden. The cabinet, which was obliged to review each capital case, commuted his sentence. The consequent public outcry made it clear that my constituents didn't agree with commutations. Then there were the Raymond Cook murders in Stettler. Cook had gone to school in Hanna with the young fellow who worked for me at the time, and he had been sentenced to hang for killing his father, his stepmother, and their five children. The current topic was whether the Diefenbaker government would commute Cook's sentence. When Cook escaped custody and terrorized our entire area, this question took on a particular urgency. I wrote a formal letter to Dief, stating that commutation could not be justified. As a result, he attempted to change my views, telling me great tales about the people he had saved from the gallows who later became model citizens. But in most of his stories the murder had not been premeditated, so his clients wouldn't have been sentenced to death under the new law. When I pointed this out, Dief walked away: "Oh, I can't convince you anyway!" All the same, Raymond Cook's sentence was not commuted. His was the second-last hanging in Canada.

It's hard for people to appreciate how upsetting a thing it is for someone in a position of responsibility to cast his vote in cabinet on whether a man should die. George Nowlan, the minister of National Revenue, was a good example. An abolitionist, he couldn't understand why, if Cook was guilty, he didn't confess to his crimes when he went to the gallows. George was deeply upset by this. I remember telling him that Raymond Cook wouldn't confess to anything, that he wouldn't give you the satisfaction of knowing you were right, that he was that kind of person.

In Transport, J. R. Baldwin ran the show. He was George Hees's deputy minister. Much has been made of the qualities of Hees's executive assistant, Mel Jack, but not even Mel and George combined could move Baldwin on most issues. Thus, we weren't overly impressed with Hees. But he wore well. He may have been a glad-hander, but he recognized that Hugh and I were separate people: we both gave him marks for that. David Walker in Public Works never did. He would call me "Doctor", "Hugh", "Jack", "old chum, old buddy, old boy". He received the poorest marks, however, for not knowing how to get his estimates through the House. Walker was so abrasive that he antagonized the Opposition at the wrong time, every time.

By contrast, Donald Fleming, in Finance, was a guy who really paid attention. His behaviour over a small matter like the John Deere cabs was typical. An implement dealer from Morrin had written to me complaining that whereas a John Deere combine with the cab already on it came in duty free from the United States, he had to pay 22.5 per cent duty on the cab — an extra $126 — if he bought the combine and then ordered the cab. The John Deere representative was appearing before our Agriculture Committee, so I asked him if this was true.

"Absolutely."

"Who are we protecting?"

"The cab makers in Canada."

Well, this seemed wrong, because a John Deere cab can't be used on anything other than a John Deere combine. It has to fit tight. Before the next meeting of the Agriculture Committee, I had the John Deere rep bring me some big glossy prints of the combine and cab. When I told him I was going to show them to the Minister of Finance, he was a little sceptical. He told me that John Deere had been trying to get the regulation changed for years. Nevertheless, I thought Fleming would listen, so I went to see him to explain the problem.

"You've never run a combine," I told him. "A lot of farmers fifty, sixty years old can't take the dust. If you take a look at these pictures, you can see how the cab has to fit tight to keep it out. You can't put any old cab on that combine. I think you should let them have this without charging them the extra $126."

Well, lo and behold, when Fleming brought in his next budget, he turned to me in the middle of his speech to announce the removal of the duty on combine cabs. I, of course, pounded my desk in thanks. At his reception following the budget, Fleming wryly remarked, "I guess now your dad can put a cab on his combine." For a moment, I imagined he thought I'd been arguing for myself, which annoyed me. I told him we didn't have a combine with a cab on it and weren't going to get one either. What truly amused me, though, was that at the end of the year the Alberta Farmers' Union and the National Farmers' Union and everybody else checked this off on their list of accomplishments, though they hadn't a clue how it had happened. It had been accomplished because a hard-working and busy Finance minister took the time to hear me out.

Given the absence of genuine agronomists in the Diefenbaker government, the West was strongly represented with Harkness, Hamilton, and Churchill, to say nothing of the Chief himself. And after October 1960 there was Walter Dinsdale. Dinsdale is a nice man. But, so far as I could see, Parks Canada ran him. Northern Affairs and Natural Resources was a department that needed a tough minister. Dinsdale wasn't. It didn't seem to make much difference whether he was there or not; his officials carried on and operated as they thought best. This was one of the fundamental problems we encountered with many departments.

I remember one occasion when we even had trouble with the officials in the Department of Agriculture. The problem was that sheep were selling well below the stabilization price and the department should either have been buying them or paying compensation. It was doing neither. I went down to see Alvin Hamilton as a back-up to Deane Gundlock (Lethbridge), who had been getting the bureaucratic double-shuffle in response to representations on behalf of his constituents. Alvin had his deputy and assistant deputy ministers there. Deane, who was considered a pretty quiet guy, wasn't getting any satisfaction at all at this meeting. Out of the blue, he let out a few choice swear words and threw his huge file of letters on Alvin's floor. Well, I'll tell you, those civil servants jumped a foot. Shortly thereafter, the lamb industry started to receive help. In fairness, I wouldn't short Alvin. However, the details of any program were really too minor to hold his attention. Fortunately Roy Faibish, his executive assistant, was aggressive and hard-working, though Dief didn't think much of him.

As for Dief's Quebec ministers, they were a pretty weak lot. Léon Balcer was no more than a figurehead in Transport. Noël Dorion was a stuffed shirt. Paul Comtois and Henri Courtemanche made hardly an impression. Raymond O'Hurley in Defence Production was probably the hardest working and the friendliest. Pierre Sévigny would likely have been the best, had he not been overtaken by misfortune. He was a stately kind of person, carried himself well. He thought he was pretty capable, and was. He was a real old-style Quebec politician. Tough. There weren't many other members from Quebec who could have done well in the cabinet. Old Duplessis had swung his team behind Dief, and in 1958 a lot had been elected who didn't expect to be. Of the better ones who come to mind, there was Georges Valade, an honest broker who always got elected but for some reason or other never received any recognition. And there was Charles Campeau, probably as shrewd a politician as there was.

As for the members of the Opposition, I remember when Paul Hellyer came into the House in early 1959. He had been in Parliament from 1949 to 1957, had been defeated twice, and was now back in a by-election. Hellyer stood as tall as he spoke, but he read his speeches off cards! He was a real disappointment to me in my search for performances to emulate. On the other hand, I learned a lot from watching Paul Martin. He was a past master at handling the Speaker. Paul would smile — and then completely ignore the Speaker or turn his back on him. Everyone would be hollering, Mr. Speaker would be standing. . . and Paul would be coming on, making his points one by one, seemingly oblivious to the uproar. In those days, the Speaker couldn't kill your microphone to prevent you being heard, and Paul took full advantage of this. He could talk on any subject. Paul Martin talking about wheat made about as much sense as Jack Horner speaking on fish, but Paul could do it. Even if he didn't know a subject, he knew its political implications. One may not have liked his style or the way he went about things, but as a politician he was superb.

After the 1958 election, when the Liberals were reduced to forty-eight members and were suffering spiritually, they were kept going by the "four horsemen": Paul Martin, Jack Pickersgill, Lionel Chevrier, and of course Lester Pearson. Paul Hellyer was considered an important addition to this foursome when he came back to Parliament in 1959. Judy LaMarsh was an important supplement too. Like Hellyer, she came into the House in a by-election, and she struck me as a very sharp-minded person. But she was overwhelmingly partisan: there was no Conservative with an ounce of good in him. Not in her early days, at any rate. Often her partisanship destroyed her logic and warped her judgement.

Pickersgill was the sharpest debater of the group. When Pic was at his best, he was fearsome. He was said to be the only guy that Dief was leery of, and this is probably true. But one never knew when he was ready for the attack; he was a kind of on-again off-again individual. Chevrier, on the other hand, was a consistently hard worker. He always appeared slightly annoyed with everything and everybody, but this probably helped him in his criticism of the government. I came to know him a little better after he was out of politics, and found him a very pleasant person.

I have left Mike Pearson to the last because, of the four horsemen, he was the most difficult to understand. He was a nice man. I really believe this, but I don't think he was suited to be party leader or prime minister. I don't think he was tough enough. He didn't have the necessary inner core of strength. He had made his mark in the world of diplomacy, in the art of compromise, of agreeing and not agreeing, or not quite agreeing. This isn't a good school for a leader. A leader, in my opinion, has to have the core that will not bend or detour. Pearson lacked the necessary character and conviction. Consequently, he did things he ought not to have done. He accepted solutions for their own sake, because any solution to a crisis was acceptable, given the absence of criteria derived from principles encompassing long-term national interests. He allowed his ministers to get into policy or other troubles which resulted in their downfall. I doubt if any of his colleagues were confident of his personal loyalty. No doubt he meant well, but this is not enough. Watching him over his ten years as leader of the Opposition and prime minister, I found it hard even to believe that Pearson was the keen athlete he was reputed to have been in his younger days. He showed nothing of the tough, hard, competitive spirit one looks for in an athlete. Others have judged him and still others will. I think Pearson was the wrong choice for leader of the Liberal party. They chose him because he won the Nobel Peace Prize.

Important far beyond their numbers on the Opposition benches, between 1958 and 1962, were the eight CCF members: Argue, Fisher, Herridge, Howard, Martin, Peters, Regier, and Winch. There was a great deal to be learned from them — how to badger, attack, filibuster, how to bring Parliament to a virtual standstill. I remember Arnold Peters giving a speech on grain marketing. I was quite concerned that he didn't have his facts straight on permit books and delivery quotes, things that can seem complicated unless you grew up on a farm in western Canada. Consequently, I brought in one of my old permit books for Arnold to look at and tried to explain a little of the detail of marketing grain on the prairies. The next day, Arnold made virtually the same speech. Again I went over to him.

"Arnold, I explained it to you yesterday. You're all wrong about permit books."

"Jack, don't worry about it," he replied. "My job is to hold up this bill. I'm not interested in your permit book."

I couldn't believe it. Here was I, a serious-minded and dedicated (if inexperienced) member of Parliament trying to help, and old Arnold blithely says, "Don't bother me with the facts." I looked at him and blinked.

"Think about it," he said, and went on to point out that the CCFers were not going to let the bill through until they had got whatever it was they wanted from the government. It was a rude shock to me, but I learned an important lesson. As the years passed, Arnold and I became very good friends and we worked well together: the Socialist and the arch-Conservative. Not as odd as it seems. It was a natural development of our relationship as individuals and a consequence (once I had learned my lessons) of each of us understanding the system and knowing how to make it work for us.

Frank Howard, more than any of his CCF colleagues, tended to make the government side nervous. He had an established reputation as a determined, mean, tough fighter with a fine command of the English language. The first time I tangled with him, he accused me of being so narrow-minded that I could look down the neck of any medicine bottle with two eyes at the same time. I responded by suggesting he was a Communist.

"You're nothing but a dirty liar!" he shouted.

We had a fair verbal Donnybrook going when the Deputy Speaker intervened. Howard had to withdraw "dirty liar". The rest stood.

If I learned anything from the CCF members, it was that an individual MP can bring the government nearly to a halt if he stays at something long enough and hard enough. The CCF brought our government to a standstill on the divorce bills and nearly to a standstill on a number of other measures. For instance, there was the occasion when Frank Howard was holding up the estimates that Harkness, as Agriculture minister, was putting before the House. Day after day, Howard would rise to his feet, shuffle his papers, and argue point after point. He exhausted not only the patience of the minister but that of the House too.

Gordon Churchill was the government house leader at the time, and one evening he passed the word around the dining room that we should be in the House "sharp at eight o'clock tonight" as soon as the bells began ringing. (The bells of the Commons ring until there is a quorum of twenty members. Generally, it takes three to five minutes for a quorum to assemble, but if the necessary number of members arrive in the first minute, then the bells cease and the House gets down to business.) As instructed, we were there at eight o'clock sharp. By the time Frank Howard arrived three or four minutes later, we had passed the item in the estimates that he had been belabouring. When Howard stood up to continue his filibuster, the Speaker said, "I'm sorry, that estimate is passed." Well, Howard sat down. I don't think he knew just how he had been beaten, but he knew he had.

Hazen Argue was another aggressive fighter, but he fizzled out of the limelight. My first experience of winning the admiration of my fellow members came as a result of an unplanned intervention in a debate against Hazen Argue. He had been badgering Harkness over the support prices for hogs, and in the course of his remarks had revealed that he didn't know much about the industry, not even that a hog was sold rail-grade and that a good pig grades 75 per cent of its live weight. I was rather sarcastic in putting him down. He became so incensed that he stomped out of the chamber. Later in the day, at a reception for Princess Margaret at the Chateau Laurier, various members came over to pat me on the back: "Boy, did you ever silence Argue!" It was a good feeling.

As a matter of fact I had already discovered, as a result of my committee work, that if I did enough study on any subject I could understand it and meet the best of them. I first proved this on the Agriculture Committee in a meeting with the "greats" of the Canadian Labour Congress — Claude Jodoin, Stanley Knowles, and Eugene Forsey. At the time, Jodoin was president of the CLC, Knowles was executive vice-president, and Forsey was research director. Based on a comparison of the five-year periods 1947-52 and 1952-57, they had presented a brief, arguing that labour was not the cause of increased prices for farm machinery: management and profits were the culprits. We received this brief a week in advance of the CLC's appearance before the Agriculture Committee so that we would have the opportunity to study it. I took it home, checked out the CLC's research, and discovered a serious error. In the 1947-52 period they had included the value of inventory in their calculations of costs and profits. In the 1952-57 period they had not. As a result, they showed a 100 per cent profit increase in the second five years when in fact they should have shown a 35 per cent profit decrease.

I went into committee armed with my various reference books. I had so many that Hugh had to help me carry them in. Everyone wondered what on earth I was up to. They soon found out. When I pointed out the error, the CLC officials were reluctant to admit it, and even more reluctant to admit its implications (though they did correct the figures in the annual brief they submitted to the cabinet a couple of weeks later). The committee room was lined with union people from the manufacturing plants in Hamilton, and a number of them came up to me when we adjourned.

"Horner, we'd like to get you alone. We'd certainly straighten you out on the cost and manufacturing of farm machinery."

"Don't try and brand me anti-union," I told them. "You look at the record. My approach to the machinery companies is equally critical."

The annoying thing about all this was that earlier that day I had attended a Broadcasting Committee meeting on CBC expenditures. Canadian content was as much an issue then as it is today, and I had questioned the need to have Lady Astor on "Front Page Challenge" at a cost of a thousand dollars and expenses. "What on earth is the use in paying this kind of money to bring over crackpots from other countries?" I had asked. That evening, the Ottawa *Citizen* ran a headline: HORNER SAYS CBC BRINGS OVER CRACKPOT.

In the same edition of the *Citizen* there was an article by Charles Lynch contending that the MPs who came in on Dief's coattails were a sorry lot, not worth the money, and that higher salaries should be paid so we would get more members the calibre of Doug Fisher. The *Ottawa Journal* contained a similar article by Gordon Dewar, though he at least didn't mention Fisher. But he too was a strong advocate of higher pay to attract better and higher-quality MPs. Blair Fraser had written the same thing in that month's *Maclean's*. These people hadn't any idea of the work an MP does. Here I had just stumped the Canadian Labour Congress, and I received not one line of ink for all my labours, because no press were at the meeting. Yet I had got headlines for one idle question in the Broadcasting Committee, a question that had cost me no work, no effort, and no time. I was about ready for a row with someone.

I couldn't locate Charles Lynch, but I got hold of Bruce Phillips, a young reporter for the *Citizen*. Bruce was a good friend, and he offered to relay my message. Well, I laid into Charles. I remember saying, "Doug Fisher is so impractical, he couldn't track an elephant in six inches of fresh snow." Then I phoned Gordon Dewar and gave him the same blast. The next day, Dewar's column in the *Journal* gave an account of my telephone call. I was sitting in the House when Fisher came over and suggested I read that day's *Ottawa Journal*. This was twenty years ago. I've been watching Fisher ever since: although he's great on theory, I haven't changed my mind about his practicality.

While I'm on the subject of Doug Fisher, I remember a furious battle in committee between him and Donald Gordon, the president of the CNR. Gordon always put on a great show. He would pound the table with his big hairy hands. His wife would cry in the background. The Railway Committee room would be filled with people. On this particular occasion, Doug Fisher had a document from the accounting files of the CNR dealing with the financing of its trucking business. He was making the case that the government, through its subsidization of the CNR — and thus of the CNR trucks — was putting private truckers out of business.

Gordon demanded, "Let me see that paper you're reading from. Let me see those figures."

Fisher made the mistake of giving it to him.

"Fine," said Gordon. "This is a CNR document. Either you stole it or somebody close to you stole it. It's home now and it's staying there."

Well, Fisher was struck dumb.

"I'm tired of you MPs attacking me in the House of Commons," roared Gordon. "Attack me here! Attack me right now so I can answer you."

Well, there was one scene! A flurry and scutter as MPs began to apologize for attacking him in the House. Of course, Fisher wasn't about to apologize. Neither was I.

I told Gordon, "I made a speech in the House of Commons in which I said, 'What have we got? We've got a losing team. The CNR is losing money. It's losing business to CPR. The morale of the team is down. You can't win when the morale of the team is down. What do you do? You fire the coach.' I said this in the House of Commons, Mr. Gordon, and I'm saying it now."

Gordon thundered and snorted. "What do you know about the CNR?"

I replied, "I just ride your trains. I've talked to your workers."

Those sessions with Gordon used to last all week. At the end of that particular week, when Gordon arrived back in Montreal, two thousand CNR workers were out to welcome him. This great rally was staged to demonstrate the high morale of the CN team and show that they all loved their coach. Doug Fisher has rarely had anything good to say about me, but standing up to Donald Gordon prompted the exception.

Most committees did their work very quietly. We carried out detailed examinations, made recommendations, but only on a couple of occasions in my experience have committees developed, in essence, policy.

One instance involved the feed mill question in the early days of the Diefenbaker government. The cabinet was betwixt and between. At issue was whether feed mills should be allowed to continue to buy off-board grain. The government didn't know what should happen. In consequence, they turned the whole matter over to the Agriculture Committee. We heard many witnesses. J. E. Brownlee, head of the UGG, appeared before us. Don MacKinnon of the XL feed mill in Bassano was another. Finally, after long haggling and with I suppose a little bit of steerage from myself and Ged Baldwin, we decided that the existing practice should continue. This was one policy decision which the government accepted from a committee. Indeed, it is still in effect and still considered wrong by the National Farmers' Union. It resulted, nevertheless, in the rapid expansion of the feeding industry in western Canada. In consequence, the slaughter industry expanded. Years ago, beef was 60 per cent slaughtered in eastern Canada; now it is 60 per cent slaughtered in western Canada. To me, this was a move towards increased efficiency in beef production. But it was a rare thing to have a policy referred to a committee for examination.

Committees have become much more political in recent years. I remember when the Wheat Board came for an entire week to make its report to the Committee on Agriculture. We dealt with every paragraph of its annual report. Each paragraph would be read, every question in relation to it answered, and then we would go on to the next until we had systematically examined every aspect of the Wheat Board. As the years rolled by, the practice gradually changed to where the Wheat Board only stayed one day. Naturally, the questions became purely political, an exercise in scoring points. On one occasion, I put up a formidable stand against this practice and wouldn't let the chairman proceed. My point made, I relented, but the whole thing is wrong. Members of Parliament require an adequate chance to examine the Wheat Board's operation. If they don't do it, who will?

As I mentioned earlier, besides serving on all the committees I could get onto I was also speaking in the House as often as possible. One of my major speeches during my parliamentary apprenticeship was the one I delivered on the Hutterites on March 22, 1960. The Hutterites were quite an issue in my constituency: there was a neighbouring colony which operated a farm of some 22,000 acres, and it was said to be exempt from taxation. From the time of my election in 1958, I attempted to discover the details of any taxing arrangement with the Hutterite farmers in western Canada. National Revenue wouldn't tell me; it was a closed matter. Eventually I discovered why information was so hard to come by. Until 1939 the Hutterites had paid no income tax. During the war they had paid, like all other citizens. Thereafter, they lobbied Ottawa for total exemption on the basis that they were in essence a charitable organization, and in 1947 officials from Ottawa reached an agreement with them that those living in colonies would be subject to special assessment for income tax purposes. An individual over sixteen years of age was given an exemption of $1,000. Anyone under sixteen was given an exemption of $500. At the time, the law provided that dependent children under sixteen were exempt $150. These civil servants acted illegally. In a Hutterite colony with $100,000 taxable income, the consequence was that fifty adults and one hundred children would eliminate all taxes.

When I went to George Nowlan, the minister of National Revenue, he told me the whole thing had been settled in the Supreme Court of Canada. I phoned the clerk of the Supreme Court to ask for the rulings. There weren't any. Nowlan was giving me the runaround. When I brought this up in caucus, he said, "Jack, your fight isn't with me, your fight is with every Roman Catholic in this room" — which was untrue, unfair, not relevant, and downright dirty. I was just a little angry.

"All right, Mr. Nowlan, I'm bringing this up on the floor of the House."

In those days, votes on Supply were scheduled for 8:15 on Tuesday evenings. If the vote took half an hour to run off, this left an hour and a quarter of House time for a member to bring up grievances, a provision which no longer exists. I announced my intention to speak. Marcel Lambert, who was at this time Nowlan's parliamentary secretary, approached me.

"Jack, you can't speak tonight," he said. "It'll embarrass the Prime Minister."

"I'm going to," I replied. "I don't think it will embarrass the P.M., but if you think it will, I'll send him a note to ask him." I did.

Dief looked up from his Commons seat and beckoned me out behind the curtain. "Now look, I've got your note. I don't mind you raising the Hutterite income tax problem tonight at all. But for heaven's sake, take one of those governors off one of your dad's old tractors and go about it slowly, carefully."

I laughed and assured him, "Don't you worry, Mr. Diefenbaker. I've been preparing this speech for two years. I have all the relevant court rulings from Manitoba, New Brunswick, and the Supreme Court of Canada. It is carefully prepared. I'm not going to speak angrily nor too fast."

"Well," he said, "all right."

I told Marcel, who never liked the Chief anyway; he went away, grumbling and mumbling that I was going to hurt his minister.

The way the grievance period worked, the question for debate was established by the first person to get the floor. Then there could be as many subsequent speakers on the same subject as time allowed. So, if I weren't the first person up, I might not have an opportunity to speak. To make certain some other donkey didn't get recognized before me, I went and had a word with the Speaker, Roland Michener. Michener was at great pains to explain there was no order, that he recognized whoever stood up first.

"I fully believe you'll be fair," I told him, "but if you happen to be looking at the wrong corner of the House, you're not going to see me. There'll be nobody up before me, I just want to make certain you're looking in my direction so you'll recognize this."

Well, he smiled and agreed. "Okay. You don't have to worry. As soon as the vote is over, I'll be looking in your direction. But don't let anybody beat you because I don't want to look as if I'm showing favours." All the groundwork was in place.

That evening I made my speech. I made it coldly and slowly, and quoted the court rulings. (For those interested, it is reproduced in Appendix 2.) To this day, it stands as a pretty good speech on the subject as to whether or not Hutterite colonies are charitable organizations and should be considered as such. I began by stating that I wanted to make it abundantly clear that I had no grudge whatsoever against these people but that I felt they were receiving a subsidy from all the rest of the tax payers in Canada, and that was my only grievance. I pointed out that the Hutterites were exempt from income tax under section 62(1)(e) of the Income Tax Act which read as follows:

> A charitable organization, whether or not incorporated, all the resources of which were devoted to charitable activities carried on by the organization itself and no part of the income of which was payable to, or was otherwise available for the personal benefit of, any proprietor, member or shareholder thereof.

I then pointed out that, according to the *English Law Dictionary*, a charitable organization is one that has no capital stocks and no provision for making dividends and profits but derives its funds mainly from public and private charity. The same dictionary defined charity under four principal divisions: the relief of poverty, the advancement of religion, the advancement of education, and other purposes beneficial to the community. I pointed out that although the Hutterites relieved the poverty of their children, just as we relieve the poverty of our own children, they contributed very little to the relief of poverty in the community as a whole. Religion, of course, they did advance within their own communities, and I had no objection to that whatsoever. As for the advancement of education, I cited figures which showed how behind in their grades Hutterite children were compared to others in Alberta. However, the main point I made throughout was that by being exempt of tax, the Hutterite farmers had an unfair advantage over their competitors — the many individual farmers of western Canada.

I hadn't been deceiving Diefenbaker when I told him I'd done a lot of work. Anyone who takes a look at my speech will see that I had given the matter much consideration. It made a lot of people think. Mind you, there were those who branded me as a bigot, a racist, and all sorts of other things. But National Revenue realized that some changes had to be made, and George Nowlan told me he was prepared to consider the question.

"If you want to go the deduction route, fine," I said to him. "If I pay my sons wages and claim this as an expense on my income, I have to be able to prove that the money went from my bank account into theirs. Income tax inspectors have made many a farmer prove this."

"All you're saying," replied George, "is that you want the Hutterite colonies to pay their people wages."

"That's right. I don't care if they give the money back to the colony, but the money has to move from the colony to the people."

"Well, that's a new angle. I'll take a look at it."

When the department took some action in 1961, the Hutterites immediately began legal proceedings to have these regulations set aside.

The sequel to this story happened in 1977 when I was a cabinet minister in the Trudeau government. The minister of National Revenue, Joe Guay, came to me one day and asked what I thought he should do about the $54 million owing in back taxes on the Hutterites. Trudeau had told him that I knew more about Hutterites than anyone else on Parliament Hill.

"Joe, you've got no choice," I said. "We're so short of money we had to turn down an increase in veterans' pensions. You've got to go after it."

He did, but without result. Twenty years after my original speech in the Commons, the issue remains before the courts. But at least I made it an issue and brought it to the notice of the government. I took a fair amount of abuse for my trouble, but I would do it again.

In one way and another, I managed to achieve a good deal during those first learning years in Ottawa. When in April 1962 Parliament was dissolved, I wasn't particularly worried — not for myself and not for the party. In 1958 we had won 208 of a possible 265 seats. In the coming election we could afford to lose some seats, and it was obvious that we would. Such strength as we had in Quebec had been dependent on

Duplessis. He was dead. So was Sauvé. It seemed more than likely that we would lose most of our fifty Quebec seats. What I didn't expect was that we'd lose almost as many in Ontario.

In my view, the government had done a good job. We were a small country and Diefenbaker, as prime minister, was making an immense impression internationally. I was proud of his attack on Soviet imperialism at the U.N. in September 1960 and of his role in forcing South Africa out of the Commonwealth when it refused to alter its apartheid policies. And I thought he was right to attempt to diversify our international trade.

On the domestic front, we in western Canada were growing rapidly. We were benefiting from improved agricultural conditions and legislation. Grain sales to China had begun. We were further buoyed by the practical consequences of Diefenbaker's Northern Vision, his Roads to Resources, the Pine Point Railway, and new oil and gas legislation. The South Saskatchewan dam was equally important in this respect. As a water project, it didn't have any effect in my area, but it showed that there was federal money to be spent in the West.

From a water conservation point of view, I agreed with those who contended that the project to divert the Red Deer River should have taken precedence over any development on the South Saskatchewan. It was only logical to proceed with upstream development first. But the Manning government said no, they didn't want to go ahead, they wanted no federal interference in the management of Alberta's natural resources. (In this sense, Lougheed is Manning's natural heir.) The Saskatchewan government, on the other hand, always keen to exploit any federal initiative to the full, responded positively. Given this situation, plus a prime minister from Saskatchewan who had spent years railing against the inactivity of the King and St. Laurent governments on this project (and who was not impressed by the cost-benefit studies of his predecessor), the South Saskatchewan dam was quickly given the go-ahead. We are still waiting for the Red Deer diversion.

The irony is that the money would have been better spent in Alberta. Saskatchewan has done very little with this important resource. It has not built the envisioned system of auxiliary waterways to distribute to farmers the water stored in Diefenbaker Lake. Irrigation is alien to Saskatchewan. But not to Alberta! There are some 800,000 acres under irrigation in Alberta. If one considers, however, that there are 48 million acres under irrigation in the United States, this gives some idea of how far we have to go. Of course, in 1962, the South Saskatchewan dam had not been completed; Diefenbaker Lake did not exist.

Unfortunately, from a political standpoint, the fact of anything being done for the West fostered the popular notion in the East that Dief was doing everything for the West and nothing for Ontario. To the press, this meant that the Diefenbaker government was rudderless, that it had no national policies or objectives. To this very day, one hears the same thing. From where I sat (and that was in the Conservative rump which found itself for seating purposes on the Opposition side of the House) most of the government's major initiatives, as always, involved the advancement of central Canadian interests. The problems that eventually undid Diefenbaker were equally central Canadian: the Avro Arrow–Bomarc controversy, the Coyne affair, the devalued dollar. More important than any of these, of course, was the posture of the eastern establishment, as manifest in the cabinet, the civil service, and the press, which was reluctant to accept a small-time prairie lawyer as prime minister. Peter Newman, in *Renegade in Power*, demonstrates this attitude again and again. The establishment made absolutely no effort to admit Diefenbaker to its ranks. Of course, he eventually reciprocated in kind, creating a stand-off.

Dief's slide in Ontario began with the cancellation of the Avro Arrow in January 1959. It was a difficult decision. Twenty years later we were still looking for a fighter very much like the Arrow. Should the government have kept pouring money into its development and production? Possibly. Without foreign sales, however, the government could not proceed without incurring huge deficits: something considered unacceptable at the time. These sales were not forthcoming; the United States was not buying. Perhaps the best idea would have been to put the whole project in mothballs until a later date. In any event, the decision to scrap the Arrow began a Conservative decline in Metro Toronto from which Dief was never to recover.

The high unemployment which plagued the government from 1957 to 1962 I blame on Coyne. I don't blame Dief. I don't blame Fleming. I don't blame Mike Starr. Clear and simple, I blame the then governor of the Bank of Canada, James Coyne. Tight money is not compatible with a high level of employment. There was a period from August 1959 to September 1960 when the money supply in Canada actually decreased. Its effect was to curtail our growth and increase our unemployment. This tightening of the dollar also tended to increase its value, placing it at a premium in relationship to the United States dollar, thus adversely affecting our exports. Once Donald Fleming announced in his 1961 budget the intention of the government to bring about devaluation, it was evident Coyne had to go. I remember saying to Fleming, "Here's the Bank of Canada annual report. Am I reading this wrong, or did our money supply actually decrease in those months?" He replied, "You're not reading it wrong. I can't comment on it, but we're going to take some necessary action." A month or two later, the government moved to fire Coyne.

Diefenbaker, in my opinion, bungled the operation. He made a serious mistake in not allowing Coyne to appear before the House of Commons Finance Committee. Not that I had, at the time, sufficient seniority to have expected a place on it, but I would have loved the opportunity to tear into Coyne. Diefenbaker did not trust the capabilities of his own members of Parliament. There was nothing to fear. The Chief has blamed Fleming for the failure of the government in this regard, but the decision was strictly Diefenbaker's. When I talked with Fleming, I gathered he would not have objected to having Coyne appear before the Commons committee. Regardless, whether it was Dief or Fleming, it was a mistake.

The government's decision to deny Coyne his "day in court" created a false issue and, in the eyes of the public, enhanced Coyne's stature. He was popularly portrayed as a fighter for what was good for the country. The government was seen as trying to hide its erosion of the dollar and so on, when in fact their decision happened to be correct. Coyne was the stick-in-the-mud: an antiquated financier at best, a deliberate politician at worst. He appeared before the Liberal-dominated Senate Finance Committee, where his success was assured. I carefully prepared a list of questions for Dad to ask. Not that I expected him to follow my list, but I thought, what the heck, I might as well give them to him. In launching into Coyne, Dad wasn't as sharp as he should have been. Consequently, he didn't corner him as well as he could have. The whole affair rebounded to the political discredit of the government, benefiting the Liberal party in the short term and no one in the long term. It convinced the people that devaluation was wrong. When devaluation suddenly became an issue during the 1962 election campaign, the voters, especially in Ontario, were much more apprehensive about it than they would have been had they been presented with the opportunity to understand what the Coyne business was really all about. Over and over again in my political experience, the critical policies affecting this nation — be they devaluation, bilingualism, metrification, or whatever — have not been subjected to the kind of public examination and debate necessary to a popular understanding of what is involved. The consequence has been public reaction. And, in 1962, a swing away from Diefenbaker.

3/Fall of the Chief

There's nothing like an election to bring a politician down to earth. I thought I'd been a pretty good MP. I had worked hard and enjoyed some success, I had received some attention in the national papers, and I thought all this would be recognized back home. Well, I got the nomination all right, but five candidates challenged my re-election: a Liberal, an Independent Liberal, a Social Crediter, an NDP, and an Independent. What's more, the Social Crediter — a fellow by the name of Hewson — came within nine hundred votes of beating me. Elections don't come easy in my constituency.

Still, I did better than many of my colleagues. Instead of the 208 seats we had had in the previous parliament, we now had only 116. In September 1962, when we assembled in Ottawa for the opening of Canada's twenty-fifth parliament, the members of caucus I knew were not optimistic. Neither was I. I hadn't been at all impressed with Diefenbaker's August cabinet shuffle. I couldn't believe it when I heard that Donald Fleming was being replaced in Finance by George Nowlan. It was obvious that Dief was not functioning clearly. He had had a rough time. His greatest majority ever had been reduced to a minority. And he had fractured his ankle. We were sympathetic, but his cabinet didn't make sense. If anything, it was worse than the one he had taken into the election. We went along with it, accepted it, but had we made the choice it would have had a considerably different look.

The major surprise in Dief's new cabinet was the appointment of Wallace McCutcheon, via the Senate, as minister without portfolio. Unfortunately McCutcheon, a gruff old financier, was ineffective in politics. Dief had sought him out in an attempt to win back a following in the financial community in Toronto, but although McCutcheon was respected by the business community, he was never popular with it in the sense that the business community would follow him. All the same, he certainly knew his stuff. I went to him for advice on more than one occasion. If you could get to him before 5 P.M., he couldn't be shorted.

Apart from our phenomenal losses, the surprise of the 1962 election was the success of twenty-six Créditistes under Réal Caouette in Quebec. With Bob Thompson elected in Red Deer and Bud Olson in Medicine Hat and a couple more in B.C., Social Credit thought it was on the march nationally. The CCF-labour New Democratic Party elected its first members, nineteen of them. The Liberals, however, with a fifty-one-seat increase over their 1958 total of forty-eight, could smell our blood; they were really gung-ho.

The 1962-63 parliament was the least productive I've ever seen. The session was so short the committees didn't even begin their work. The government was never off the ropes. From the Cuban Missile Crisis in October until our defeat in the House in February, there was a constant squabble within the party over nuclear weapons. This seemed to occupy cabinet to the exclusion of everything else. There was no legislative program evident, no budget. Such legislation as was introduced ground to a halt in the face of Liberal obstruction.

Diefenbaker's and Howard Green's handling of the Cuban Missile Crisis, with whatever justification, only served to increase the disillusionment of the Toronto power brokers. Diefenbaker, to the end of his political career, remained popular with a lot of the rank and file in Ontario, but his refusal to lend immediate and unconditional support to Kennedy over Cuba ended any chance of his ever recovering support in the influential spheres. When Pearson made his switch on the broader question of Canada's acceptance of nuclear weapons for the armed forces in early January 1963, and when the United States openly supported the Liberal position, the fate of the government was sealed.

As a government back-bencher, I could see what was happening on the outside, in the Commons, and in the party. But none of us in caucus had any idea of the impending revolt in cabinet. We knew that Harkness and Diefenbaker weren't getting on. Beyond this, we didn't know much. Thus, on Monday morning, February 4, 1963, as I was driving to work listening to my car radio, I didn't believe it when I heard the news reports of Harkness's resignation and the demands in the cabinet that Diefenbaker step down as prime minister. When I arrived at the House, I checked with the other guys. They had heard the same stories. We sat around and talked. It couldn't be! That George Nowlan, of all people, was to be interim prime minister — it was hard to accept. But no one in the cabinet considered it necessary to tell us anything. We had no source of information other than the news reports. I always bowled on Monday mornings at eleven, and there was no point in not going. When I came back at one o'clock, everyone was still standing around talking about what they had heard on the news. So I said, "Well, let's go find out. Alvin Hamilton will know." Sure enough, Alvin said it was true: Hees and Fulton had been to see Dief on Sunday to ask him to resign.

Back in Hugh's office on the fifth floor of the Centre Block, I began to stir up support for Dief: "He's going to be feeling pretty low when he comes into the House at two. When the bells start to ring, we'd better have the troops down there to give him a rousing hand."

I undertook to rally the Ontario members, most of whose offices were on the fourth floor of the House, while Hugh and the others said they would look after the western members, most of whom were on the fifth floor. In consequence, there was a big crowd waiting for Dief when he emerged from his little office behind the Commons chamber. This cheered him up immensely. When we walked into the government lobby, Theo Ricard jumped up on a table and started to sing "For he's a jolly good fellow", and the whole gang joined in. Of course, the rebels were there as well. I tell you, there were some pretty strong words said to Hees and company. Hugh, for one, gave Hees a real tongue-lashing, but it was Lawrence Kindt who threatened Hees: "When Dief speaks this afternoon, you'd better bang your desk at every opportunity or I'll break your arm." (I was accused of this because in one popular account the MP is an unnamed "burly Westerner".)

When Pearson moved want of confidence in the government that afternoon, the critical question was how the Social Credit–Créditiste combination would vote. Dief's speech in response to Pearson's motion did not go as far as we thought he might in reaching out for the support of Thompson and his Social Crediters. Thompson got up and waffled. Everyone thought he was going to say something definite before six. He didn't. After the supper hour, Thompson continued his speech, more or less stating that when the vote came the next day his supporters would bring down the government. Whoever had got to him between six and eight, I don't know. Pat Nicholson, the newspaperman, was lobbying hard with Thompson, whether on behalf of the Chief or Nowlan wasn't clear. The Liberals were making promises they'd never keep. There was every kind of speculation, every sort of rumour. The big boys were playing and one didn't know just who was winning.

My only criticism is that the Diefenbaker side didn't play it well. The following day — Tuesday, February 5 — the government was defeated. All day, the hallways and corridors were filled with argument. I remember Dad asking Hugh and me, "Are you sure you're right in supporting Dief?" Our reply was a definite yes. "There's going to be an election, and we're going with Dief." We knew his campaigning ability. If we had to go back to the people, we wanted to go with him.

On Wednesday morning the caucus call went out. It was a tremendously soul-searching experience. George Hees came in and, as caucus chairman, made his pitch. He showed a lot more guts than I would have given him credit for, but he went on far too long. He got a few boos and catcalls from the members. Then they began to yell, "Let's hear Dief!"

The Chief started to interrupt George. He then got up and cut him to ribbons. George broke down. When caucus got into the act, Alf Brooks made an outstanding play on behalf of Diefenbaker and unity in the party — that we had to go into an election which would be the political fight of our lives, that in fighting each other we were cutting our own throats, and so on. Angus MacLean and Grattan O'Leary also made speeches. The press gave O'Leary credit for unifying caucus, but I think the major credit should go to Alf Brooks. His speech was far more effective. Finally, Dief brought caucus to an end with a rousing speech, saying he could forgive Hees and the rest of them. When he demanded to know how many of us were with him, only Harkness and perhaps Balcer and Sévigny remained seated. With George Hees cheering "Bring on the tigers", we went out of the door united.

We thought that the wounds were patched up and that we were in the best condition possible, given the circumstances, to fight the battle. But on Saturday, February 9, Hees announced he was quitting and going skiing. This was a shock the troops didn't need. In the midst of all this, Sévigny's resignation was hardly noticed. I don't know whether Diefenbaker could have won the election had Hees stayed — I don't want to rate Hees that highly — but his decision to quit certainly demoralized those of us on the hustings.

Hugh and I and the rest of our gang had lined up pretty hard behind Diefenbaker, and this began the legend of the "Diefenbaker cowboys". Cousin Albert (Albert Horner, the Battlefords) was always with us; he was our silent strength. We continued to fight Dief's battles as long as he was leader. He never had to worry about where we stood. Dief quickly grasped the extent and significance of his support in caucus, which he effectively used time and time again to thwart those seeking to overturn his leadership. It is a fact that caucus remained overwhelmingly loyal to Diefenbaker until this ceased to matter in 1967.

There were important exceptions, of course, notably Doug Harkness who now had publicly challenged Dief. Harkness, long since, in my opinion, ought to have been fired from the cabinet and replaced by Art Smith. But there couldn't be two ministers from Calgary, and in Dief's view of things, Harkness's seniority guaranteed him the job. A mistake, as I've suggested before. The best Dief could do for Art Smith was to send him to the U.N. as a member of the Canadian delegation. Art became pretty dissatisfied with his lot — the poor pay, the $10-a-day living allowance in New York — and in consequence he became pretty dissatisfied with Diefenbaker as well. On that February 5 vote of confidence, he had been one of the few back-benchers to align himself with Harkness and the cabinet rebels against Dief, staying outside the

Commons chamber rather than vote to sustain us in power. In any event, he didn't run in 1963. His failure to do so allowed the Liberals their one success in Alberta with the election of Harry Hays in Calgary South. Had Art Smith decided to continue as an MP and had he sided with Dief, his star would have risen quickly in Opposition, with whatever future result. Instead, he lent such influence as he had within the party to the "dump Dief" cause.

The shocker to me, however, came after the 1963 election when Ged Baldwin joined the ranks of the rebels. One had to wonder how the man who had been Dief's parliamentary secretary, how the one Alberta member who could actually point to something achieved for his constituency — the Pine Point Railway — could have the gall to demand that Dief step down. Of the '58 crop of MPs from Alberta, Baldwin had been the one to receive the most recognition from Diefenbaker. Yet he was one of the first to turn against him. In doing this, he isolated himself from the rest of us. If Baldwin had come within earshot of me, I would have given him both barrels. To my knowledge, he never came near any of his fellow Alberta members, except for Doug Harkness and Marcel Lambert. He seemed to associate mainly with Gordon Fairweather. Fairweather, of course, never came near the rank and file of caucus at any time. He was above that.

Around Ottawa one gets to thinking everything that happens there is so important. When I came home to campaign, I thought the election was going to be worse than anything I'd ever faced. It wasn't. The people still liked Diefenbaker, although they couldn't understand what had happened to the party. Why had Harkness resigned? Why had Hees? It was easy here in rural Alberta to say, "Well, let's not worry about Colonel Harkness: just a hidebound army type who refused to change his mind." I had no trouble in Acadia with that one; my constituents didn't particularly like army colonels. Hees was more difficult. I explained this apologetically: he and Diefenbaker couldn't get along; Hees quit, went skiing. Later on in Hees's political career, he arrived at the stage where he liked to report to caucus that he had sinned and knew how bad this was, urging the rest of us never to do the same. Too bad he couldn't have seen this at the time!

The nuclear arms question was the big issue in the national campaign. It didn't occur to me that this would not be the same everywhere. I wanted to go on television immediately to explain the Conservative position. In those days, you could book five minutes on Red Deer television for seventy-five dollars; this was live, not videotaped. We had booked a series of five-minute weekly broadcasts for the election, and I had a great row with my campaign manager, Spike Donaldson, over what I was going to say. Spike contended that maybe by the third or fourth week of the campaign, when saner minds had prevailed and tempers had cooled, I might be able to talk about nuclear arms. But not yet. He won the argument. Consequently, for my first five minutes I fell back on what was becoming my traditional "What Are Political Parties Made Of?" broadcast. I would begin, "Let's look at the political parties. What are the differences? In Alberta we have a Social Credit government. In B.C. they have a Social Credit government. In B.C. they nationalized power. In Alberta they didn't. It's the same party. What is the difference? The difference is the men who make them up. In one party you have W. A. C. Bennett; in the other, Ernest Manning. Two different people. Same party, but they do different things. Now, let's look at the Conservative party. Diefenbaker, Alvin Hamilton, Gordon Churchill: Westerners in key places in government, prepared to make certain that western Canada gets a fair shake. What do you find in the Liberal party? Pearson, a former civil servant. Mitchell Sharp, a former civil servant. Guy Favreau, a former civil servant. Jack Pickersgill, a former civil servant. If you want more bureaucrats, vote for Pearson. That's what you're going to get. That's what his party is made of." This, essentially, was the message of my first five-minute talk.

Spike was right. The campaign did level off. It was much the same as any other. There were no ban-the-bomb demonstrations in Acadia. It was true that Diefenbaker was losing popularity in centres like Stettler, where the daily newspaper exposed people to a steady barrage of anti-Diefenbaker stories. It wasn't any one thing that stuck in their minds, it was "Well, we don't know about Diefenbaker; he seems to have a lot of trouble with his cabinet" sort of thing. It was the same with Trudeau in 1979, the daily onslaught of anti-Trudeau stories. People finally said, "I don't like the guy." When asked why, they said, "I don't trust him; he's a Commie." Or, in Dief's case in 1963, "He's a one-man government." The trickle of water on stone eventually wears through. This is the power of the media.

The biggest danger in the 1963 campaign was the growing feeling that Diefenbaker wasn't going to win. This had to be fought because people like to be on the winning side. A good friend of mine who was drawmaster of the Stettler bonspiel suggested that the best thing I could do was get in the bonspiel. I did. There were six events. We took the third. More important, I got into a lot of discussions about nuclear arms and Diefenbaker. It turned out to be a pretty good thing to do — just curl a little in February.

To state the obvious, my activities in the 1963 election were limited to the riding of Acadia. I was concerned lest my Social Credit opponent gain advantage from the 1962 re-emergence of his party, so at every opportunity I differentiated between Thompson as the leader of four English-speaking Social Crediters and Caouette as the leader of twenty-six from Quebec, pointing out that while Thompson might be able to relate to Manning, Caouette didn't care to. I had to be very careful not to appear to be running against Manning. As I mentioned earlier, my margin of victory in 1962 had been less than 900 votes. Against the same Social Credit candidate in 1963, this increased to 5598. Nationally, the Conservatives lost. My surprise was that Pearson didn't get a majority. In my opinion, Dief did very well to hold on to ninety-five seats; anyone else but Dief would have been absolutely decimated. This is what the would-be power brokers and rebels within the party never seemed to grasp. They thought they could dump Dief and have the power of his office pass unaffected into their hands.

The election of the Pearson government in 1963 opened up a whole new ball game for me. In government, the theory is that legislation is examined before it is presented. They don't need back-benchers to scrutinize it publicly. But the Opposition's job is to make certain the people understand what the government is attempting to do and why, if for any reason at all, it's going to be detrimental to them. Therefore, there were all kinds of opportunities for an interested MP to make speeches. I told Gordon Churchill, our house leader, "Any time you need a speech on anything, give me a ring." This got me into the occasional awkward situation, because I was now involved in debates a good deal more important than talking out some private member's bill. I recall once being called to hold up the Finance estimates because George Nowlan, our critic, was away from the House that day. The argument I pursued was what, for the purpose of customs duties, should be defined as an agricultural machine? I spent a great deal of time on items like water troughs, truck boxes, steel boxes. I even got around to the question of lariats. Pickersgill interjected, "If you just shut up, we'll buy you a couple of lariats!" I heard about lariats until they were coming out of my ears after this. But I held up the estimates as requested.

Gordon Churchill was the strategist who got Dief through those difficult years, both in Parliament and in the party. Gordon was not an easy person to communicate with. This was reflected in his relations with the media. I don't think he ever received good press. To a newsman with a question, Gordon invariably gave a curt reply. As a result, the press never came to understand him. Until I learned to persist in my dealings with him, his gruff exterior turned me aside as well. Working with him in Opposition, however, gave me a chance to know him. He was an untiring house leader. On any question of what was happening in the

Commons he knew to the last word exactly how many days such-and-such a debate had gone on or how many hours, and how long it would continue. He was responsible for every detail. He must have had some difficult times trying to convince Dief to do things, attempting to harness Dief's ability in the best interests of the party. Without a doubt, Gordon was one of the unsung heroes of those ten years, from 1957 to 1967, within the Conservative party. He was greater than Alvin Hamilton or Waldo Monteith or Howard Green or any of the others. Also, and so important to Diefenbaker in Opposition, it was Gordon who always made certain that I or Terry Nugent was at caucus when there were rumblings against the Chief. Gordon contributed more than anyone to the party's stability. Yet, to my knowledge, nobody gave him full marks.

It was a very difficult time for the Conservative party. After the 1964 annual meeting, when Dief was given an overwhelming endorsement by the membership, one might have expected the party outside of caucus to line up behind him. But Dief's victory at the meeting meant about as much as Léon Balcer's elevation to deputy leader. I doubt if Dief ever intended to share his leadership with Balcer, although things might have worked out differently had their personalities not been as incompatible. If one was around Dief very long, he wanted you talking; he wanted to know your views and he wanted you to listen to his. Balcer, by nature, was reticent. Nor do I think he was particularly interested in Dief's views. The whole thing was a bad idea. It did little to placate the Quebec wing of the party and it laid the groundwork for future trouble.

The most important event, by far, in 1964 was the election of Dalton Camp as president of the party. In 1956, Dief had wrested control of the party from the eastern establishment. He then set about the party's democratization, which in effect meant broadening its base support to include all peoples at all levels. Through the introduction of annual meetings, he sought to give his new membership, which was by definition anti-establishment, a predominate voice in party affairs. Camp was the vehicle for redressing the balance in favour of the party's traditional forces.

No doubt, because Pearson was in little danger of being defeated in the House, it was expected that Parliament would run the normal four years before another election. Dief by then would have passed his seventieth birthday and it was reasonable to expect that he would step down, whether voluntarily or under pressure. Camp, as president, would be in position to assure the establishment an acceptable new leader.

The pattern established by Camp was there for those who would see it. First: win the presidency. Second: organize the party youth. (The Student Federation and YPC delegates are the closest thing to a voting bloc in any convention. They love to flock together, have no established personal loyalties, and are easy to control. Further, their enthusiasms are often contagious and they are good convention troops.) Third: attempt to control the development of new party policies. (For Camp, the Fredericton and Montmorency conferences are examples of this.) Fourth: control the timing and location of any convention and especially the leadership convention. Finally: control the selection of delegates, so far as this is possible.

The proof of the importance of the Camp example, however, lay in the period after 1967. Stanfield proved so inept a leader in Opposition that the presidential races were hotly contested because each would-be successor to Stanfield wanted to get his man in position. John Robarts wanted to keep the door open for his entrance into federal politics, so he encouraged Don Matthews to seek the presidency. Camp attempted to keep control of the National Executive by promoting Roy Deyell and Roy McMurtry as his team. In 1974, Joe Clark, in making his move toward the leadership, successfully manoeuvred Michael Meighen into the presidency, albeit by a mere sixteen votes. The oddity here was that the day before Meighen's election, thirty-seven last-minute convention delegates were named, none of whom appeared to be supporting Don Matthews's re-election. Matthews, at this time, had the support of over ninety per cent of caucus. Malcolm Wickson, on behalf of Stanfield, approved the credentials of the delegates in question.

I certainly never envied Diefenbaker his leadership in the period following the 1963 election. He had always to be looking over his shoulder to see who was doing what to undermine him. The pressures must have been enormous. Nor had any public figure in our history been so maligned by the press. This was a process epitomized in Peter Newman's *Renegade in Power*, which was published in the fall of 1963.

Newman's book prompted my brother Hugh to issue his "orange juice" theory in rebuttal. As Leola and the boys were now permanently at the ranch, Doc and I were sharing my house in Ottawa, and one evening I asked him if he had ever noticed, when we were in government, which cabinet ministers got good press and which didn't.

"What are you getting at?" asked Hugh.

"Well, Hees got good press. Fulton got good press. So did Nowlan. Dief was getting pretty good press until he cut off the booze at 24 Sussex. Donald Fleming never poured a drink for a newsman in all the years he was around. Mike Starr once told me about the tremendous press coverage he and United States Secretary Goldberg had received during a meeting in Washington." I speculated, "I'll bet they filled those newsmen full of booze. The orange juice and lemonade treatment doesn't work."

This became Doc's "orange juice" theory. When Newman came up to see him about it, Doc, who had little time for the press in any event, told him what he thought of him in pretty short terms. Dief was a bit upset about Doc's release at first, but after a few months he changed his mind, thought it was a great stroke of business.

It was always those of us in caucus, rather than the party establishment, who rallied round. In the House, this was easy because Dief's leadership was often inspiring. For example, the 1964 debate on the Canadian flag was initially a good one for caucus. Diefenbaker really kept his troops in there fighting. Personally, I was not caught up emotionally in the flag debate. I participated only twice. My view was that if Canadians wanted a truly distinctive flag, I'd go along with it, although I was never certain whether a majority of Canadians did. Of course, Diefenbaker was a stout defender of our British heritage. He wanted the Union Jack on the flag. His emotions came into full play on the issue, and this gave him a purpose to stay. It was the length of the debate that became the problem. Support in caucus began to drop off. The press and the public wearied of the arguments. Fortunately for both Dief and caucus, the Rivard affair broke before the flag debate ended: Erik Nielsen came to the fore in the House and the press with his great discovery of corruption in high places. Pearson was in a shambles. Dief was in his heyday cutting up Guy Favreau. This served to restore our spirit.

What those counting on Dief's early retirement could not have calculated was the total ineptness of the Pearson government, which proceeded from disaster to disaster, creating every opportunity for Dief to re-establish his credentials as leader. Nor could they have calculated that Pearson was planning an early election from the moment he was sworn into office. That's the obvious conclusion if one considers the more than $2 billion increase in the money supply from April 1963 until the calling of the election in September 1965. Having created an immediate economic ebullience, Pearson had to go to the people before rapid inflation destroyed his artificially based political advantage. Typically, he was caught in his own web. How else could one explain calling an election with the Dorion Report on the Rivard affair hanging over his government's head? From coast to coast, Dief crucified him with "It was on a balmy night such as this that they let Rivard out to flood the rink."

Meanwhile, Dalton Camp and company had their problems too. Having failed to dump Dief at the National Executive meeting in Ottawa in February 1965 (this time using Balcer as the catalyst), they faced the intolerable prospect of the party under Diefenbaker actually winning the November election. What were they to do? In addition to everything else, they were now convinced that Dief was in a state of mental and physical breakdown. There was no way they were going to allow him to become prime minister again. Consequently, Premier John Robarts's "big blue machine" was not put in gear in Ontario and, more important, Manitoba's Premier Duff Roblin refused to run in Winnipeg. We had all privately hoped that Roblin would run. We knew that Diefenbaker was counting heavily on him. Had Roblin joined, and joined early enough, the '65 campaign could have been won. Duff was a tremendously good stump speaker. He had a fine command of the English language and was very fluent in French. If Dief had been able to present him as his heir apparent, people in Toronto would have seen some hope in the Conservative party down the road. I recall one Créditiste, who later switched to the Liberals, telling me that he would have gone Conservative if Roblin had been leader. So we might have done better in Quebec if Roblin had joined the campaign and gone to work hard. And we could have put Dief in a minority government position in 1965. No question about it.

The main problem in the 1965 election was that the party wasn't pulling together. Not only were many of the Conservative establishment not helping Dief but they wanted him to go down in defeat in the worst way. The story went around that Eddie Goodman jokingly threatened to jump out of the window of the Chateau Laurier Hotel if Diefenbaker did win. (It was kind of amusing to see that lot in power for a few months in 1979 and then to see them lose power without Dief to blame for their ineptitude.) Once again, one must conclude that Pearson would have achieved a majority if it hadn't been for Dief's great campaigning.

A good example of Diefenbaker on the husting was his appearance in Stettler. I was looking after the arrangements, and I stopped in to see Ernie Salt who ran the travel agency, hoping that he would lend his car. I had to get twenty cars to the train station at Alex to bring the Diefenbakers, their entourage, and the press into town.

"Somebody said you might be interested," I told Ernie, "you've got a good car."

"Well," he replied, "I've got a good car, but I'll tell you, Jack, if I do it, I'll do it for you, not for that S O B , Diefenbaker. I wouldn't walk across the street for him."

"Ernie, right about now I don't care who you're doing it for. You don't have to have Diefenbaker in your car, you can have some bloody newspapermen."

Well, Dief arrived. The Memorial Hall was packed, loaded, standing room only. People came for miles. We couldn't even begin to serve them coffee or tea. George McTaggart had been renting the hall for a showing of new G.M. cars (he was a Liberal but he had agreed to let us use the hall for our meeting) and he had cleared out his cars except for one on the stage. I thought Dief would just walk around, shake a few hands, talk to a few people. He decided to speak. Luckily we had a microphone. Without warning, I had to make the introduction. It had been such a rush to get the meeting going that I hadn't had time to think properly, and I offered this as reason for stumbling a bit in my remarks. Dief responded, "Oh, don't worry about that, Jack," and went on to tell his story about once being introduced as Mr. Studebaker (using the car on the stage as a prop). He brought down the house. Who would have believed Mr. Diefenbaker could laugh at himself? For fifteen or twenty minutes that audience stood enthralled. Afterwards, this same Ernie Salt came up to me: "Jack, take me to your leader. I want to meet him. He's quite a guy. I never thought I'd ask, but I want to meet him."

In contrast, when Pearson's Agriculture minister, Harry Hays, came into the town of Trochu, which was considered a Liberal bastion in my constituency, everyone thought he was a joke. He told the people, "I don't care who you vote for. If you can't vote Liberal, vote against that fellow Horner. He's a curse in Ottawa." They just laughed. Thought it was pretty good that Harry had singled me out. He helped rather than hurt me. This was Pearson's problem: he didn't have any appeal in the West and he had no one in his cabinet who did.

During the campaign I spoke in Avonlea, Saskatchewan, for my friend Lawrence Watson who was seeking re-election in the riding of Assiniboia. Hazen Argue had held that seat for the CCF from 1949 until he switched to the Liberals in February 1962. Successful as a Liberal in the 1962 general election, he had been defeated by Lawrence in 1963. In 1965 all the pundits said that Lawrence was in trouble, that Hazen was the sure winner. Well, I spoke for Lawrence on a Saturday night. I was to make another speech in the southern part of his riding on Monday. The problem was that I was speaking to the converted; the people I spoke to on Saturday had long since decided to vote for Lawrence. I was wasting my time unless I could reach the uncommitted voters.

On Sunday morning, Lawrence showed me some old newspaper clippings on what Hazen Argue had said about Pearson prior to 1962.

"This is great stuff!" I told him. "What you ought to do is take a full-page ad. Put 'What does Hazen Argue think of Pearson?' in big bold headlines, and then just print a few of these."

Lawrence's wife objected. Well, we argued a bit. I didn't want to push them where they didn't want to go, and as we weren't campaigning that day, I thought I'd better get out of there. So I went to visit my brother Byron who lived in Regina. While we were watching football on TV, I told him my idea about the advertisement. He thought it was a good one.

"Who do we know with the Regina *Leader-Post?*" I asked him. "Isn't there a Wade around here?"

"Gerry Wade," Byron replied, "one of the Wade kids from Leask, about twenty miles down the road from where we grew up at Blaine Lake, not a bad fellow."

So I phoned Wade and told him my problem: "I know in the political game you have to print who's sponsoring the ad. Can I put 'The thinking citizens of Assiniboia'?"

He didn't know. This wasn't his end of the paper. He gave the name of the managing editor and suggested I ask him. I phoned the managing editor and explained the situation. He was ready to oblige. Although he was a Liberal, he didn't like Hazen Argue.

"Cost you four hundred and ninety-five dollars," he said. "You can put 'The thinking citizens of Assiniboia' if you like, but you'll have to give us a list of these thinking citizens in case there are any law suits. Otherwise, it's okay with me."

I told him that I didn't want the ad on any of the back pages. I wanted to buy a right-hand page. I wanted the person who opened that page to have read it before he could turn it over. He agreed. When I went back to Lawrence's that night, I told him what I'd done. Lawrence was all for it, but his wife still had doubts. Monday morning, Lawrence and I talked to his campaign manager. He thought it was one heck of a fine notion. It would really rock Argue.

"Don't worry about the money," I told Lawrence. "I'll put up the five hundred dollars. I like the idea so much, I'll put the damn thing in myself."

Finally, even Lawrence's wife agreed. We ran that ad a few days before the election in both the daily Regina *Leader-Post* and the *Assiniboia Times*, the local weekly.

Tuesday morning, I went back to my own riding. From what I heard, Hazen Argue hit the panic button when he saw Lawrence's ad. With good cause, as it turned out. Lawrence attributed his re-election (by a narrow 619 votes) to its effectiveness. And, to put a little icing on the cake, following the election, Dief, with no knowledge of who was responsible, told caucus that our advertisement in the *Leader-Post* was one of the smartest things he'd seen in the whole campaign. (I might mention that when I first ran as a Liberal in 1979, I expected someone to pull the same sort of thing on me, but no one did.)

It is a fact that once an election campaign begins, the candidate is so busy tending to the practical matters necessary to convince his constituents they ought to return him to Parliament that he loses touch with what is happening in the national campaign. Certainly, that's the way it was in 1965. I may have seen something in the paper that suggested all was not right at National Headquarters, but that was it. The problems that Eddie Goodman or Flora MacDonald may have been causing did not directly affect what was happening in Acadia. After the initial questions of how much money one was going to get and which nationally prominent politicians would come into the riding to help, contact with the national campaign managers was limited to the cartons of leaflets and flyers received from Ottawa, which were either useless or too late.

I once made the mistake of distributing, as a householder-mailing, a newspaper-type campaign piece sent out from headquarters. Its claims that we were winning everywhere were so extravagant it made me look foolish. Consequently, I began the practice of publishing my own newspaper a week or so before each election, setting out those things in which I believed. To give my constituents an idea of what I had taken an interest in during the past parliament, I would include the relevant portions of the indexes from Hansard. Thus, the voter could run his eyes down the list, year by year, of the debates in which Jack Horner had participated. It was a good thing to do. Also, I would buy an ad in each issue of the weekly papers, as large as I could afford — perhaps a quarter page. These didn't read "Elect Jack Horner" but "DID YOU KNOW?" In each one I would list four or five facts in which I thought people would be interested. This worked, and I felt comfortable with a campaign designed to inform the voters. They would look them up: "Well, what are we supposed to know this week?" This sort of thing was far more effective than material from headquarters.

I think it was in the '68 election that we burned literally barrels of material, the product of some eastern ad agency, containing favourable mention of Dalton Camp. I took one look and said, "This isn't going to my constituents." It only proved how far out of touch National Headquarters most often was with what was happening in the West. Dalton Camp had led one of the dirtiest political coups ever. Given the absence of guns, it was as bad as anything you might find in a banana republic. John Diefenbaker's leadership was destroyed. Yet it was expected that we, who had become Conservatives because of Dief and had remained loyal to the end, would simply forget what had happened.

But I'm anticipating. In 1965, Camp was still in the early stages of his step-by-step campaign to topple Dief. In Ottawa, with Pearson running a minority government, most western members didn't have time to pay much attention to what Camp was doing. We had the serious business of the nation to attend to. For example, the National Transportation Bill, legislation of vital importance to all Westerners, was brought before the House in the fall of 1966. In the Transportation Committee we would hear brief after brief on this — some three thousand pages of evidence in all. There is no question that my part in the transportation debate saw me come of age as a parliamentarian.

It was in September that the Conservative caucus met to decide how we would handle the bill. Alvin Hamilton took charge, aided by Ged Baldwin. Alvin explained that the bill "naturally divides into five parts." (Clearly it did: there was Part 1, Part 2, Part 3 . . . .) Listening to Hamilton and Baldwin as they began to allocate responsibility for each section, I knew that neither had studied the bill; they were going on their past knowledge. Alvin thought we should kick it around a bit, then let it pass without serious challenge. Gordon Fairweather agreed; said it looked like a good piece of legislation to him. Finally, I interjected, "It's a bad piece of legislation. I'm going to oppose it. I'll take responsibility for it all."

Transportation is a very difficult subject for the average person. If one asks a Westerner, "Why are you mad at the East?", a common reply is "Look what they've done to us in transportation." If one takes this a step further and asks, "How do freight rates affect you?", ninety-nine out of a hundred Westerners don't know, but they do know there's something wrong. Prior to this debate, I was like most people. However, I had done enough work to grasp the basics.

There are four kinds of freight rates: competitive rates, agreed charges, class rates, and non-competitive rates. The competitive rates pertain to most of the freight hauled where there is competition between railways, trucks, and water transportation. Thus, competitive rates apply mainly to central Canada. These aren't frozen, they are regulated by the market place. As for the agreed charges, they are rates negotiated between the shipper and the hauler. These give the hauler guaranteed volume and the shipper the lowest possible rate. Generally, only large companies generating a lot of traffic can obtain them. Of course, the big companies in Canada are mostly in Ontario and Quebec. In consequence, a furniture industry starting up in Calgary has difficulty competing with the furniture industry in central Canada. Agreed charges allow the eastern manufacturers to penetrate the western market. The western manufacturer, however, doesn't have the volume to negotiate a similar agreed charge. It is interesting to note that in the United States agreed charges are against the law. In Europe they have a different name for them, and there too they are outlawed. Canada is one of the few countries which permits agreed charges (to the benefit of central Canada).

As for class rates, they apply most often to very expensive goods on which the shipper is prepared to pay a premium to guarantee safe delivery. Only 4 or 5 per cent of railway traffic, however, involved class rates in 1966. The non-competitive rates, on the other hand, amounted to about 26 to 28 per cent of the traffic. These applied to the long hauls in and out of western Canada and in and out of the Maritimes, where there was no competition from trucks or water. Non-competitive and class rates had been frozen by Diefenbaker under the Freight Rates Reduction Act. Jack Pickersgill, as the Pearson government's Transport minister, was attempting to take off this freeze, which pleased the CPR. Further, he was going to give the CPR a study of the Crowsnest Pass rates to prove they were losing money, so as to justify a government subsidy in compensation. Finally, Pickersgill was going to diminish the power of the National Transportation Board by changing the right of a shipper to appeal a given freight rate under what was commonly referred to as "the captive shipper's clause". For all this, the CPR had agreed to pay municipal taxes on its land. Until this time, the CPR didn't pay the city of Winnipeg or Vancouver or any other municipal government taxes on the land built up around its right-of-way. So the deal was that, starting in 1967, the CPR would pay these taxes. But what the CPR lost to the cities and in new contracts with its employees, it would more than make up through the National Transportation Act.

On September 6, 1966, in my first speech on Bill C-231, I cast my net for support in caucus.* Having stressed that our policies should be fair and just, I spelled out the percentage of railway revenue derived from the four different types of freight rate, pointing out that class rates and non-competitive rates together accounted for 33 per cent of the railway's revenue. These two rates would be allowed to rise if the bill was passed — and it would be western Canada and the Maritimes that would bear the burden, since they were the regions where most commodities were shipped under these rates. Eighty per cent of the railway's increased revenue would come from western Canada and the Maritimes.

"The transportation policy was the Magna Carta of the West," I told the House, "and a basic reason for confederation in the Maritimes. This policy had a great deal to do with the uniting of Canada. What does this present bill do? It puts aside those historic facts and, to use a common expression, throws the Maritimes and the western part of Canada to the wolves."

I then moved on to the study which was to be made of the Crowsnest Pass rates: "I look at this particular clause of the bill and consider how it will affect me or any other member of the House in running an industry when we realize that within the next three years the government is going to have the commission make a study of that industry and ascertain how

*An excerpt from the speech is given in Appendix 3.

large a subsidy, if any, is to be paid after the three-year period has expired. I know what I would do. I would try to minimize my efficiency in the next three years. I would try to paint a picture of dire need of a subsidy as huge as I could logically expect to be paid. This clause is suggesting to the railways that they should be inefficient for the next three years and they will be compensated forever from that time onward. This clause should be taken out of the bill completely."

That evening, Alistair Fraser came up to me in the parliamentary restaurant. Before becoming clerk of the House of Commons, he had been Pickersgill's executive assistant, so I knew I was on the right road when he said, "Your speech this afternoon was a pleasure to hear. You really knew what you were talking about." If I needed assurance that I could handle the bill, this was it. To my surprise, Pic, in response to a subsequent speech, confirmed Fraser's judgement, noting my remarks as "one of the best speeches I have heard in the House on a very complicated subject."

Pic was obsessed with the idea that the transportation bill had to be passed by the end of 1966, and he threatened to keep us sitting through Christmas. In fact, we sat until December 21 and were called back January 9. In the continuation of the debate in January, I remained most concerned over what appeared to me to be the thin end of the wedge with regard to the Crowsnest Pass rates.

The Crowsnest Pass Agreement between the government and the CPR had been in effect, except for one brief period, since 1897; and in return for public subvention for the construction of the Crowsnest line it had provided substantial reductions in freight rates between central Canada and the prairies. In the bill we were debating, the provision for a new study was a ruse to cover the government's intention to abandon the Crow rates. There was no question in my mind about this. Gordon Churchill, seconded by myself, moved that the section providing for the study of the Crow rates be struck out. We were in Committee of the Whole studying this legislation clause by clause, and we wanted our troops there for the vote on this amendment. In Committee of the Whole, there are no bells. The members have to be there. (For normal votes in the House, the bells ring to summon MPs.) When it appeared that we would come to this vote on a Tuesday night, about five to ten, I talked it over until Wednesday.

In caucus on Wednesday morning, I used the oldest ploy in the book. I lamented that the eastern members of the Conservative party had done nothing for western Canada. I told them, "All I ask is one thing. Stick around for this vote. You don't have to say a word." I was to have the floor on Wednesday after the Question Period, and I promised that I would speak briefly, for maybe seven minutes. I said that I would outline about nine succinct points as to why we didn't want a study on the Crow rates. My assessment of the mood of the House was that, immediately following, there would be a vote on our amendment. All that the members of caucus had to do was to stand and be counted. They could then go about their business. They assured me they would stay.

Question Period passed fairly quickly. I spoke probably for nine minutes and made seven points, instead of the other way round. When I concluded, up jumped Tommy Douglas, in effect to reiterate what I had said. David Lewis was taking over the leadership of the NDP and, wanting to be on the safe side of motherhood in western Canada, he jumped up to repeat what Tommy had said. Our members were beginning to float away. Back of the curtains which separate the Opposition lobby from the Commons chamber, I urged them to wait. Our seats were pretty empty. Pickersgill and the government house leader George McIlraith were hollering, "Come on, let's vote, let's vote," thinking they had no problem. But Lewis kept talking. Finally he stopped. In Committee of the Whole, when the Speaker calls the vote, the Clerk of the House counts the members row by row. Consequently, there is a moment or two to step through the curtain. Lo and behold, when the smoke cleared, we had beaten the government fifty-nine to fifty-eight.

Pickersgill was beside himself. The next day he brought forward his own amendment, providing in essence that all statutory rates (which would have included the Crowsnest) be reviewed. The standing rule of the House is that once a matter has been decided, another vote cannot be taken on the same issue that session: certainly a very necessary rule. We got into an awful procedural argument on whether Pickersgill's amendment was in order. I put the issue clearly:

"Mr. Chairman, if I may add a word on a point of order . . . the committee has already voted on the question of a review of the Crowsnest Pass rates and has decided not to permit such a review. If the amendment before the committee is accepted as being in order, it could mean that an amendment could be proposed to it and the committee once again could vote on the very question it decided last Wednesday. If this happens, we can see that on other pieces of legislation there will be amendments to amendments to amendments, and votes on votes. In fact, this would destroy our parliamentary procedure in committee."

The Deputy Speaker, Herman Batten (Humber-St. George's) was in the chair. He said it was a difficult question, he wanted a day to consider it. Perhaps unfairly, I felt he would rule in favour of Pickersgill as both were Liberals representing Newfoundland constituencies. Consequently, I prepared myself fully for some wild outbursts against him. I didn't care if I was thrown out of the House. (As a point of explanation, a member is thrown out of the House if he fails to obey the Speaker.) I knew that if I said what I thought, I would be asked to withdraw my remarks. Well, I would refuse, and I would have to leave. I thought this a pretty good way to go. If I was thrown out fighting for the Crowsnest Pass rates, this would help the Conservative party. Conversely, it would damage the Liberals. And it would demonstrate fully to western Canada the Liberal intention to destroy the Crow rates.

The next day, as I expected, Deputy Speaker Batten ruled in favour of the government. Churchill appealed his ruling to the Speaker, at which point Batten left the chair. Until the Speaker was located, the House waited. Thus, my remarks were not recorded. So even though I accused Batten of rank partisanship, of being a tool of the government, I couldn't be thrown out because technically the House wasn't sitting.

In the meantime, I walked across the floor to talk to Pickersgill. By this time, he and I had become fairly good friends. We had fought tooth and nail, but instead of becoming lifelong enemies, we had developed a mutual respect. I laid a copy of his amendment on his desk. Pointing to it, I shook my finger, saying this would be in order if it said "all statutory rates except the Crow". (The press, observing this, wrote up the incident as: "Horner walks across the floor of the House to shake fist at Pickersgill.")

After about half an hour the Speaker took the chair. Realizing the gravity of the situation, he too wished a day to consider the question. We went on to an examination of other clauses — the captive shipper or whatever — while we waited, but we were in a state of suspended animation until we had his ruling. To our satisfaction, the following day he overruled his deputy and decided against the government. A momentous decision, a momentous victory! Churchill and I and a member by the name of Reg Cantelon (Kindersley), who had helped us carry the bill during this debate, were pretty happy. In fact, we were overjoyed. But these had been as tension-packed a three days as I can remember in Parliament.

It was then that Jimmy Walker (York Centre) came over to suggest I apologize to Deputy Speaker Batten, telling me that I had hurt Batten badly and that some of them on the other side had spent a difficult night with him. Batten was thinking of resigning. Jimmy was government whip at that time and a nice person. I wasn't much inclined to apologize. My remarks had not been made on the spur of the moment; I had come to the House fully prepared to make them. But Jimmy was persuasive. Finally, I said, "Well, Jimmy, I'm going to speak as soon as we get back to the business of the Transportation Act. Leave me alone for a while and I'll think about it." Well, there was no doubt that I could afford to apologize.

The Speaker, in his ruling, had offered reasons parallel to the arguments I had used in speaking against Pic's amendment. I was flattered that the law clerks of the House (who advise the Speaker on such rulings) and I had been thinking along the same lines. Nevertheless, I was not convinced I was wrong. Some people may be able to apologize when they don't feel they should. Not me. I grudgingly did as Jimmy asked, but it was a poor, backhanded effort: "Mr. Chairman, first of all I should like to say I was recorded yesterday as saying some words in the heat of the debate which I now wish I had not said. I do not deny having said them but I would like to apologize to you, having had my faith in democracy restored by what might be termed the Supreme Court's ruling on the case that was before the House. I should like you to know that the remarks I made were in the heat of battle and I would not like you to consider them to be as harsh as they sounded at the time. I should like to make that apology to you, Mr. Chairman."

Pickersgill immediately got to his feet to respond for the government side: "May I say, sir, how pleased I am by what the Honourable Member for Acadia said today. I think he has revealed to me and to a lot of us that in the consideration of this bill about which he felt very strongly and to which he has applied himself with great diligence — and I would say has had some influence on — he has revealed to us a new side and has gained stature and new respect in the House. We all do things in the heat of battle."

Jimmy Walker sent a note over to thank me. So did John Turner. Paul Martin, of course, was the most gracious in writing: "It is the mark of a true parliamentarian to be able to apologize in the House to a fellow member . . . " and on and on, but it was pretty nice. This was an important step in my development as a House of Commons man, and it gained me new respect in the House, with the Liberal party, the Speaker, the whole lot. The fact is, no matter what the issue, one has to go on living with the other members in the House. One has to go on asking them to listen. Apologizing to Batten was a necessary courtesy, whether I wanted to do it or not, and I didn't. Later, I was thankful Jimmy Walker had convinced me to make amends.

Along with my apology, I gave notice that there was one further small amendment I wanted to move and that I would then stand aside and let the bill pass. This amendment came about in a curious way. During the debate on the Crow rates, Bill Hussin, a representative of Canada Steamship Lines, had come to see me. He wanted me to take up his company's battle on the Transportation Act. I was rather brusque.

"Why are you coming to see me? My constituency hasn't got a finger in steamships."

"Oh," he said, "you have. I'm from Edmonton and we freight water, rail, and truck. Half of it is water, but we give an all-inclusive rate quite often and it affects freight rates in western Canada. This transportation bill is adversely affecting us."

It turned out that Diefenbaker's Freight Rate Reductions Act to roll back freight rates 17 per cent had used the wording "transportation companies". The new Transportation Act said that phasing-out subsidies would be paid to "railway companies". Well, the point was, did it mean transportation companies? Canada Steamship Lines weren't sure. They wanted that one word changed from "railway" to "transportation". At stake was some $400,000 per annum. It meant a lot to them. After Bill Hussin explained this to me, I said I'd take a look at it. But I was curious. Why had he come to see *me*?

"We were told you were the only one in the House that Pickersgill will listen to."

"With that kind of flattery I'll have to take a look."

Thus, when I apologized to the Deputy Speaker, I knew Pic would be amenable to a final request. And he was. He was most receptive. At five o'clock that afternoon, he called me over.

"Jack, here's the best we can do with your amendment. Will this accomplish it?"

I took a look. "Well, I think so, but I'll let you know at eight o'clock. I think you can have your bill tonight."

I showed Pic's proposal to Bill Hussin. He thought it would do the trick. I said, "It's the best I can get you. I would guess if they didn't pay you the subsidy now, you'd have a pretty good law case." I never so much as let Hussin buy me the dinner he wanted to, but of course we became good friends. I went back to the House at eight and told Pic it was okay. One of his foot soldiers moved it.

It was at this eleventh hour that Lawrence Kindt tried to get in on the act, realizing that I was making some headway and that, given redistribution, he might have to run against me for nomination in the new riding of Crowfoot. Consequently, he started to ask Pickersgill questions about this and that aspect of the bill. Pic responded with great patience until I sent him a note: "I promised you could get this Act through tonight, but if you keep on answering Kindt you're never going to get it through. For heaven's sake sit down." Pickersgill looked at the note, looked over at me, and made one of his great slouches into his seat, pretty nearly sliding out of sight, never to get up again no matter what Kindt said. It was most comical.

It had been quite a debate. In my experience, with the possible exception of the 1964 flag debate, I don't think there's been one to take up as much House of Commons time. It didn't solve the transportation problems of the West. I told them it wouldn't. One last point: the press coverage of the transportation debate was abysmal. When I had the government on the run, the press didn't know what I was doing. It was a complicated issue, and it would have caused some of them to do some work. As they didn't understand what was going on, they didn't report it. I took the opportunity in the last of my remarks to let them have it between the eyes:

"We in this House of Commons have been told time and time again by the news media that we should get down to work, that it is a terrible thing the way the members project their petty conditions, their petty jealousies, and fight for personal gain.... The bill before us was described by the Minister of Transport as the most important piece of legislation that this House will be dealing with this year. We have spent two weeks debating it here and we spent six weeks studying it in the Transport Committee. We moved seventy amendments in the committee and we have moved something like seven or eight amendments here during the last two weeks. Do you know what I heard on CTV news last Sunday evening? In a report on what was happening in Ottawa it was stated that Ottawa has been rather dull during the last two weeks, that not much has been happening but that the weeks ahead look good because there is a fight developing in the Conservative party over whether there should be an early or late leadership convention. Who is it who projects across the country the image of members not working? It is the vultures who sit up there....

"The vultures sit up there waiting to see whether or not a member is going to be in a dangerous position. Then they flock in and feast upon the bones. If we are all healthy and working, there is nothing sensational about which they can write so they circle high and stay away. They know nothing and care nothing about a parliament which is working. They want sensationalism to sell their newspapers and capture the imagination of the television and radio audiences. They have agitated the public and discredited the House of Commons all across Canada. They alone are responsible for the disrespect in which this House is held. It is high time that they educated themselves."

At the time, there was only one newsman in the gallery, a very good guy, Dave Davidson. He wrote this up in great style: HORNER CALLS PRESS VULTURES. Naturally, it got national attention. It was a good line, very true, very apt. The press, by and large, are a pretty shallow lot.

It was true, however, that throughout much of the transportation debate we had been involved in fighting a rearguard action against Dalton Camp's final assault on Dief's leadership. This had begun in May

74

1966, and it took the form of a demand for a leadership review. Inseparable from this issue was Camp's campaign for re-election as party president. Aided and abetted by the so-called Red Tory group of Flora MacDonald, David MacDonald, Gordon Fairweather, and the rest, with their strategic connections across Canada, Camp was able to dominate the National Executive and thus manipulate events to the advantage of the anti-Diefenbaker crusade. For example, had the annual meeting of the Conservative party been held in March 1966 as originally called for, instead of November, Camp could not have got his campaign off the ground. By the time those loyal to the Chief made any move to counter Camp, it was virtually too late. His gang had its men in place and all the corners covered.

Three or four weeks before the annual meeting in November, Gordon Churchill phoned and asked me to come over. Mike Starr was there. So was Donnie MacInnis (Cape Breton South).

Gordon said, "We've got to put up somebody against Dalton Camp. Mike's going to see Arthur Maloney. He's the one man we can rally the troops behind." I agreed.

Mike explained that he'd seen Arthur the previous week: "Arthur said he might consider it, but he wanted to know where the Horner boys and Donnie MacInnis stood."

Doc wasn't in town, but I pledged us both: "You've got the Horner boys. Get Arthur."

When Doc hit town at the first of the week, he asked, "What are we doing? Dief should retire."

"Sure," I said, "everybody says Dief should retire, but you and I know he's not going to, particularly when he's got a fight on his hands. Here's the story. We're trying to get Arthur Maloney to run against Camp, and I've assured him that the two Horners will be right behind him."

"You did the right thing," was Hugh's reaction. "No question. We can go with Arthur."

Before the 1966 annual meeting, Acadia had never been fully represented at a national convention. I certainly wanted a full contingent at this one as I knew it was going to be the roughest thing ever a man got into. So I called a meeting to choose delegates. Well, there was one person there who looked as if he was going to volunteer as a delegate, and I knew he definitely wouldn't support Dief. I jabbed one of the others in the ribs and suggested he nominate Lloyd Duncan. Lloyd wasn't keen. Said he didn't know enough about it.

I had a private meeting with him in the washroom. "Look, Duncan, I want you in Ottawa. I don't care whether you want to go or not. Go in there and say you will. I've got to have Diefenbaker supporters. I'm going down there to fight, and it's going to look sick if I have anti-Diefenbaker delegates coming from my own riding." Duncan got the message.

The convention was being held at the Chateau Laurier, and I got there Sunday morning. The excitement on Sunday was the National Executive meeting: Whose agenda would the annual meeting follow — the national director's or the national president's? Jimmy Johnston's or Dalton Camp's? Camp wanted the voting to take place on Tuesday afternoon, while Johnston recommended it should be on the last day, Wednesday, according to practice. I wasn't at the meeting, of course. I stood around outside and waited with the press. As soon as it was over, Terry Nugent came out and gave me the report. Terry told me that Bob Stanfield and John Robarts's representative Stanley Randall had sided with Camp against Jimmy Johnston, and that both were ready to oust Dief. Johnston had lost: the vote was to be on Tuesday. With it coming that early, I couldn't see how we could achieve anything. There wasn't enough time.

Nugent disagreed, "Don't worry. We can still beat them. Let's go to town." We really did. Lloyd Duncan had come to the convention, just as he said he would. He was a big fellow, not quite as tall as me but a little thicker in the shoulders. When we paraded around that convention, anybody who wanted to mix it with me looked over my shoulder and saw Lloyd. We bluffed our way through an awful lot. But it was a heavy go!

There was no use spending much time with the western delegates because they were either solidly for Dief or solidly against him. You couldn't budge them. So I spent a lot of time with the Youth and Ontario delegates. We were into some great arguments. I remember one group of Torontonians telling me, "We don't care if we lose two seats in the West for every one seat we gain in Toronto. It'll be worth it." I was infuriated. We were walking down the hotel corridor towards the elevators at the time. There were about six of them.

I said, "I'm worth six of you."

They thought I wanted to fight.

I was willing. "I'll take you one at a time if you think you're so smart!"

Just then, I looked over my shoulder and there were three elderly ladies, delegates from Lethbridge, one head on top of the other, looking around the corner. I recognized them and apologized. By this time, the hotel had sent a man up to quiet us.

The next day I saw the three ladies again. "Oh," they said, "Mr. Horner, you were terrific! We just wish one of those fellows had taken you on."

In the meantime, we argued and we argued. Camp had recently made a speech on Canada's defence role. His views didn't make an ounce of sense. In the House of Commons we had just concluded the long debate on armed forces unification. We had nearly defeated the government when Edgar Benson, the Finance minister, appeared to run out of Supply. Thus, I was well acquainted with the various defence arguments. I kept asking the young delegates, "Why are you voting for Camp? We stumped the government in the defence debate, but if we'd taken Camp's line we wouldn't have done anything. For heaven's sake, aren't you proud of the way we've been fighting?" In fact, most of the delegates were proud of the show we were putting on in the House.

We were making progress in wearing away Camp's support, despite his infamy on Monday night, November 14, in the ballroom of the Chateau Laurier — a night I'll never forget should I live to be a thousand. Carried live to the Canadian people via the broadcast facilities of CBC and CTV, the national leader of the Conservative party, Leader of Her Majesty's Loyal Opposition, the Rt. Hon. John G. Diefenbaker, was subjected to the humiliation of his life. It was a scene that literally made me ill. I wasn't seated inside with the rest. I was too nervous and upset by what was happening. I was sitting in the corridor nearly parallel to the stage, watching the audience, trying to get a reading on where the bad apples were and who was organizing them. The Harkness crowd was right down in front. Pat Nowlan was over on the side, making a lot of noise. Jean Wadds, Earl Rowe's daughter and MP for Grenville-Dundas, was there; a fellow by the name of Al Heisey; and of course the bunch from Toronto. These people sat and booed and heckled Dief as he tried to make his speech.

Dief believed in his powers of persuasion, in touching the hearts of his audience. This had always stood him in good stead. Somehow or other he believed he'd rise to the challenge again. Granted, his powers had faded a little, but in normal circumstances they would have been good enough. In these circumstances, they weren't. He had to reach for his audience and he didn't do very well. He spoke for longer than he should. The crowd became increasingly noisy and insulting.

I looked around and saw people going by me with drinks. This was too much! I went to find out what in the world, and sure enough there was an open bar at the back of the ballroom.

"Who gave you permission to open?" I asked the bartender.

"The manager."

"That's the leader of this party up there speaking. I think it would be only polite if you shut down."

He looked at me. "Who are you?"

"I'm Jack Horner. Now, you take those tablecloths and you cover up those glasses and put that liquor stand below the table, or I'll do it for you. And if you don't like it, go tell your manager Jack Horner's shutting down your bar." He did both, and the bar stayed closed until Mr. Diefenbaker finished speaking.

The entire affair was soul-destroying: the planned annihilation of the man who had brought our party out of twenty-two years in the political wilderness. I felt that, sure, Dief was getting old, but we all owed him more than this.

Somewhere in the midst of all this I had to prepare the program for the western members' luncheon on the Tuesday. Ernie Pascoe, member from Moose Jaw, was helping me. I had lined up a group of entertaining speakers for the head table, someone from each western province representing a particular industry to show that there was more to the West than cowboys, Indians, and wheat. Following the outrageous treatment of Dief on Monday night, everyone began to back out: "Look Jack, I don't feel up to it." "I'm sick." "What they're doing to Dief, I can't participate." Warner Jorgenson, one of the greatest storytellers ever to hit the House of Commons, told me he just couldn't carry on. I finally shored him up and kept him there. Then Davie Pugh backed out. Davie was from B.C., a great Conservative, a great Diefenbaker supporter. Finally, Ernie Pascoe came to me and told me he was through.

"Ernie, you can't!" I said.

Well, he wanted me to get Diefenbaker to come to the luncheon.

"There's no way I can get Diefenbaker," I said. "He doesn't come to the western luncheons at these conventions because he believes he's not a western MP. He's the leader. He's MP for all of Canada. If he came, then he'd have to go to the Quebec dinner and the Ontario breakfast and the Atlantic provinces' fish bar. You're asking the impossible."

"Jack, you've got to phone him."

So I phoned Dief. Of course, he explained why he couldn't attend — exactly as I'd told Ernie. This was about eleven o'clock on Tuesday morning. Dief was really low and he had every reason to be.

"Well, Jack, I guess we're going to lose and lose badly," he said.

I disagreed. "No, it's not going to be that bad. Camp might get re-elected president, but it's going to be mighty close."

Dief didn't think so. He thought it was going to be terrible.

Searching for something to cheer him up, I said, "Just remember, Mr. Diefenbaker, we may lose the battle on the plains, but we'll cut them off at the pass." He laughed, thought that was pretty good.

The election for president came at two-thirty that afternoon. Camp won; Maloney lost. Thus, Dief lost. But the difference was only thirty-two ballots! The rest of the votes during the meeting were largely automatic and anticlimactic, including the one on leadership review.

Word quickly came from Gordon Churchill to meet in Eric Winkler's office. Eric was the whip. Gordon had called together those loyal to Dief to swear allegiance to our leader. Gordon's strategy was that the elected members would run the party the way we wanted, and to heck with Camp as president. The problem was that if taken to its logical end, we would have had two Conservative parties. In which case, we ought not to have attended the annual meeting nor engaged in the dispute over Camp's call for a leadership convention. Eventually, we had to accept that Camp was going to have a leadership race whether we liked it or not. Unfortunately, caucus members most often are too busy with House of Commons work to handle the machinery of a national political party.

Camp and his followers believed that the main direction of the party should be determined outside of caucus by the non-elected Conservative establishment. As far as they were concerned, any donkey could get elected. One of the Camp crowd actually stated, "If the jackass MPs could only keep their mouths shut during an election, we'd have a better chance of re-electing them." Somehow, they actually believed the national party organization got MPs elected. The rise of Dalton Camp as president and his attempt to diminish the influence of the caucus had begun a running battle from about 1964. It was still going on when I left the party in 1977.

Of course, the advice of the rank and file of caucus never seemed to be sought on anything. From time to time, I had as many as six MPs living at my house in Ottawa (there was plenty of room and the fellows enjoyed rent-free accommodation), and many a discussion took place there, the products of which could have been some value. But as there was no established channel to the top and as Dief appeared decreasingly interested in anything that couldn't be hit on a high emotional plane, we tended to stand back and watch, rather than participating. I began to realize that this was not the way to do things. If I had a view I thought worth while, it was up to me to bring it to the fore. Consequently, I was making myself heard as never before — in caucus, in the House, and at conventions.

Over the 1966 Christmas recess, I sat at home wondering what I was going to do about the leadership race. Recognizing that there was going to be one — just as sure as guns, no matter what I or anyone else liked — early in January I stopped in Toronto to talk to Arthur Maloney. Arthur was a likeable person and I could trust him far more than any person I knew from Ontario. Also, he was bilingual. As Dief was from the West, the next leader might well come from Ontario. I decided to see if Arthur would allow his name to stand. He didn't turn me down absolutely, but there was no way I could entirely convince him. Back in Ottawa, the thought still plagued me, and one afternoon I took a few minutes to see Mr. Diefenbaker. We had always enjoyed a good relationship. In a sense, it was a rare relationship. If I went about it with a certain amount of tact, I could tell him things he didn't want to hear and still escape with my hide, to be welcomed back the next day. He more or less came to expect my straight approaches. From time to time, he even sought them out, hoping of course that they were favourable to his point of view, and most often they were.

Anyway, I went in to see Dief. To get him in the right frame of mind, I said, "During the last convention, Mr. Diefenbaker, I was terribly hurt. When you got hurt, I got hurt. But I guess whether we like it or not, this guy Camp is going to have a leadership convention."

Well, Dief refused to think about it.

I continued, "Remember when I said, 'We may lose the battle on the plains, but we'll cut them off at the pass'?"

Yes, he remembered. "What have you got in mind? Get to it."

"Just a minute. We lost the battle on the plains. Now we have to make certain we're ready to slaughter them at the pass. First, however, we've got to do some planning. If we don't, they might take some other pass; we might miss them."

"What are you getting at?"

"First, let's agree there's going to be a leadership race. Second, I don't want to see you hurt again because it hurts me too much. I don't think you should run because they'll cut you down."

Dief was becoming a little impatient. "Who have you got in mind? Out with it! Let's hear it."

"Just let me tell my story the way I want to," I answered. "If we all get behind one person right now, and if you support this person, Mike Starr and Alvin Hamilton will follow you. Then we can begin the groundwork."

"Who have you got in mind? Who have you got in mind?"

Finally, I had to admit I had Arthur Maloney in mind.

Dief cut me dead. "I talked to Maloney yesterday and under no circumstances will he allow his name to stand."

I stared at Dief. "Are you sure?"

"Are you questioning my word?"

"No sir," I said, and got the heck out of there as quickly as possible. I went up to Hugh's office. I thought I'd at least accomplished something by telling Dief he shouldn't run. When I told Hugh about the conversation, he said I was lucky to get out of there with my skin.

"Where are you going now?" he asked.

"Back to my office to phone Arthur."

"Then you don't believe Dief?"

"Oh yes, I believe Dief, but I also believe in my strong powers of persuasion."

But Arthur was through with politics. Although he didn't say so, I believe his reasons were those of family and that the outcome of the convention had nothing to do with his decision. But it was too bad he wouldn't run. Had we been able to get behind Arthur, we would have beaten Camp in 1967.

During 1967, as the leadership question built up, my brother Hugh briefly considered running. Very dissatisfied with his lot in Ottawa (he wasn't working nearly as hard as I was), he had gone back to a fairly heavy medical practice in Barrhead. He told me that he had to quit either politics or medicine. And if he was going to quit medicine, it had to be for something more than being a back-bencher in Ottawa. It was this kind of thinking that prompted him to enter the leadership race on the spur of the moment — and certainly without my advice. I tried to help him, but he soon changed his mind, realizing that he had a third option: provincial politics. Lougheed had talked to him and wanted him in the worst way: Hugh had the sort of political experience and credibility that Lougheed needed if he was going to pose as a reasonable alternative to Manning. So Hugh quit federal politics in May 1967 and ran in the provincial riding of Lac Ste. Anne. It was a brave stroke of business because only six Conservatives were elected, and Hugh was the only one outside Calgary and Edmonton.

As Hugh was out of the race, there was no question where my loyalties lay. I supported none of the declared candidates. I was committed to supporting Dief, and until he declared himself one way or the other there was nothing I could do. It was with a pretty jaundiced eye that I watched Camp form his policy committee and call his "thinkers' conference". Lo and behold, if I didn't receive an invitation to attend the Montmorency meeting in August. I went, prepared to watch carefully what was happening.

Maison Montmorency was an old Dominican retreat and the beds were terrible. But as it was completely separated from the "whirly burly" of the city, one was isolated and could think; Montmorency Falls were the only outside attraction. This was my first chance to participate in a so-called "thinkers' conference", thus I was alert to what was happening around me. For example, it was here that I heard first mention of the guaranteed annual income concept within the party. This was rampant socialism, appropriate to the NDP, not the Conservatives. This kind of thinking became increasingly prevalent in some party circles around Ottawa and of course it spilled over to the Liberal side to be advanced by

Marc Lalonde a time or two in the years ahead. After Montmorency, my antennae were up and I was prepared to fight this wherever it appeared.

At Montmorency, I met Richard Rohmer for the first time, heard about his plans for the development of the subarctic reaches of Canada — his so-called mid-Canada line — and had a chance to discuss this with him. His was the impractical dream of someone working in an air-conditioned office in Toronto. Academic and theoretical, it did not answer the practical questions of how one got the people up there, how one provided the envisioned services, who would do the work. In discussing it with him, I could see he had spent a great deal of time in developing the concept but that it wouldn't work in practical application at all. I think I told him so.

The other interesting person who came to my attention was Marcel Faribault. He was the instigator of the "two founding races" or *"deux nations"* theory of Confederation which later was to prove a curse to poor Stanfield. Faribault was a big man, with a commanding presence. He looked just like the wealthy financier from St. James Street in Montreal that he claimed to be. He spoke very passionately of the desires of French Canada as he argued his case. Dick Bell (Carleton), who apparently had known him before, and Faribault got into a fierce shouting match during one committee meeting. Mary Southern, a lawyer from Vancouver, attempted to take Bell's argument and make some sense out of it, to put it forward in a manner in which it might be debated. But this was a waste of time. Faribault was the chosen one of the party outside caucus; *deux nations* was adopted because there was no way in which it could be stopped. An interesting exercise to witness!

There was no question that Dalton Camp was the dominant figure at Montmorency. A keynote speaker, he participated fully in every important discussion. Odd as it may seem, very few of the leadership aspirants made their presence felt at all. Duff Roblin came up, and Alvin Hamilton was there, but none of the others made any more than a guest appearance. They were too busy campaigning across the country. So far as I could see, the whole conference was orchestrated by Camp and company to impose certain policy ideas upon the party. It was a clever bit of planning. Montmorency, in effect, was to be the Conservative policy conference, the decisions from which were merely to be endorsed by the policy workshops at the leadership convention. I was there because I was becoming recognized as someone who spoke out. If they encompassed me, they could smother me. Besides, they needed a token agriculturist. Jack McIntosh (Swift Current–Maple Creek), as tough a nut to crack as any there was, had also to be silenced. If they brought in people like McIntosh and Horner, they would be able to say, "Look, this all took place at Montmorency and those fellows agreed." A great stroke of strategy!

Frankly, I was unaware of the significance of the Montmorency Conference until I arrived at the Leadership Conference in Toronto in early September. Had I realized at the time that these position papers were automatically to become the policies of the Conservative party, I would have been alarmed. Contrary to Camp's belief, the members of caucus are the salesmen of party policy. It has always been my contention that the salesmen know best how to package the product; they know best how to sell it and best what should be in it. Therefore, the salesmen should have a major say in its development. At Montmorency there was a mere sprinkling from caucus. This didn't fit my concept of how the party should function. It was one more demonstration of the conflict between the elected and the non-elected branches of the party. Once more, I became convinced I was on the right side of this argument. I used to complain that NDP policies were devised by the labour unions — and here was the Conservative party on a parallel course.

Not realizing that my attendance at Montmorency automatically made me a policy delegate at the leadership convention, I was in no rush to get to Toronto. I arrived Wednesday morning. I was still in plenty of time to vote, but as I didn't know what the Chief was going to do, I didn't really want to become involved with any of the other candidates. Consequently, I missed Stanfield's supposedly good speech on Tuesday night. As well, I missed any participation in the early policy discussions. To my surprise, when I registered, I was given a special button as a policy committee member. Delegates from my constituency had been looking for me, anxious to see me get to work in some of these sessions, particularly on *deux nations* and welfare. I was, however, too late for the debate on *deux nations*.

On Wednesday evening, I went up to see Mr. Diefenbaker in his suite at the Royal York, just to check in, to tell him I was in town, see how he was doing, and so on. He had still made no decision and didn't know what he was going to do. When I went to see him the following day, much to my surprise there were hosts of people trying to get in to see him: newsmen, cameras, the whole bit. I was recognized as a friend by his assistants, Tom Van Dusen and Greg Guthrie, who ushered me in to see the Chief through an adjoining room. There was a great discussion going on over whether or not Dief should run. Most were telling him, "Yes, certainly." When Olive brought my presence to his attention, Dief parted the men around him.

"Well, here's the great Jack Horner. He'll tell us the facts of life. What should I do? What do you think? Should I get into this race?"

"Mr. Diefenbaker," I replied, "the people have come to choose a new leader, not reinstate an old one."

"You told me that last January. Go down and talk to the delegates. Find out. I don't think you've talked to them enough."

"I'll go down and talk to the people, but I'm absolutely certain the opinions I come up with will be the same. If you were going to run, you should have advertised the fact long ago. Then the delegates could have come with this in mind."

He didn't like that! When I left, I was thoroughly annoyed with those around Dief for urging him to run. I firmly resolved that I wouldn't be a party to it. He was bound to lose and get hurt. I did mix with a few of the delegates, however, to confirm my assessment of his situation. Nominations closed the following morning. I deliberately stayed in bed until they had.

The only time I had met Robert Stanfield before the convention was when he was supporting Dalton Camp at the 1966 annual meeting. Arthur Maloney, of all people, had introduced us. I was completely unimpressed. Not wanting to judge Stanfield by this alone, I watched him carefully in Toronto. He looked like an honest broker. He didn't look like a Camp product, which is what made him appealing to a lot of people. The Nova Scotia members were solidly behind him. I remember taking a Stanfield badge off Bob Coates's shirt and then putting it back on.

Coates asked, "What are you doing that for?"

"I want to see who's behind this."

"Oh no, Jack, you don't have to worry about that."

"Yes I do!"

I went to the Stanfield reception Wednesday night. I saw nothing to convince me. I couldn't share the enthusiasm of his supporters at all.

In the voting on Saturday, I supported Dief on the first two votes. Then I gave George Hees a vote because I hadn't been impressed with Duff Roblin. Hees didn't move, in fact he went down. My last two votes went to Roblin. The main thing I learned from the whole exercise was that if the House of Commons people — Hees, Fulton, Hamilton, Starr — had come together as one, they would have been high enough on the first ballot to be in a possible place to win. Instead, they spread their support and left the final round to Roblin and Stanfield. It would have been good to see Stanfield beaten because he was the choice of Dalton Camp.

It was a shame Camp had divided the party so thoroughly, so strongly, so bitterly. I've said many times that he wasn't a bad person. He was clever, a good writer. But what motivated him in politics? Many an advertising executive has been drawn into political activity on one side or another by the lure of the largest single source of political patronage in Canada: $60 million spent each year by the federal government on advertising. The first contracts to change with a new government are those involving advertising. Fifteen per cent off the top to process copy prepared by government information officers is a handsome reward for political involvement. But one has to be on the winning side. Camp and company were convinced that Dief had to go, and they made this certain at the annual meeting in November '66. This does not explain, however, Camp's decision to back Stanfield for the leadership.

There is no question that Camp packaged Stanfield well. The life-sized picture of Stanfield striding forward, with the people all following him, was a great image. By all reports, the Tuesday night speech Stanfield made to the delegates in the Royal York Hotel, written by Camp, was an excellent Kennedy-type speech. But Camp sold the convention a bill of goods, an impossible leader. Because of the effect J. F. K. had had on the style of democratic politics, the world was going to youth. The boyish appearance, the hair, the look-you-in-the-eye direct approach, the highly articulate, clear, brief speaking-style — these were the attributes of a political winner. Stanfield looked ten years older than he was; he had a hunched back, one bad eye, was bald; and he hummed, hawed, and nearly stuttered when confronted. Why did Camp, this great political mastermind, do this to us?

4/Stanfield

I was not very happy when Leola and I left Toronto for the ranch following the leadership convention. My judgement of Stanfield was not then as harsh as it would become. Yet, hard as I tried, I couldn't see anything in him. He just didn't look like a winner. I recognized I might be wrong, that possibly the best man had won, although I doubted this. I was prepared to watch him as leader and change my mind if the evidence warranted it, though I was not convinced I wanted to work for him. More important, I didn't know if Stanfield wanted me. If he didn't, I could save myself a messy fight with Lawrence Kindt over the Crowfoot nomination.

Under redistribution, both the ridings of Acadia and Macleod were to disappear. About 21,000 from my riding and an equal number from Kindt's, plus some from Bud Olson's Medicine Hat and Eldon Woolliams's Bow River riding, had been combined to create the new riding of Crowfoot. Lawrence Kindt had as much claim to the Conservative nomination as I did, and he really wanted it. He was working hard for it, too. The poor guy had a doctorate in economics but had knocked around, never really finding his niche until he became an MP. It was the best job he'd ever had. He didn't want or expect to be a cabinet minister; he just wanted to be an MP. Running against another sitting member for nomination is never pleasant. I was building a new house at the ranch, which was taking far longer to complete than I expected. I thought maybe this was as good a time as any to back out of politics.

I might add that while I had never had much time for Kindt, Diefenbaker was really mean to him. In front of a whole group of people, who understood exactly what was happening, Dief would build him up: "Doctor, you've studied the economics of this. You were working with the United States Department of. . . ." (He'd sort of run Kindt's own boasts back at him.) "You know how this should be done. Give me some notes. Write out some plans on this, what a program should include." It was cruel, but Lawrence never caught on. He would go away, happy as a lark, work out a great song and dance. I knew darned well Dief wasn't going to look at it. Chucked it in the waste paper basket most likely. No more wanted to hear from Kindt than fly to the moon. For the rest of us sitting around, it was difficult to hold straight faces.

Anyway, the Crowfoot nomination convention was set for

November 4. I came back to Ottawa, still undecided whether I would run. I flew all night. Just after I arrived at my office, Admiral Brock dropped by to say hello. Geoff Brock had been the great lobbyist against Hellyer's unification of the armed forces that year. Heavens, there was one five-day period in that debate when, at Brock's urging, I made a speech every day, arguing in one — if I recall aright — against the purchase of the CF-5 airplane (which the government eventually bought and which turned out to be a dud). Brock, among other things, was a staunch Stanfield supporter, and I thought I'd seize the opportunity presented by his unexpected visit to see what Stanfield was made of.

"Well, what has the professional lobbyist got on his mind today?" I asked. "You should be happy as a lark. Your man won, mine didn't. Is he the best man?"

"Oh yes," Brock answered, "he is."

I said I wasn't so sure. I then told him of the redistribution of the ridings and the contest with Kindt — that I had come out for Roblin in the leadership race, that Stanfield didn't impress me at all, and that I had thought it all over and decided not to contest the nomination.

"Let Kindt have the darned riding. My wife certainly wants me at home. I'd get back to ranching, something I know I can do and love."

"You can't do that," said Brock. "You've got all kinds of ability. Parliament needs people like you."

"That's all well and good," I replied, "but it doesn't win me the nomination. Besides, I don't know whether Stanfield wants me around. Maybe I'd get in his hair." I knew Brock would go immediately to see Stanfield.

At noon hour I lay down on the chesterfield and switched out the lights. I was tired after flying all night and thought I'd catch a little sleep. I had just got settled when there came a knock at the door. In came Stanfield.

"No, no, lie there," he said.

I jumped up.

"Oh, don't bother putting on your shoes."

I put on my shoes. "Well, Mr. Stanfield, I appreciate your coming to see me."

He explained that Geoff Brock had been in to see him, so I gave him the full story.

Stanfield said, "That's why I'm here, Jack. I know about you. You're a pretty tough customer, but I don't want all yes-men around me. I have to have someone to tell me what it's like and how it is. I want you to seek that nomination. We'll have to do something for Kindt, but I want you to be the member for Crowfoot."

"Mr. Stanfield, that's certainly good to hear," I replied. "Yes, I can take another look at it." I was flattered by his concern. I told him I hadn't supported him for leadership, that I had supported Roblin, but that the best man probably had won, and so on. We seemed to be off to a very good start. We had one further meeting about my nomination, at which he told me that Kindt wanted a guaranteed Senate appointment to drop out of the Crowfoot race. If we formed a government, Stanfield was prepared to do something for Kindt, but not a seat on the Senate. By this time my spirits had returned. I told him not to worry, I would beat Kindt.

In his campaign against me, Kindt committed what proved to be a tactical error. He blanketed the constituency with notices on what a great man he was, how he had started the first farmers' union in Alberta, how he'd worked for the U.S. Department of Agriculture, how he'd written the Wheat Board Act. . . . A lot of my friends and neighbours, who normally didn't take a interest in politics, started to phone.

"Jack, this guy is good. You're in real trouble. What are you going to do? What can we do to help?"

"Be in Brooks November the fourth. We've got to have bodies, lots of them. Bring a car-full."

In addition, I invited Duff Roblin to be guest speaker, and this helped draw a crowd. About seven hundred showed up, over five hundred of whom were entitled to vote. When I walked into the hall in Brooks, I knew Kindt didn't have a chance. I beat him three to one.

I felt I had well earned my rest that Christmas; 1967 had been an event-packed year — the transportation debate, the Bank Act, armed forces unification, Montmorency, the Leadership Conference, and finally my own nomination. But I suppose I had grown in political experience and stature through it all.

In February 1968 I was travelling in the Maritimes along with the others on the Transportation Committee. It was on February 19 that we crossed from New Brunswick to Prince Edward Island. Due to misinformation, by the time we arrived to catch the ferry it had been waiting nine hours just for us. There was a line-up of traffic miles long; some of the vehicles had been there for as much as twenty-four hours, including a bus full of high school basketball players, without food. We just wheeled by — the House of Commons Committee — straight onto the ferry. As we got out of our little bus, the people on board actually booed us. Were they mad! None of us had a clue as to why. (In order to avoid any conflict with his constituents, Heath Macquarrie, one of the P.E.I. members, spent the entire crossing secreted in the men's washroom.)

I sized up a couple of angry-looking truck drivers and asked, "What's going on?" They were not bashful in telling me. I said, "Look, you ever take your truck to the mechanic and have her purr like a kitten, and ten miles down the road have her start to act up again? Well, you're fortunate. She's acting up now, and you've got the mechanic right here. This is the Transportation Committee. We'll be able to study the situation properly."

On the P.E.I. side, the snowplough had been down from Charlottetown to clear the road especially for us, but there was just one cut through a six-foot wall of snow. First off the ferry, we stopped to check the state of communications between the island terminus and the mainland; we thus found ourselves behind a large transport truck — which jack-knifed, blocking the road. We sat there for seven hours in our bus. I never saw so much snow in my life. Luckily a few of the boys had brought along a little refreshment! Finally, we arrived in Charlottetown, checked into our hotel — to be told the government was defeated. This must have been about three o'clock in the morning of February 20. We'd all been asleep on the bus. Everyone stared in disbelief and said it couldn't have happened; but it had.

Before going to bed I met with the leading Liberals on the committee. They had been in touch with Ottawa to confirm what had happened. Apparently, the government had been defeated on a tax bill. Pearson was out of the country and many of his ministers had been away campaigning for their party's leadership; little Reynold Rapp the Conservative whip (whom most of the hot shots around Stanfield thought was no good at all) had done a major stroke of business in keeping our troops in there, and we'd defeated the government on a recorded vote. No one on the Transportation Committee, Liberal or Conservative, had any doubt that we were into an election. A Department of Transport Viscount was laid on to pick us up at 8 A.M.

Back in Ottawa, we had caucus that afternoon. Stanfield told us the facts but really didn't say what he was going to do. There was, however, an inkling in his remarks that he would let Pearson off the hook. I was pretty tired, I suppose, but I immediately got up.

"If you've beaten them, then take over! This isn't a boxing match when you stand back and let the fella up so you can hit him again. You're fighting for keeps. You get them down and you kick them."

"Yes, and with hobnailed boots to boot!" bellowed Donnie MacInnis from the back of the room.

Stanfield thought he would have to discuss the problem with Pearson: "We have to be patient, we have to see." He and Pearson had developed quite a relationship by this time. It was an odd thing to witness. Diefenbaker could always put the hex on Pearson, and Pearson returned the favour with Stanfield. In the first vote of confidence after

Stanfield entered the House, he was paired with Pearson and couldn't vote. (Pairing is a convention whereby a government member due to be absent will arrange [pair] with an Opposition member, or vice versa, not to vote. This prevents the numerical balance of the House from being upset.) We forgave Stanfield, thought he didn't know any better, but none of us could have imagined Diefenbaker pairing with anyone. For heaven's sake, Dief wouldn't have paired with the whole Liberal party!

We caucused every day. Stanfield got worse instead of better. It became obvious he was going to give in. Apparently, Pearson had Stanfield talk to Louis Rasminsky, the governor of the Bank of Canada, and, I suppose, to a number of other people. They convinced him that it would be disastrous for the Canadian economy, that a serious run on the dollar would result, if the government were to be defeated and an election called. Stanfield erred greatly in not taking this argument to caucus to let us shoot it down. He told us nothing. He owed it to caucus to tell what he knew. (And, if this information was given him in secret as a privy councillor, he erred in accepting it.) Pearson suckered him! I spoke in caucus every day. I remember saying, "You people think you've the right to govern. You think that because Pearson and his government have collapsed, you're automatically going to win whenever an election is called. Well, the Liberals are going to have a leadership convention in April and a fellow by the name of Trudeau is going to be their new leader. He will go to the people immediately. You will not win. He will. Take your government now." But I couldn't convince Stanfield.

Pearson went on national television. Stanfield should have gone on before him to tell the nation the significance of the government's defeat on the tax bill, to explain how our parliamentary system works. Pearson had but two legitimate choices: to advise the Governor General to dissolve Parliament and call an election, or to advise that the Governor General ask someone else within the Liberal party to form a government. But Stanfield gave Pearson a third option.

Thursday night, February 26, Gordon Churchill told me he was going to resign.

"You can't, Gordon!"

"I can. The party's never going to fight under Stanfield, and I refuse to belong to a party that won't fight."

"You're judging Stanfield too early," I argued. "He's going to fight, he's going to stand."

"No, he isn't."

"Why don't you tell Stanfield you're going to quit unless he stands and fights?"

Gordon refused. "I will not resort to blackmail."

I told him I'd resort to almost anything to win this battle. "Will you at least hold your decision until after caucus tomorrow?" I asked.

He agreed. "The House doesn't sit until after caucus anyway, and that's where I'm going to make my announcement."

The next day I went a terrible hard lick at Stanfield, urging him to stand, to tell Pearson he was finished. I deliberately tried to provoke him. Stanfield became a little angry and took a pretty fair verbal roundhouse or two at me. I was so surprised, all I could say was, "Well, Mr. Stanfield, you're good when you're mad. You ought to get mad more often." The net result, of course, was that Gordon was right, Stanfield never fought. Pearson was allowed to save his government, and constitutional practice affecting responsible government in Canada was sacrificed to political ineptness on our side and to expediency on Pearson's. My interest in Stanfield as leader went all the way down to ziltch, never to recover.

I made a last-ditch play to convince Gordon Churchill to stay. We needed him. He was a pillar of strength. But it was no use. At 2 P.M. that day he moved to sit as an Independent Conservative. No one seemed to appreciate the loss of the best House of Commons strategist around, a man who had proved time and again his effectiveness as a hard-nosed poker player in the difficult job of house leader. Stanfield and his advisers were almost jubilant at Gordon's leaving; and, to the press, Churchill was just one of the hard-line Diefenbaker crew who had outstayed his time. It was a shock to discover how small a ripple his resignation made on the surface of the party. When Jack McIntosh threatened to leave with Gordon, only a lot of talking on my part kept him back. (I might add that if Joe Clark had had a Gordon Churchill as house leader, the 1980 election would never have happened.)

It was to become quite common to hear otherwise intelligent people say, "Bob Stanfield may be hard to get elected, but he'd be a good prime minister." Repeatedly I responded, "No he wouldn't. He'd be a poor prime minister. The man can't make decisions. He can't see down the road. To be prime minister, to be a leader, one has to be able to look ahead and judge the effects of any action." Dief, for all his faults, had a vivid imagination. He could see quickly where a decision or policy was likely to lead. It didn't take him a minute. But not Stanfield. He might have been able to get by in Nova Scotia, but it was a good thing he didn't become prime minister of Canada — though I certainly never stopped him from succeeding. In fact, I tried to help him, the dumb cluck!

When looked at coldly and objectively, Stanfield was snookered from the beginning. The first vote of confidence told the story. I've curled a lot, played a lot of other games. In curling, if your opponents think they're going to lose, you've got the advantage right off the bat. I've established a pretty good name in the bonspiels around here, and when anyone comes up against Horner, they know they're in for a pretty tough match. I have the advantage if they haven't ever beaten me. It was the same with Diefenbaker and Pearson in the House. Pearson knew Dief could beat him. Dief had the advantage. He just had to point his finger, and Pearson quivered. Stanfield, on the other hand, came in not knowing anything about the antagonistic game of politics in Ottawa. Right off the bat, Pearson got the jump on him. He invites Stanfield in for lunch and a nice quiet chat about all the difficulties Dief had caused in Parliament and how Stanfield wouldn't want to be like that. First vote of confidence? Holy mackerel, Stanfield has to sit there and say, "I'm paired." It was the slickest snow job I'd ever seen. After Trudeau took over and thoroughly trounced him in 1968, Stanfield learned to hate Trudeau and tried to fight back, but it was no match. Trudeau treated him with deserved disdain. A very, very sad choice, Stanfield. Had Duff Roblin won the leadership in 1967, Pearson would have stayed defeated in February. Roblin might not have beaten Trudeau in '68, but he would have been prime minister in '72. It's just that simple.

The only apparent logic in Stanfield's leadership is that he was a caretaker for Dalton Camp. Camp was a close confidant of Stanfield. He knew Stanfield's capabilities. I think Camp harboured the illusion for a while that Stanfield would serve as a blind until he himself could weather the storm he'd caused in dumping Dief. Camp didn't realize the lasting animosity his actions would engender, that he would be so completely ostracized by the party rank and file. Of course, old Dief stuck around to make certain Camp didn't weather any storm.

I might note, I was annoyed in the early part of Stanfield's leadership to be regarded simply as Diefenbaker's thrust. After I gave up on Stanfield completely, I didn't mind one way or the other. It is no secret I liked Dief, liked his company, liked his humour, liked his mind. After Dad died in December 1964, I suppose Dief became a political father figure of sorts for me. I always went in to tell him what I was doing or what fight I was in. When my fights gave Stanfield trouble, as they so often did, Dief loved this, at least secretly. Although he never said so exactly, I knew he had no admiration whatever for Stanfield, and less, if possible, for Joe Clark when he came on the scene. The point is, though, that it was on my own that I began whatever I happened to be in. I would check with Dief to confirm I was on the right road and occasionally he would provide a useful tip-off or lead, but mainly I went to see him for the pure pleasure of it.

Although many observers thought Dief should have left Parliament after Stanfield took over, a fair number of the younger members found him a source of inspiration and encouragement. Charlie Haliburton (South Western Nova) often used to go in to see Dief, and one day I asked him why he didn't go to see Stanfield.

"He's our leader," I said.

"Oh well, Jack, yes, but Stanfield doesn't do the same thing for you that Dief does."

John Lundrigan (Gander-Twillingate) felt the same way. When I asked why someone like him from Atlantic Canada didn't go to Stanfield with his problems, he said, "Fiddle! If you go to see Stanfield, you've got to carry the conversation to him. At least Dief will give you a clue. Tell you where you're wrong. Oh, he'll pick your brain too, but . . . ."

And, really, that's what Dief did. This was a side of Dief that wasn't very well known. When I was interviewed at the time of his death, I said, among other things, that Dief had continued to play a very worth-while role in the party even while Stanfield was leader. I might have added that press criticism of his failure to attend caucus under Stanfield was unfair. Had he done so and taken a position, he would have stolen its support from Stanfield in an instant. Dief knew this and stayed away.

Coming back to the events of 1968, the Liberals had their leadership convention in April. When Trudeau won, he did exactly what I thought he would do, he went to the people. In the election, Trudeau stood for One Canada. Stanfield's easy slogan *deux nations* wasn't that bad, but you had to listen to his explanation of it. Trudeau wasn't listening, he had no cause to. That's the game of politics. I didn't accept *deux nations* however understood, nor did it become an issue in Crowfoot. Marcel Faribault became the issue. Touted as Stanfield's Quebec lieutenant, he did Stanfield more harm than good when he came out to Winnipeg to campaign. Not only did he bring his constitutional theories to the attention of the western voters, he talked so long that poor Stanfield lost his network television time. Stanfield, or his advisers, should have had the foresight to see what would happen, another Stanfield weakness.

Faribault had to be explained very delicately in the West. "Who is this guy Faribault and is he going to run Stanfield?" This came up at a joint party meeting in Meadowlark Hall, west of Hussar, some fifty miles from Calgary. My principal opponent was the Liberal candidate, Noel Sharp, Mitchell Sharp's son. He was a high school teacher in Bassano. A confident speaker, he didn't shy away from an audience. He knew how to organize a meeting, and he'd brought a lot of his supporters up to the meeting in Meadowlark Hall. They jumped all over me on Faribault and the *deux nations*. I came back the only way I knew, that I didn't know much about Faribault, but at least I could say this, that he'd fought for our country in the last war. "Need I say more?" A hush fell over the hall. A few Conservatives from Calgary came up to me later: "You certainly handled that question better than any of our candidates."

Bassano was new territory to me. Before redistribution, it had been in Bud Olson's Medicine Hat riding. Good cattle country; I thought, surely to goodness a rancher shouldn't lose here. Noel Sharp, however, was confident; Bassano was his base. I drifted into town one day about noon to have a chat with the owner of the tire shop. (Fellow by the name of Husband. Did a commentary about the community on the local radio station: "Best town by a dam site" was his motto.) If anyone wanted to spread the word, Husband was the key. As I always drive around on worn tires, this seemed a good time to get a couple of new ones. While we were chatting, I mentioned I thought Bassano was in for a surprise.

"It's kind of amusing, folks hereabouts thinking that Noel Sharp, if he goes to Ottawa, will look back to see only this town and work to make it grow like no other. They're badly fooled. I've got a ranch about sixty miles from here. My roots are here. I look at every town, Bassano, Hanna, Brooks, each equally. Noel Sharp hasn't any roots here; he doesn't even own a lot in this town. When he goes to Ottawa, he'll forget all about Bassano."

Well, sir, at the next forum, Noel announced he had purchased a lot and was building a house in Bassano. He has lived there ever since. I probably helped him out in the long run. It was kind of a mean trick, but on election day I not only won in Bassano, I beat Noel overall in Crowfoot 16,518 to 4,783.

Nationally, of course, Trudeau whomped Stanfield. We lost twenty-five seats, reducing our number to seventy-two. Of these, twenty-five were from the prairie provinces, twenty-five from the Atlantic provinces, seventeen from Ontario, four from Quebec, and one from the Yukon. We were overwhelmingly rural and small town, to the despair of Dalton Camp and the others surrounding our leader. They were interested in finding the electoral key to the cities and to Quebec. Consequently, they were content to be monumentally uninformed about agricultural issues and to frown upon any efforts in this direction.

I was determined that agriculture and other matters of concern to the West should be given due attention. Over the years in Ottawa, I had established a certain credibility. I wasn't a Mr. Nicey who apple-polished to win favours. I was tough, hard-nosed, and didn't take no for an answer. I knew the departments my constituents needed me to deal with, and through my work in committees I'd met most of the senior officials in them. Not one of those senior civil servants wanted me on his back very long; he wanted to satisfy me if he could and be rid of me. When anthrax broke out in part of my constituency and I phoned Dr. Wells, the chief veterinarian, he acted immediately.

"Yes sir, Jack, make this call collect. I'll contact the rancher. I'll look after it. Leave it with me."

That was the response my constituent had the right to expect, but this sort of thing doesn't happen automatically. For example, Heward Grafftey came up to me in the hallway of the House of Commons one day in 1975 (by which time he had been around, off and on, for seventeen years) and lamented, "Jack, what can I do? There's a very important question affecting my riding. I can't even get the deputy minister on the phone. I have to have an answer today. What do you do in situations like this?"

"I just leave my name and number."

"Oh," he said, "I've tried, but they never return my calls." Heward was as excited as could be. "What would you do in my case?"

"I think I'd go over and park myself in the deputy's office, until he showed up, but I've never had the problem."

I remember going into my office, laughing, to tell this story to my secretaries. I asked, "Do you ever have trouble like that? Does a deputy minister ever not return your call?" They replied that once they mentioned they worked for Jack Horner, they generally got whatever it was they were looking for.

Fortunately, part of my reputation was that I didn't fly off and raise Cain over nothing. I only went to the departments or, later on, to their ministers when I had a substantial case. The fastest way to destroy one's credibility in Ottawa or anywhere else is to go to bat over something frivolous. I recall Dan McKenzie (Winnipeg South Centre) coming to see me with an article he'd picked up that said metrification would result in a ten-hour day. He even had a picture of the new clock.

"Jack, you're the critic on metric," he said. "You have to ask a question on this in the House."

The whole article was a joke, of course. He was quite annoyed with me when I pointed it out. A year or so later — it was after I'd joined the Trudeau government — Dan himself put the question about the ten-hour day. I couldn't ask a question like that, couldn't possibly.

Steve Paproski (Edmonton Centre) was equally frivolous — the court jester of the Commons. When Steve stood up in the House he would be greeted with roars of laughter, because the members knew he was going to come up with some kind of joke or other. All the while he was in Opposition, even as whip, I don't recall him ever asking a serious question. Back in 1958, Diefenbaker had told us: "Make all the jokes you like outside the House of Commons, but this is not the place for humour. Tomorrow, or five years from now, your jokes will not read well in Hansard. Laughter isn't recorded, and the funny side isn't generally obvious. Do not use humour to make your points in the House." I wasn't the type of person to do this anyway, but what Dief said is certainly true. When a member acts as entertainer or flies off at everything, what happens when he has something serious to say? Nobody takes any notice. Everyone has long since ceased to listen closely to what he says.

In caucus there is greater latitude for a member, and I never felt at all limited there. Of course, back in the days when there were 208 Conservative members, you didn't make an ass of yourself by bringing up trifling matters. You hit your points — hit them hard — and sat down. During Stanfield's days I used two approaches. I had what I called the "dumb farmer" approach, in which I would wonder aloud about something; for example, the legislation to increase unemployment insurance benefits. Is this the way we should be going? Is this good for the country? What is the party's position on this? I through feigning ignorance, I would draw out the establishment around Stanfield as to where they stood on a given issue, and then I would play my trump. My other approach was to come on hard to give them the facts or to create hell over some position they'd taken. As will have been gathered, I took caucus very seriously. It was the place for wide-ranging discussion and argument. I should mention that caucus used to cheer when David Mac-Donald and I happened to be on the same side of any given issue. Some actually worried about me when I agreed with David, which happened more than once. It amused me to note that caucus seemed to know we ought not be together on ideas.

For the first year or so of Stanfield's leadership, he appeared to make some effort to develop a close liaison with caucus. He failed. After a while, his chairmen's lunches at Tuesday noon were largely devoted to matters relating to the control of caucus, which met on Wednesday morning. Stanfield felt more comfortable with those outside the elected wing of the party, people like Dalton Camp, Flora MacDonald, and Malcolm Wickson.

As I mentioned, this group was more interested in urban rather than rural support, and it was especially interested in Quebec. In this latter respect, on a matter as critical to national unity as the Official Languages Act, Stanfield and his crew — so desperate to make some gains in Quebec — abdicated all democratic responsibility by not publicly ventilating the bill's every facet. I appreciated that the language question was a sensitive area, but I was convinced that Prime Minister Trudeau was moving well ahead of the people in his desire to end the dialogue between

French and English, and legislate a solution. I could see this leading to nothing but trouble down the road. To my mind, the Conservative party had to keep its options open.

The official languages legislation of 1969 should have provided one of the most important debates ever to face us. Instead, all Stanfield could see were the difficulties that any legitimate discussion might cause him. Without benefit of advice from caucus, he decided that the party was going to vote unanimously with the government. I felt that the best he could do would be to call a free vote. The more he emphasized that the party must be united, the more difficult it became to cover the fact that we weren't. There was no way he was going to get a unanimous vote. My private calculation was a maximum of twenty-six against, possibly twenty-one, but more likely seventeen. The rest would fade in the stretch.

My name was on the Speaker's list before the party attempted a rigid control over who would speak in the debate. I wanted to make certain the vote didn't come on a Friday or a Monday, when governments in the past had slipped contentious pieces of legislation through, such as the public service right to strike. Thus, I jockeyed for position so that I would be able to use my forty minutes, if necessary, to hold the debate over until a Tuesday when most of our members would be present. I discovered that I could keep shifting my friends ahead of me in the debate without consulting the Conservative whip. An interest began to develop in what I might say. Indeed, Liberal members started sending me notes inquiring when I was going to speak.

When I did speak on May 23, it was to a full House. This fact is important because, on the basis of my remarks, I was labelled an anti-French bigot. I doubt if the members who heard me could support this contention. I leave it for my readers to judge.

"Mr. Speaker," I said, "in rising to take part in the debate on this important piece of legislation, I wish to say that I believe it to be a continuation of the dialogue that has been going on for some time in Canada. I also say with no hesitation that the government is rushing this dialogue, has come to a conclusion on it, and in fact is forcing a decision far too soon before the people all across Canada have had ample opportunity to become fully involved in the dialogue and to understand the full meaning and logic of the aim of the legislation, which is that Canada should become a truly bilingual country. If Canada and Canadians accept this decision, then I have no hesitation whatsoever in saying that I also fully agree with it."

I went on to say that in my opinion the bill was poor legislation and that it would not, as Trudeau contended, create greater unity in Canada. It would have the very opposite effect. My reasoning was as follows:

The Shawville Horners. From left to
right, top: Norval, Alex, Byron (Jack
Horner's father), Henry. Bottom:
Asa, Margaret, William (grandfather),
Gladys, Cecilia, Sarah (grandmother).

The Blaine Lake Horners, 1943. Left
to right, top: Bill, Jean, Jack, Ruth,
Hugh. Centre: Byron, Byron senior
(father), May (mother), Norval.
Bottom: Bennett, Kathleen.

"Stars" of tomorrow. Left to right:
Jack Horner, Hugh Coflin (who
played professionally for Chicago
1950–51), Alex Atamanenko.

Jack Horner's wedding, with brother
Hugh as best man and sister Ruth as
bridesmaid.

The Horner sons in 1958. Left to right: Brent, Craig, Blaine.

Four Horners in Parliament, 1958. Cousin Albert (the Battlefords) is at centre back.

Mr. Diefenbaker at Senator Horner's 80th birthday celebrations in 1964.

Supporting Arthur Maloney for the presidency of the Progressive Conservative Party of Canada, 1966. Left to right: Hugh Horner, Terry Nugent, Jack Horner.

"Must you go? Here's your hat."
Cartoon by Rusins in the Ottawa
Citizen, August 16, 1974.

In the House of Commons with (left
to right) Bill Skoreyko and Stan
Schumacher (front), John Wise and
Craig Stewart (back).

At the ranch with sons Blaine, Craig,
and Brent, 1976.

"My job is to make the delegate's
choice easier." — Jack Horner.
Cartoon by Macpherson in the
Toronto Star, January 12, 1976.

Leadership convention, 1976, with
wife Leola.

Leadership convention, 1976. Stan
Schumacher and Bill Skoreyko are
front and centre. The Horner family
are above the sign.

Leadership convention, 1976.

With Claude Wagner at the leadership
convention, 1976.

Cartoon by Donato in the *Toronto
Sun*, February 1976.

With the Chief.

Worst photograph ever, used nine times by the *Calgary Herald* since 1976.

At the Calgary Stampede in 1978
with Prime Minister Trudeau and Les
Blackburn, president of the
Stampede. Premier Bill Davis of
Ontario and Roy Bennett, president
of Ford of Canada, are in the
background.

Signing the Northern Pipeline
Agreement in 1978 with (left to right)
Alastair Gillespie, Allan MacEachen,
and Bob Blair of Foot Hills Pipeline
Ltd.

With China's Hua Kuo-feng in 1978.

Former Hanna Hornets hockey
players at Queen's dinner in
Edmonton, 1978.

Tall in the saddle.

Whether we like it or not, this bill will become part of the life of Canada. I accept without hesitation the principle that confederation in 1867 was the coming together of the two founding peoples, the French and the English. I accept this readily. But we must not make it difficult for other people to become full Canadians. If it is the intention of the government that Canada shall become a fully bilingual country, I would have no hesitation about getting on with it. But in this case the government should have announced, as a first step, that it was prepared to contribute toward the cost of sending additional teachers to the vast area of western Canada, to Newfoundland, and to every nook and cranny of this country where people have no opportunities to learn the other language. In Quebec the same course should be followed. . . .

The bill before us would prevent the people of Newfoundland, for example, from making the contribution they would like to make within the next ten or fifteen years until they become proficient in the other language. It would have the same effect upon the people of Quebec who have not learned the other language. This bill will do the same thing for the people in that vast area west of the Lakehead. . . .

In that wonderful area west of the Great Lakes the people will find themselves having to fill out forms to determine what kind of Canadians they are. This practice will once again become evident. We will find people in that particular area being referred to as hyphenated Canadians. There is no doubt in my mind that the people in western Canada today are already what they regard as the best kind of Canadians — only one kind. Whether people are born Canadians or are naturalized Canadians, their citizenship is accepted and that is all there is to it. I suggest that this bill will put us back to that difficult period of the late twenties and middle thirties so far as this particular issue is concerned. To introduce this bill at the present time is, to me, a mistake.

I made it very clear that it was the timing of the bill I objected to as much as anything. Canada could be a great country if we were all bilingual. No question about it. But until everyone had been educated to this — with sound financial backing from the government — the proposed legislation would put a great many people at a disadvantage.

I then commented on the way English Canadians had been treated in Quebec in the previous couple of years. While educational authorities in Alberta were trying to begin the teaching of French in Grade 1 (and would do so if only they could be helped with the cost of the program), studies were being undertaken in Quebec to determine ways in which

French could always be maintained as a major language there. "That sort of action," I said, "does not suggest that both languages will enjoy equal status in that province as this bill suggests they should."

Much fear has been expressed in certain quarters that civil servants will be affected by this measure. The Minister of Justice (Mr. Turner), in several soothing, reassuring statements, has said that it will not affect civil servants. What poppycock is this, Mr. Speaker? Of course they will be affected. Bilingual civil servants now receive a premium of 7½ per cent of other salary. The Minister of Justice said, "But you need not be individually bilingual; we are thinking of institutional bilingualism." I ask, if a bilingual public service is not the ultimate aim of the government, why is it paying a premium of 7½ per cent of their salary to bilingual civil servants? We all know that the government prefers to have fully bilingual heads of departments....

The people of western Canada complain that the federal government pays inadequate attention to a whole gamut of problems. They ask, how will it help us if top civil servants must be bilingual? They fear that few from western Canada will be promoted to the top ranks of any agency or department of government, since few of them speak French. Many of our people have not had the opportunity to learn the other language. Only about 3 per cent of the population of Alberta is French speaking, the figure being lower for British Columbia. Less than 7 per cent of the people of Manitoba speak French, and only a nominal number in Saskatchewan speak the language.

After some further reasoning in this vein, I concluded my speech by saying: "Let us continue the dialogue, be frank, above board, and open with one another. All Canadians should understand and know the full implications of this bill."

Afterwards, Louis Comeau (South Western Nova), one of our few French-speaking members, came up to me and said he could live with my speech without any trouble. But, for some reason, the press just assumed that because I was against the language legislation, I was against French Canada. If they had listened, even to my opening remarks! It was so easy, of course, to label me "the big tough rancher from the West" who shot first and asked questions later. I fitted this image so well. Maybe, if I had been smaller and a little less aggressive, I would have got away with being a rancher. But the combination of the two was too much. Stanfield listened to my speech, as did a number of his inner group. I guess the best I can say is that they didn't believe me. They thought I was a bigot even though they heard me speak in different tones.

If nothing else, by manoeuvring myself back on the Speaker's list, I successfully held off the vote until the Tuesday of the following week. The Monday night, May 26, a group of us gathered in my office to determine whether we were really going to force a recorded vote on second reading. It required five members to rise in their seats to call a vote, but Tom Bell (Saint John–Albert), one of Stanfield's intimates, had in his own cunning manner thoroughly implanted in the minds of most of caucus that it took ten. I had to phone the Speaker to confirm that it only took five. I didn't tell him, but he probably surmised what we were about. I didn't want all five members to come from Alberta, so I approached Doug Alkenbrack from Ontario and George Muir from Manitoba. Monday night, they both said they would stand. Tuesday morning early, they were quick to tell me they had thought it over.

Muir didn't want to do anything that would make bilingualism an issue in the Manitoba provincial election, but he said he would vote against the bill if the vote was called. There was no question about this, he said. Alkenbrack had talked it over with the Ontario boys who had convinced him he'd better not be one of those to stand. I didn't really mind. I didn't want anyone to do anything he didn't feel right about. (I was a trifle vexed in later years when Alkenbrack acquired some notoriety as a critic of bilingualism, because when it came to the crunch he didn't even vote.) When my brother Byron called me from Toronto to tell me the *Globe and Mail* said it looked as if the Official Languages Act would receive a nearly unanimous vote and that Horner's group had collapsed, I gave him my figures. "It will rock in pretty tight around seventeen," I told him.

I then proceeded in my own way. I phoned Arnold Peters to see what the NDP was going to do.

He said, "Why should we call a vote? My constituency is half French and half English. I'm going into the French area to say I'm all for the bill. I want to go into the English area and say they're going about it the wrong way."

"Arnold, for heaven's sake!"

"That's politics, Jack."

When I went up for lunch, I met Dief. "We're not going to call a vote on this are we?" he asked.

"We're not, but the NDP or the Créditistes might."

Dief didn't think so. "And I don't think you should either," he added. I thanked him for his advice and said I'd think about it.

However, I determined to call for a recorded vote. I knew Jack McIntosh was going to stand, and I wasn't going to let him stand alone. That was two of us. So I needed three more to do the same. I went to see Cliff Downey (Battle River).

"Are you a man or a mouse?" (This was the best approach with Downey.)

"I'm a man. What do you want?"

"We need five guys to stand. It's going to take a lot of strength, the pressure's going to be great."

"I'll stand," said Downey. "You and McIntosh, me, and who else?"

"I think Skoreyko and Harry Moore." (Harry was the member for Wetaskiwin.)

I went down the hall. It was two o'clock and the bells started to ring. Harry Moore came out of his office.

"Harry, I've got to see you."

"Jack, the bells are ringing."

"I can hear them. Get into Skoreyko's office. I want to talk to you two guys." Inside the office, I told him and Skoreyko the story: that five of us had to stand. None of us could leave the House until the vote. (When Harry did leave for a minute or two, I nearly panicked, but he got back in time.)

The vote came. We stood.

The Speaker said, "Call in the members."

Well! You never saw such animosity and anger. While the Commons bells rang, the five of us waited in one corner of the Opposition lobby with the rest of the Conservative party cursing us. The vote was just as I'd predicted: seventeen Conservative members rose in opposition to the Official Languages Act. Hansard records their names:

Messrs:

Cadieu (Meadow Lake)	Horner	Schumacher
Coates	Korchinski	Simpson
Diefenbaker	McIntosh	Skoreyko
Dinsdale	Moore	Southam
Downey	Muir	Stewart (Marquette)
Gundlock	Ritchie	— 17

This was nearly one quarter of our membership in the House, which wasn't bad. We had registered a strong protest on behalf of the silent majority of Canadians who wanted a better explanation of why and how we were to become a bilingual nation. In the circumstances, this was all I could do.

The bill was now referred to a Special Committee for study. Here again I was disappointed in Stanfield. There were eight Conservatives on this committee, yet not one of the seventeen who had voted against the bill was appointed to it. This is not the way Parliament should function.

Stanfield deliberately stroked out any contribution we might have made. He gave us no chance whatsoever to work to change this bill so that we might vote for it on third reading.

Stanfield then laid down the law in caucus that there would be no amendments by our party unless sanctioned by caucus and by himself. If any were proceeded with independently, the member responsible would be ostracized. He didn't want any more "stupid actions". (Stanfield loved to use the word "stupid". It didn't bother me, but a lot of members hated to be called stupid. Every time Stanfield said it, he went down a peg in their minds.) I had first thought of tabling a hundred amendments in an attempt to filibuster the bill, but listening to Stanfield's tirade, I decided I would come up with just one amendment — one that they couldn't help but support. If Stanfield was going to set the rules, I'd learn to play by them.

I had to be on my toes because once the Special Committee reported back to the House, I would only have forty-eight hours to file my amendment, and there was no way to tell when the committee was going to report. Mel McQuaid from P.E.I., a very fine individual and very fair, had been assigned by Stanfield to lead the Conservatives in that examination. From time to time, I went in to talk to Mel about how it was going.

Finally, I came up with an inoffensive amendment which, while not altering the bill in any fundamental way, might help set aside some of the fears surrounding it. Also, it was consistent with the views expressed in my speech. I had contended that the demand for bilingual senior civil servants would further shut out the voice of western Canada. In essence, I had argued, "If all senior civil servants are to be bilingual, notice must be given to the next generation of Westerners desiring a public service career to allow them time to become fluent in the second language. Then there will be deputy ministers, assistant deputy ministers, heads of branches, and so on, reasonably representative of all parts of Canada." To my mind, this was vital, because so many policy ideas come from the senior ranks of the civil service, and quite often the way in which policy is administered depends on the interpretation of these same officials. Western Canada was already too isolated from Ottawa. If our important bureaucrats were to come exclusively from eastern Canada, our isolation would be most serious indeed.

I cut things pretty fine. At a Tuesday's chairmen's luncheon, I caught Stanfield's attention. My amendment had to be filed by six that evening. I read out my draft: "Notwithstanding anything in the Act, no person shall be refused employment or promotion within the public service of Canada on grounds alone of inadequate acquaintance with either of the official languages mentioned in this Act, provided that the applicant has declared his intention and willingness to learn the other official language."

Luckily, it was George Hees's birthday, and he was in particularly good spirits. Before Stanfield could respond, George said, "Jack, there's absolutely nothing wrong with your amendment. We can support it." Lincoln Alexander agreed. Stanfield was more cautious.

"I don't like the sound of it," he said. "It seems to go against the principle of the bill, but I want more time to think about it. However, in fairness to you, Jack, I think you should go ahead with it. Caucus may or may not ratify it tomorrow. If they do, it'll stand. If they don't, you'll have to withdraw it."

"Fine. That's all right with me," I replied.

In the meantime, Walter Dinsdale was trying to get Stanfield's attention. The bells rang and the meeting adjourned before he succeeded in doing so.

The next morning in caucus, Stanfield started to give Walter a severe tongue-lashing for filing an amendment without approval. I thought for a minute he was talking to me, until he reassured me he wasn't. I wouldn't have taken that kind of abuse from anybody, and I think Stanfield knew this. Unfortunately, I was sitting a fair distance from Walter and I didn't know what he had filed. As it turned out, he had moved that, in the spirit of federalism, proposed bilingual districts should not be set up in a province without the approval of the provincial government. Given that, to date, no bilingual districts have been set up anywhere, Walter was certainly on the right track. But, once again, Stanfield was not open to ideas. He wanted no changes. He didn't care how the bill affected Canada. This was a dangerous subject politically, and he didn't want it discussed. He called Walter everything that was possible without using a profanity. I felt sorry for Dinsdale, but as I didn't know exactly what he had done and as my amendment was coming up next (and I wanted it accepted), I didn't rise to defend him. When Stanfield finished with Walter, he called on me to explain my proposal. Then he told the caucus he guessed he could live with it but he didn't like it. Caucus, in a mood of general reconciliation, proved more than willing to endorse it.

Before it was debated in the House, I spoke privately to John Turner. My amendment applied directly to the merit principle about which Turner, who was piloting the legislation, had done a lot of talking. He said, "Look Jake," (he always called me Jake) "it's the best amendment on the books, but the word is that we can't support it." I was not surprised therefore when, during the debate, Turner stated the government's line in response to my amendment: "We contend that the honourable member's solution would be impracticable, one not capable of realization."

The whole question of bilingualism should have been debated much, much more thoroughly and for much, much longer so that the people of Canada could have been aware of what was happening. If the people are not given information on all sides of a question, how can they be expected to understand it? The constant lesson is educate, don't legislate. Even a very little knowledge sometimes helps perspective. (Ask any ten people, for example, who it was that introduced bilingualism to our airlines. Invariably, the answer will be "Trudeau". In fact, this came under Léon Balcer, the Transport minister in Diefenbaker's government.) If the caucus had followed my lead in the discussion of the language legislation, there's no question in my mind that we would have come out far stronger and far the better both as a party and as a country. Again, I was thoroughly disappointed with Stanfield's leadership.

The second round came in May 1973 when Bud Drury, the president of the Treasury Board, put before the House a resolution outlining nine points which would be taken into consideration in the application of the official languages legislation. On May 7, I asked a series of questions which shocked the Conservative party. Shivers of fear went through Stanfield and his confrères. Here was Horner again on the official languages issue. My questions, however, were very carefully thought out and very carefully presented.

"Does the Prime Minister envision an act or a bill following this motion which will place binding authority either on the Treasury Board or the Public Service Commission?" I asked.

"No legislation is contemplated at this time," replied Trudeau.

I asked a supplementary: "Can the Prime Minister assure the House that the nine points outlined by the president of the Treasury Board will have lasting effect and be carried on by another president of the Treasury Board in subsequent parliaments, or for that matter this parliament?"

Trudeau said he failed to understand the meaning of my question.

I got up again: "I could explain it a little better. A resolution passed by this or any other body is an expression of that body's opinion, but if the Treasury Board, the government, the cabinet, or this group of members of Parliament should change, that resolution would not necessarily be binding on a subsequent body of men or women. What means of conveyance of that authority does the Prime Minister have in mind for subsequent parliaments?"

The point I was attempting to make — and it was a very valid one — was that a resolution by a body of men and women in any given society merely resolves that they will do something, but it does not become a binding piece of authority.

While the Conservative party shuddered and shook at me asking all these questions without their consultation, I was laying the groundwork for a defence. I wanted the nine points the Treasury Board chairman had introduced encompassed in the bill so that they would be part of a lasting authority. Stanfield, of course, wouldn't allow himself to reach my conclusion. On June 1, I made a speech in this debate in which I drew a comparison between my amendment in 1969 and the proposals of the chairman of the Treasury Board, which read "that competitions for bilingual positions will be open to both bilingual candidates and unilingual candidates who have formally indicated their willingness to become bilingual." I said, "On July 4, 1969, I moved an amendment that parallels this point almost to the word. Many people in my constituency do not think an Opposition member can find his words in legislation. This is not legislation, but my words are there." I then went on to quote what John Turner had said of my amendment: "We contend that the honourable member's solution would be impracticable, one not capable of realization." If it was impracticable and incapable of realization in 1969, how would it be capable of realization in 1973? I pointed out that Mr. Carson, head of the Public Service Commission, had clearly stated he took his authority from the law and nothing else. These resolutions were meaningless unless encompassed in the bill.

The position I had so carefully laid out was perfect for the Conservative party. If Stanfield had decided to fight for this, if he had had the nerve, the people of western Canada — for that matter, of English-speaking Canada — would have found a source of new strength and confidence. It was a government resolution; the government might have been forced to put it into law. Stanfield appeared to me to have no other course. But I was wrong. He wouldn't touch the bilingual issue with a ten-foot pole. After the 1972 election, with 107 Conservatives to 109 Liberals, and 31 NDP holding the balance, Stanfield could smell power. He certainly wasn't going to take any chances, which meant he wasn't going to provide any leadership. Consequently, the Conservative party once again went through a heart-rending exercise on the official languages question, which in my opinion was completely unnecessary.

I believe that when you get into a fight, you should carry it to the end. You don't walk away. Thus I had to vote against the resolution. Although there were only five members left from the original seventeen who voted against the Act in 1969, sixteen Conservative MPs were to vote against this resolution. As a point of interest, a fair number of Albertans were amused that Eldon Woolliams, who loved to give the impression that he was the big brave fighter, somehow missed both votes on the language question. The afternoon the second vote came up, he talked to me on the telephone at ten minutes after five. The vote was to come at

5:30 or 5:45. Eldon fell asleep in his office, despite the bells, which ring pretty loudly to summon the members.

After the vote, Steve Paproski joyously informed me that he was very, very happy my numbers were diminishing. I was surprised actually that through two parliaments and with changed representation, there was still this much resentment against the way the government was handling the bilingual question. Again, anyone who wanted to look at my participation in this debate would fail to find evidence of bigotry. Of course, the press, as usual, paid no attention to what I had said. To them, I was the supreme reactionary.

Coming back to the early years of Stanfield's leadership, I think it would be fair to say that Stanfield really didn't have any particular philosophy or strong conviction on national goals. I found myself seriously questioning his concept of what he wanted to achieve as leader. Indeed, I often remarked that if Stanfield was given Canada on a platter, he wouldn't know what to do with it. The man simply searched blindly in every direction for something, anything, which would lead him to power. This led him to grab at the guaranteed annual income idea in the fall of 1969.

What he wanted was an endorsement of this policy by the party's Priorities for Canada thinkers' conference at Niagara Falls that October. One delegate from each constituency, plus the elected representative or defeated candidate, plus about three or four hundred others chosen by Stanfield and the group outside caucus were invited to debate those policies preselected to assure our urban electoral success. As I mentioned earlier, Stanfield and his crew were mainly interested in the urban vote.

In a number of speeches prior to this convention, Stanfield had come closer and closer to advocating a guaranteed annual income. He had made one such utterance during the '68 election which sent my constituency into a tizzy. If you read this speech carefully, however, you realized he had limited its application to those unable to work due to disability or age. But the very thought, the very words "guaranteed annual income" sent chills down the spines of most Westerners. Was the Conservative party about to deny the validity of the work ethic? At Stanfield's behest the party's research bureau issued a report on a minimum income plan of $2,030 per annum for a family of four. This was not *noblesse oblige*. Neither was it going to stamp out poverty. Instead, it would institutionalize indigence and indolence. Naturally, I believe that we have an obligation to help those who can't help themselves. But self-sufficiency should be the goal, not dependence on the state. Through education and relocation, we should help people to help themselves.

At a special caucus prior to the Niagara Conference, I asked Stanfield for assurance that the positions devised there would in no way automatically become the policies of the Conservative party without ratification by caucus. He replied they were simply to be policy recommendations. Thus did I file my caveat against these proceedings. I then went on to state how deeply disturbed I was to see the leader support a guaranteed annual income without discussion in caucus. Stanfield denied ever advocating any such thing. By genuine coincidence, I discovered in my pocket a newspaper clipping of a speech he had recently made in Lloydminster. According to the account, he had unequivocally supported a guaranteed income for all. I read the newspaper account to caucus. Stanfield claimed to have been misquoted. I wasn't reassured. I told caucus I was going to Niagara Falls for one reason only: to kill any guaranteed income proposals.

Don Mazankowski (Vegreville) and I were to go to the conference together. We rode with another member as far as Oshawa, where Don was to pick up a new car. Unfortunately, it wasn't quite ready, so we had to sit around all afternoon. The consequence was that by the time we arrived in Niagara Falls, they'd let my room go. There was no way I was going to stay anywhere except at the convention site. I'd come to work and my place was right there, not halfway across town. I was fuming over this when a TV reporter by the name of Terry McInnes grabbed me: "Horner, there's only one piece of news going to be made here and you're going to make it in your fight against guaranteed annual incomes. Come up to the room, I want you to do a TV clip." I thought, "Well, if everyone knows why I'm here, this is as good a time as any." Having lucked my way into a free hotel room, courtesy of the party's finance chairman (a stroke of business in itself!), I then went down to the convention hall, where Bruce Phillips wanted to do an interview. I led off with a quote from Abraham Lincoln: "If you do for others what they should normally do for themselves, in the long run you do them more harm than good." It went national. We were in the swing of things.

The next morning, Peter Lougheed was to speak to the social justice committee. I was right on time and eager to listen, interested to see where Lougheed stood on guaranteed incomes. He passed the test. I felt relieved. The discussion became pretty free-wheeling in this particular workshop and I found quite a few allies. In fact, Jean Wadds looked as if she was favourable to my reasoning.

That afternoon, the centre stage for this discussion moved to a larger convention room where four experts were each to give a twenty-minute lecture. They were Professor Robert Clark from the University of British Columbia (whom I had met and who had done a study on pensions for Dief); Reuben Bates of the Canadian Welfare Council (now a minister in the Davis government in Ontario), with whom I had tangled before; Ed Black, the research director for the Conservative caucus; and Dr. R. W. Crowley, a Queen's University economist. After each speaker, there was a discussion from the floor. By this time, I knew who my supporters were. Few of them had previously known one another; they had come to see me independently, saying that they were on my side and asking how they could help. I placed them in various parts of the meeting room so that as soon as someone spoke in favour of guaranteed annual incomes, there was one of mine to speak against. David MacDonald was working the other side of the street; he knew what I was doing and I knew what he was doing.

When we broke at three o'clock for coffee, Ed Black came up to me. He was thoroughly put off, and when he was annoyed he stuttered, but he got his message across. He told me I was a very negative person. Why, he asked, was I always against things, couldn't I be *for* something? I pointed to my wristwatch as if I had timed him. "You see this watch? You took nineteen minutes and two seconds of your twenty-minute delivery at the podium. You give me twenty minutes, and I'll give you more positive thinking than you've heard all afternoon. From the floor, I have only one minute and I have to be careful how I use it." He just threw up his hands and walked away.

I was to win the debate that afternoon. Jean Wadds recognized this. "Jack, I've got the difficult job of being the raconteur for this panel," she told me. "I've listened earnestly to this debate and I'm inclined to agree your side has carried the day."

"When do you have to report?" I asked.

"Sunday evening."

"Let's have breakfast tomorrow morning and we'll discuss this."

I didn't want to be seen spending too much time with her, because Jean normally belonged on the other side. If she was going to favour my position in her report, fine. Of course, pro-Stanfieldites told me I was a tremendous embarrassment to the leader, that I was making it impossible for him to carry on. I told them that this was not my intention. My intention was to prevent the Conservative party from being destroyed.

Certainly, the Camp forces were badly demoralized. At the Saturday night reception in the hotel, Camp could only attract about three people to him. Most of us were gathered around the bar in the centre of the room. On Sunday morning, Jean Wadds and I had breakfast as scheduled to decide what she could say and what she couldn't say in her report. Naturally, I went out of my way to make certain it didn't sound like an absolute put-down of Stanfield. But it was.

A curiosity in the planning of the convention organizers was their decision to bring Arthur Maloney back into the fold. Arthur was to be one of the guest speakers Sunday evening. He searched me out when he arrived and asked me to look over his speech. So we went up to his room, ordered steaks, and I read the speech through. It seemed to be fine, a nice flow of words, and not notably controversial until the top of page five, where he supported a guaranteed annual income.

"Arthur, where have you been?" I asked.

"I just got here. What's been going on? That's why I wanted to see you."

"This conference has taken a position against guaranteed annual incomes."

"Don't you think it's coming anyway?"

"No. And if it is coming anyway, so is death, and I'm not going to die tonight. I don't like this kind of argument. Who suggested you put this in?"

He didn't want to admit that anyone had given him the idea, but there was no question in my mind that this had been orchestrated as part of a general strategy.

"Jack, if you don't want me to say it, I won't, but how do I get around it? It's in my text."

Knowing that Arthur always had copies made for the press, I asked how many.

"About half a dozen."

I said, "I can't just rub out this paragraph. The press will notice." I went back to page four and carefully read the last line or two. It seemed to me he could jump right from the bottom of page four to the second paragraph of page five. When I pointed this out, he agreed.

"Art, I just happen to have a little penknife here. I'll cut this inch or so off the top of page five. Some astute pressman might notice page five is a little shorter than the others but he won't know why if I make a neat job of it."

Art's speech that evening didn't stir up any trouble at all.

Before that final session I met Jean Wadds again. She wanted me to read her report. I told her this wasn't necessary, that I was confident we were in agreement. I then met two of the opponents of guaranteed incomes, Don Blenkarn from Mississauga and a doctor from Qu'Appelle Valley, who said they were prepared to move a vote of censure against Stanfield if there was any endorsement of guaranteed annual incomes in Wadd's report. There were real rumblings of discontent on both sides of this issue, and Stanfield was having trouble with the non-elected wing of the party. Well, I didn't count on the famous George Hees offering me any support. But at the final session on Sunday evening, as soon as Jean

Wadds moved the acceptance of her report, George, in his desire to smooth things over, jumped up and said, "Great report, Jean. I second it. Let's make it unanimous." All I had to do was say, "I agree." And it was so. What Hees had done was prevent any comeback attempt by David MacDonald.

Stanfield spoke quite late in wrapping up the convention and he once again referred to guaranteed annual incomes. Some of the press came over to me afterwards.

"Horner, you've won the debate with the delegates here, but you don't seem to have convinced your leader."

I replied, "I've heard that Wacky Bennett has claimed he and God are working hand in hand. So far as Stanfield is concerned, I've done the best I can. I'll leave the rest to God."

Back in Ottawa, Stanfield set up a committee of members to study the question further — really an attempt to devise a way to get around his defeat. David MacDonald, for all my disagreements with him, told me about it and said he had protested to Stanfield the unfairness of excluding me from this committee. Apparently, Stanfield had replied, "Horner is a completely negative person. I don't think he's got any good in him at all. I don't want him on this committee under any circumstances." I checked this out with Monteith, who was also on the committee, and while he wasn't as clear on the matter as MacDonald, there was sufficient agreement to substantiate the story. I accosted Stanfield with this, but he slid away.

From this point, confrontation was inevitable. I had a role to play in protecting the Conservative party. I would fulfil this, with or without Stanfield's co-operation.

5/My Own Brand

In May 1970, the *Federal Task Force Report on Agriculture* was released. This was a detailed assessment of where we were and where we ought to be going in agriculture. The task force had been headed by Professor D. L. MacFarlane from Macdonald College at McGill University in Montreal. The only Westerner on it — one out of five — was Clay Gilson from the University of Manitoba. A task force heavily loaded with eastern experts in a country where the agricultural industry is predominantly western made me very suspicious of its findings. At this time, 50 per cent of hog production was in the West, to say nothing of the West's domination in grain and beef production. The effects of agricultural policy on the economy of western Canada were far greater than in Ontario or the Maritimes. I looked at this report very carefully indeed. I was deadly afraid of its implications because I believed it would become a bible to the Department of Agriculture for many years to come. It recommended, among other things, that production should be reduced if necessary to control surpluses, that younger non-viable farmers should be moved to other sectors of the economy, and that every public policy should embrace the principles and procedures of "management by objectives, program planning and budgeting, cost-benefit analysis" and the adoption of other management techniques.*

In conjunction with this report, the government introduced two pieces of legislation: the Canada Grain Act; and an Act to establish a National Farm Products Marketing Council to authorize the establishment of national marketing agencies for farm products. There was a great deal of support in the Ontario wing of the Conservative party for the latter, as far as livestock marketing was concerned, but I was suspicious of it. Basically, this bill was alien to my every belief. It proposed to set up an agency which could control where a product would be grown, who would grow the product, where it would be processed, how it would be processed, and where it would be marketed. The establishment of the party had let the word filter through that this was a good piece of legislation and that we ought to let it pass without serious debate. As even some of the western members were in favour of the bill, I had to proceed very carefully indeed in my opposition to it. My speech

*See Appendix 4.

113

on the subject was therefore rather mild mannered. In fact it began quite whimsically.

"A strange situation is developing in Canada," I said. "On the one hand we have the Minister of Agriculture (Mr. Olson) and on the other we have a minister without portfolio in charge of the Wheat Board (Mr. Lang). I wish the phrase 'without portfolio' meant 'without power'. The point I am making is that the whole of agriculture is now divided under two ministries. The farmers of western Canada are looking to one or the other minister for guidance, for legislative help, and for assistance in the marketing of their products. They are searching for leadership. As I travelled across Canada I was struck by how much western Canada needs leadership in this field, yet we in Canada have two ministries, two vast departments supposedly trying to help the farmer market his products. This dual situation reminds me of the cross-eyed rooster and the hens. Farmers are like hens in the barnyard which do not know at which hen the cross-eyed rooster is looking."

To emphasize my point — and add a little light relief — I read the House a poem on the cross-eyed rooster:

I'm having lots of troubles,
And I think I'll quit the farm.
It's not just like it used to be,
It's losing all its charm.
The hens have slacked off laying,
And the cows are going dry,
And the poor old cross-eyed rooster
Is just about to die.

I sent away and got him;
He's a cross-bred as you know,
And according to the catalogue
Should make production grow,
But when I turned him with the hens
They wondered what was cooking,
For they just couldn't figure out
At which one he was looking.

Then two old biddies started out,
With him in hot pursuit,
And side by side they raced along
Were keeping pretty mute.
The one old hen just turned her head
And with a muffled oath

114

Said, "We had better spread apart,
Or he will miss us both!"

Now he is chasing all day long;
He can't make up his mind,
And instead of being cross-eyed,
Would be better being blind.
He's getting thinner every day,
And always out of breath,
And I know within a fortnight
He will run himself to death.

I then moved in and pointed out the pitfalls of the bill: "The legislation will provide for the appointment of inspectors who will have broad powers to search: they may examine any books, records, or documents in the possession of a farmer who does not comply with the regulations of the marketing agency. Furthermore, any farmer who does not comply with the regulations emanating from the marketing agency is liable to two years in jail. That means he will be out of production for two years. Why not jail a farmer for twenty years? Because, if the government wants to take him out of production, it should do so. This and similar pieces of legislation are putting the small farmer out of business."

I concluded my speech by making the point that the farmers themselves should be allowed to say whether they wanted an agency. "Without question it is a basic principle in any participatory democracy espousing free enterprise that producers have a voice in whether they want a marketing agency or not."

I remember John Wise and Bob McKinley saying it was a good thing I didn't go any further in my speech or I might have created trouble for them in Ontario, because this was really good legislation and we had to support it. Their remarks confirmed what I already knew, that my main problem was with caucus: how to change the minds of those in my own party who were interested in agriculture. As I came to look closely at the *Federal Task Force Report on Agriculture*, I found a substantial likeness between it, the marketing bill, and Trudeau's major speech on agriculture during the 1968 campaign. It was then I realized that we had to study the task force report very carefully.

Luckily for me, the Grain Act (C 196) had gone to committee before the Marketing Act (C 197) which passed through the House relatively quickly after my contribution to its debate. Had the government been thinking, they would have dropped the study of the Grain Act and gone ahead with the Marketing Act. The mood in caucus was so favourable to it at first that I wouldn't have been able to stop it. But because it sat second in line, I was able to hold it back by holding up the Grain Act.

But I'm getting ahead of myself. My problem in June was not how to hold up the Grain Act, I knew how to do that, but how to change the minds of those in caucus interested in agriculture about the National Farm Products Marketing Agencies Act.

On St. Jean Baptiste Day, 1970, there was a bombing at National Defence Headquarters in Ottawa, not far from the apartment that Mazankowski and I were sharing. When Maz and I went up to our offices in the West Block that morning, we were told by the security staff they had had a bomb warning there. At that moment, they were carrying out a search of the premises. Maz and I looked at one another and decided not to stick around. The House of Commons wasn't sitting that day, so I suggested a golf game up at Shawville where we wouldn't be bothered with crowds.

On the course, I began to tell Maz my concerns about the Marketing Act and the task force report, coupling these with my total disappointment in Stanfield's leadership. Maz agreed there was no question that the report was going to be the bible from which future agricultural legislation would flow, and he suggested that we organize a meeting later in the summer to study it. The idea of a meeting of western MPs had not occurred to me. I liked it right off the bat.

"We could invite the defeated candidates as well," I said, "because more than likely they'll be running again." (It should be remembered that in 1968, Trudeau had got more members from the four western provinces than the Conservatives.) June 24, however, was pretty late in the day to start organizing anything. As we golfed, we kept on talking. Finally, we decided to go ahead; but first we would sound out the rest of our western rural colleagues.

After Maz had checked out accommodation and location, we decided to hold the meeting in Saskatoon. (The Bessborough Hotel had the most reasonable rates in the country; they offered us rooms at ten dollars a night.) Meanwhile, I took on the task of formally notifying everyone:

OTTAWA
June 25th, 1970

Personal and Confidential

Dear

There has been a general discussion amongst western Members here in Ottawa and we have agreed there should be a get together of the western rural Members in the early fall. The suggested date is either August 26th, or 27th. The place, Saskatoon, as it is centrally located.

The purpose of the meeting would be to discuss farm problems, legislation, such as Bill C-197, the Lift Program, the Task Force Report on Agriculture, western Canada's survival, and the possibility of a campaign organizer for western rural Members.

A further notice will be sent to you very soon with the exact date of the meeting. Would you kindly let me know whether or not you will be able to attend because I think it is very important that we have 100 per cent attendance of our western rural Members.

We will arrange to have rooms reserved in block at the Bessborough Hotel in Saskatoon.

Yours sincerely

Before we could proceed much further, the House adjourned and we all went home. Stanfield went off on a trip to study the European Common Market and the economies of individual European countries to see what he could learn. It was like "The bear went over the mountain to see what he could see": about all Stanfield saw was the other side of the ocean. I continued to work on the western meeting from the ranch. I wrote to Professor Gilson of the University of Manitoba, inviting him to attend. As he couldn't do so, he suggested Professor Wilson at the University of Saskatchewan. Away on holidays, Wilson did not receive my invitation until August 29; too late. Both Gilson and Wilson, however, testified in their letters to the importance of the marketing bill. I also wrote to Dief, inviting him to address us at dinner following the first day's session. His reply made it seem unlikely he would appear:

I regret that I cannot give you a definite answer now, as I agreed some months ago, as part of the [Manitoba] Centennial Celebration, to go on a fishing trip with the Premier of Manitoba, Jack Benny, Lorne Green and other Hollywood stars, during the last week of August; after four days' fishing we are to have a two-day goose hunt.

As Diefenbaker couldn't guarantee he'd come and as I wanted some high-plane discussion of the party's future in addition to a certain amount of study, I invited Gordon Churchill, the supreme strategist, to address us on the evening of August 27. Gordon accepted.

In our first day's session, we made an excellent start. As chairman, I was able to lead our discussion very carefully. I wanted to sow the seeds of doubt about the marketing bill by going point by point through an excellent summary of the task force report which had been put out by

Unifarm of Alberta. Without this meeting, I suspect I would never have been able to convince our western members that the government's farm products marketing legislation was wrong for our part of Canada.

Gordon Churchill's remarks at the dinner on that night set the stage for the following day's events. In his own careful and dour way, Gordon gave us a pretty severe lecture on the drift of the Conservative party. In no uncertain terms, he told us that if we wanted to save ourselves and the party in western Canada, we had to address our problems squarely. He was most inspiring.

To my surprise, Dief flew in that night. Thus, on the second morning of our deliberations, I thought we might use a break to hear him and other speakers. Dr. Magnus Verbrugge, president of the B.C. party, had been invited by Bob Thompson, though he wasn't particularly interested in agriculture; and he led off the speeches, describing the poor state of the Conservative party in B.C. He said that although the public's attitude to Trudeau was adverse, the Conservatives were not regarded as an alternative because Stanfield hadn't taken a clear position on anything. Drugs, pollution, foreign ownership — nobody knew where the party stood. Verbrugge felt that the majority of citizens in B.C. would vote Conservative if we had clear policy alternatives and a real leader. Lawrence Watson, Saskatchewan's party president, then said much the same about conditions in Saskatchewan. He was followed by my cousin Milt Harradence, who spoke about the viability of a western economic unit. In conclusion, he too said that we needed a new leader — "a western leader from caucus, with drive, integrity, and guts."

Mr. Diefenbaker had, of course, been listening to all this. When he rose to speak, he said that something had to be done. There was no effective Opposition: Parliament had become Trudeau's playground. As for the Conservative party, it was controlled by the hands that had destroyed it — Dalton Camp was still directing things. Internationally Canada had become a joke. Nationally, all was uncertain.

"Where are we going?" Dief asked. "It is no longer a matter of party, it is a matter of country!"

Well, we talked it over a bit more, and Gordon Churchill said we should unite as a western Canadian group and tell Stanfield he had to get rid of Camp and Goodman. We had to lay our cards on the table. Western discontent was so pronounced, he contended, that a third party would result if we failed to take control. I wanted to get the meeting back to the remaining few items in the task force report, but Jack McIntosh insisted on hearing my views on the state of the party. He more or less accused me of organizing the meeting so that I could state them, which made me a little cross. Anyway, I rose to the bait and told the meeting how disillusioned I was with Stanfield — and gave plenty of examples. I said I knew, deep down in my heart, that I could follow but that the person I followed had to have some ability as a leader. If things kept going the way they were, I could see bigger and bigger inroads by the Liberals and NDP in western Canada. I was pretty loud. Bob Thompson, who had been out of the room, told me that my voice was carrying into the hallway and that the press were gathered outside.

Amidst more discussion, Jack McIntosh then moved, seconded by Bob Thompson, that we establish a western PC organization headed by Gordon Churchill, with one representative from each western province, in order to aid constituency organization and raise funds for western political activities and elections. Dr. Verbrugge, Jack McIntosh, Dr. Gordon Ritchie, and I were all elected to help Churchill in this. It was further resolved that a group of western members should meet with Stanfield to discuss the details of our meeting and the discontent felt across the West with his leadership and the performance of the party.

When we adjourned at 4 P.M., the press wanted to know what we had been discussing. Was this a mutiny against Stanfield? I said we'd discussed agriculture.

"What about the leadership?"

I replied that when more than a couple of MPs of any party get together, they examine themselves to some extent and I supposed we had done this, but that we had no real problems.

Whether I did a poor job of covering up or what, they were certainly out for blood. I had no sooner arrived home from Saskatoon than one of the newsmen phoned me. He said he had me taped completely, and did I want to buy the tape. (Apparently some newsmen with tape recorders had slipped into a serving room adjacent to the room in which we had been meeting.) I told the guy I had no intention of buying his tape and that if he attempted to use it I would sue for clever imitation. Well, that silenced him. But the headline next day was "Mutiny". The press paid no attention to our agricultural discussion, which they must have heard along with our discussion of leadership. The net result was a terrible furore in the party.

Stanfield was beside himself over the press reports. In Edmonton, early in September, he referred to our meeting as "stupid". I came under heavy fire as having been the organizer of a plot to dump the leader; and Stanfield was pressed (I think by the non-elected portion of the party) to call a caucus in Ottawa to demand an explanation from these "prairie radicals". When all this hit the fan, I merely drove up to Vegreville to pick up Mazankowski's notes of the meeting.

When I arrived in Ottawa, some of our caucus friends were very chilly: hardly would they speak to Maz or me. I knew I could defend our meeting without any trouble, but I didn't want any of the Westerners who had attended to run off like frightened lambs. So, the night before caucus, I gathered together as many of them as I could get.

"I don't care what you say about the meeting," I told them. "But you don't say anything until I've had my song. We go into caucus as if we've done nothing wrong. Let them make the charge. Then I'll speak to the charge. Afterwards, you can say anything you like."

In caucus next day they all held their fire. Stanfield stood up and charged us with the stupidest thing he had ever seen MPs do; it was especially stupid of the organizers, and so on and so forth. "Why was it just rural members?" he demanded. "And if just rural members, why wasn't Ged Baldwin there?"

I had been worried about Baldwin but hadn't invited him because he summered in Ottawa. I apologized to caucus for this. I then explained that our meeting was a study session on the report of the Task Force on Agriculture — which it was. I flung the "stupids" back at Stanfield, pointing out that a really stupid meeting was the one he had held in Regina the previous year, to which he had *not* invited farming MPs though he had invited farmers from their constituencies. "That's what I call a stupid meeting," I said. I admitted that our meeting in Saskatoon had tended to get out of hand when I gave the floor to Verbrugge, but Verbrugge had said nothing out of the ordinary. He had only told us of the work he was doing and the problems he was facing in British Columbia. My only mistake, I said, lay in our failure to anticipate the need to manage the press.

I spoke for about an hour; and, to a man, everyone who had attended the meeting backed me up. Stanfield and his crew couldn't and didn't argue. But, as a result of the whole affair, all my bridges with Stanfield and the party establishment were burnt beyond repair — as became all too evident during the next leadership race.

While all this was going on within the party, the October Crisis was shaking up Canada. I might mention that it came as an absolute surprise to me. I had taken one of my sons up to the Olds School of Agriculture, and I heard the news on my car radio as I was driving home. I was shocked, and anxious to get to Ottawa. It had all the appearances of a very serious confrontation. The government said there was an armed insurrection taking place, and I naturally believed them. They had the facts. I don't blame Stanfield for accepting the government's position initially. There was no way he could have known that the Bourassa government had panicked in calling for the military. Looking back, though, it's obvious that Trudeau responded too quickly. But, at the time, he was a hero among heroes for his decisive action.

Many Canadians don't realize the mood that existed in Ottawa at the time: the earlier bombings seemed to have set the stage for the armed patrols which now appeared almost everywhere. Each cabinet minister had a soldier following him around. Edgar Benson, the Finance minister, lived in the same apartment building as I did, and there was a guard outside the main door and a guard on his apartment floor. We wondered if their guns were loaded. At six o'clock one morning, when the fresh shift came on duty, one of the soldiers accidentally shot himself as he jumped from the truck. This ended any doubt in my mind. The guns were for real. It was a very, very unsettling time. I thought it odd, however, that no one was taking pot shots at the military patrols in Montreal. What kind of insurrection was this? It turned out to be no more than a bunch of bad boys.

In the House, David MacDonald stood against the government's Public Order Temporary Measures Act, and he was right to do so. I had spoken in support of his position in caucus, and so had Eldon Woolliams, but when the vote came I decided to go along with the party's wishes. My reasons for doing so were pretty weak. I was trying to gain back Brownie points by operating within the party rules. So MacDonald stood alone. Oddly enough, Stanfield didn't condemn him for not following the party line: he praised MacDonald for his intestinal fortitude. This didn't sit well with those of us who had received very different treatment from Stanfield in the past when we had voted according to our convictions. Stanfield would have been wise to pay his compliments to MacDonald privately.

With the new session of Parliament in October 1970, the government reintroduced Bills C 196 and C 197, this time as C 175 (Grain Act) and C 176 (Marketing Act). In holding up these bills, at no time did I have the sanction of the party. Indeed, no one in Stanfield's establishment ever came to me to ask what I was doing. Nor did I ever check my amendments with anyone. I think Ged Baldwin, as Conservative house leader, had a concept of what I was about and approved, but I never discussed this with him. It may be that none of them knew. Certainly, the farm organizations never did; nor did the press. Consequently, the public remained uninformed. But the people in the grain industry clearly understood what I was doing. Jack McDonald, the president of Pioneer Grain Company, and Bill Winslow, one of the key men in United Grain Growers, were very concerned about the grain bill and the government's intention to assume control over which elevators would remain in operation. Accordingly, over the summer, they had provided me with the ammunition I needed. Thus, in October 1970, I was able to propose forty-two amendments (thirty-seven pages of them) to prevent this bill being passed in the final days of the old session.

Like a lawyer using the rules of procedure in court to help him advance his client's case, I used the rules of the House of Commons to advance the interests of the grain industry. In the instance of the parliamentarian, the government is judge and jury. The trick is to make the government listen. A good Opposition can change legislation if it wants to, but its members have to be stout-hearted. Stanfield didn't understand this aspect of Parliament at all. Dief, of course, knew it very well indeed. Dief had made his name in the House of Commons. In contrast, I made my name as a parliamentarian not so much in the House as in the committees. In the Transportation Act, the Grain Act, the National Farm Products Marketing Agencies Act, I took my hard work in committee into the Commons where, through a thorough understanding of the rules, I made the government listen to me.

The government's point of vulnerability in the House is its legislative timetable. There is only so much time to pass any piece of legislation. Thus, in 1969, the government had changed the rules, with the aim of employing the House of Commons' time more efficiently. Passing a bill was to be simple and quick: introduced on first reading; on second reading a few speeches limited to principle, then into committee for detailed examination, with debate on any amendments at report stage; passed on third reading to the Senate. Effectively eliminated in this scheme, at least in theory, were lengthy debates on second reading and the long clause-by-clause debates in the Committee of the Whole. The select or special committees of the Commons were to carry this load instead of the entire House having the responsibility.

When these rule changes were first explained to caucus, I immediately asked, "Let me get this straight. Do you mean that within the first forty-eight hours of the report stage a member can file not simply new amendments but duplicates of those already dealt with in committee?" The answer was yes. "Well, this means any piece of legislation can be blocked by filibuster if one is so inclined." This proved very true indeed.

As I mentioned, I had introduced thirty-seven pages of amendments on the grain bill. Now, if the Speaker grouped the forty-two specific amendments according to particular subjects, as is his prerogative, this might have resulted in twelve separate debates. As the mover, I was allowed forty minutes per debate. Each member following me had twenty minutes. If I lined up five or six MPs to help me, I could easily use up more time than the government had to spend on the bill in question.

It is simply not possible to devise rules which at once protect freedom of speech and prohibit a determined group from filibustering a piece of legislation. The effective brake on any filibuster is the mood of the country. If a Jack Horner, or whoever, proceeds to block a piece of popular legislation, the letters begin to pour in, the press is filled with adverse comment, and there is, in consequence, the realization: "I'm losing votes back home as well as votes for the party across the country. I'd better let this thing go through."

In early December I was still holding up the grain bill in committee. Finally, Bruce Beer, the chairman of the Agriculture Committee, came to me and said, "Look, Horner, what are we going to have to do to get this Grain Act through?" There were still twelve of my amendments to be debated.

"Give me these seven," I said, listing them, "and you can have the thing." From my point of view, this was the best I was likely to get for the grain industry.

"What are you going to do with C 176?" Beer then asked, referring to the marketing bill.

I told him I didn't know, though of course I knew that I'd kill it if I could. As a result of the Saskatoon meeting, the western members of caucus had swung in behind me to oppose it. But we needed something more than this if the government was going to listen. I suggested to Beer that we take the Agriculture Committee across Canada to get the views of the people who would be affected by it, especially the farmers and farm organizations.

He was willing to go along with this, and on December 13 the Agriculture Committee approved it by a vote of thirteen to eight. Over Christmas recess, however, the government decided they didn't want the Agriculture Committee travelling with the bill. But I stuck to my guns and forced the committee to live up to its agreement to travel.

We set off early in 1971. Our first stop was Winnipeg where spokesmen for United Grain Growers, the Chamber of Commerce, and the Consumers' Association of Manitoba all condemned the bill. It was the same in Regina and Edmonton, if to a lesser degree in Vancouver. By this time, the Liberals on the committee were looking green around the gills. They had thought C 176 was a popular piece of legislation. When we got back to Ottawa, Bruce Beer admitted that it certainly appeared as if western Canada opposed the bill, and he wasn't too willing to have us travel in eastern Canada. Nevertheless, we went to Halifax, Quebec, and Toronto. The Toronto meeting was the significant one of the three: Bill Stewart, Ontario's Agriculture minister, supported the legislation.

After our travelling, there were rumblings that the government wanted early passage of the bill. I stalled it in committee. Then on March 23, 1971, we picked up a rumour over supper that the government was going to take the Agriculture Committee into an all-night sitting to break our opposition. Our strategy was simple: to appear to co-operate in committee until eleven o'clock in an attempt to win the favour of the government majority. We had been holding up a lengthy clause and still had much of it to discuss. So that evening I said to Bruce Beer, "Mr. Chairman, would it be possible, if we haven't passed clause seven by eleven o'clock, that we then do so and adjourn?" He agreed. By the designated hour, we had passed the clause in question. I reminded Beer of our agreement and moved we adjourn. At this, the Liberals on the committee voted to continue. Bruce Beer said he was going to live up to his agreement and was going home. Whereupon, the vice-chairman took over, obviously pleased with the opportunity and confident that he could do a job on us. Arnold Peters sent me a note: "We can't allow them to wear us down. We have to dig in our heels to make certain they don't make any progress. I'm going to fight with you. I hope you understand." No problem! We argued for three hours, Arnold and I, over a stupid little amendment on whether the letter "s" should be added to the word "meeting".

When the Liberals finally realized it was all a charade, tempers flew and the meeting turned hot and stormy. We persevered. As the hours wore on, some of the members slipped out for a bit of fortification, and Alf Gleave (Saskatoon-Biggar) had a snooze at the back of the room. But I daren't leave my chair until victory was secured. When the cleaning staff came in at 7 A.M., we adjourned. The Liberals knew they had been beaten.

The government strategy had completely backfired. First, no progress had been made on the legislation after 11 P.M. Second, and more important, instead of breaking our opposition, the Liberals had strengthened it. They had created the kind of fight that really does things for the troops. New members like Don Mazankowski and Cliff Downey cut their teeth on this bill. Old and new, we became a hard-hitting team who were having fun at the game. We were winning and feeling a zest for Parliament and committee work to the extent that we were unmindful of the rest of the party.

Finally, just before Easter, the Liberals again had to come to me and ask what they had to do to get me to stop blocking the bill.

"I want cattle and hogs exempted," I said. "You can do what you like with the rest of it."

Allen Sulatycky (Rocky Mountain) and Bruce Beer agreed to go along with that. They told me, "When the committee meets tonight, you make the necessary motion and we'll support it. If you have your eight members there sharp at eight, we'll make up the quorum. But, for god's sake, don't tell anyone."

It took sixteen to make a quorum, and as Roch LaSalle had quit the committee we had a Conservative vacancy. I asked Bob McKinley, the party whip who was also supposed to be our Agriculture critic, to get Craig Stewart in place of LaSalle. He didn't do so. He got Percy Noble instead. What's more, he told me that he and Percy weren't going to support me. I found this out just before the meeting, and we had a terrible row right there in the corridor. We were being pretty loud when Pat Nowlan came along on his way to the meeting. Pat had worked hard on the committee in the interests of the apple growers of Nova Scotia and he wasn't at all in favour of C 176. He pushed the three of us into an office. Finally, McKinley and Noble agreed to abstain rather than voting against me. But I couldn't have them abstain. I couldn't risk having my motion defeated.

With all this, by the time we got into committee the jig was up. Some of the Liberals like Ross Whicher (Bruce) had already arrived. I'd been hoping to get my motion passed before he came. Although Whicher wasn't necessarily opposed to getting cattle and hogs out of the bill, the battle between us had become so fierce over the months that he just couldn't let me win. Quickly, Gerry Cobbe (who was in on the agreement) moved that the committee be adjourned. Gerry was the Liberal member from Portage la Prairie — a very nice guy and a fine ball player. "I don't think we're going to make any progress tonight," he explained to the chairman.

That was Friday. On Monday morning I marched into Stanfield's office, demanding to know whether or not the Conservative party was opposed to Bill C 176. Luckily for me, Stanfield had made a speech that weekend — I had a copy of it — and there was one paragraph in it in which he opposed the bill. I read this out to him and asked if I could take it that the party was opposed to the bill. Well. . .he didn't really. . .he thought so. . .parts of it weren't too good.

"What's this guy McKinley up to, then?" I asked.

Stanfield didn't know. He'd have to talk to McKinley.

I told him straight: "Mr. Stanfield, I don't know how Mr. Diefenbaker feels about it, I haven't talked to him, but all of western Canada is solidly opposed to this bill. And if the Conservative party won't support me on this, I don't know why I don't start a Western Canada party. The Agriculture Committee sits tomorrow. If I don't get solid support from its Conservative members, I'll be announcing to caucus on Wednesday that I'm leaving the party."

Whether I would have or not, I don't know. Whenever there had been talk of a Western Canada party, there'd always been accusations that I was aiming to be its leader. But this was the first time I'd ever mentioned the subject to Stanfield.

On Tuesday in committee, McKinley fell all over me. But I wanted Stanfield to be convinced that I had the support I claimed in western Canada; I wanted him to recognize how unpopular the bill was. (He was apparently oblivious of the evidence contained in the Agriculture Committee records.) Over the Easter recess, I got together with Joe Hudson, the largest egg producer in Ontario and one of my strongest supporters against C 176. We decided to run coupon advertisements in the Ontario dailies against the National Farm Products Marketing Agencies Act. We went for a double-coupon system: "Send one coupon to your Member of Parliament and the other to Jack Horner, MP, Ottawa." I received 800 letters a day for ten days, 99.9 per cent of them against Bill C 176. In western Canada I approached the Western Stock Growers Association. As I was campaigning to get beef exempted from the marketing bill, I thought it important to have their support. Once they overcame their initial unwillingness to get involved, we were able to go ahead with full-page ads in the *Country Guide*, the *Western Producer*, and the *Free Press Weekly*. The trick in western Canada was to have the second coupon sent to Bob Stanfield. He received some 52,000 coupons. I had no more trouble with the Conservative party over this bill.

As the session wound down, C 176 got through committee. As before, I told the Liberals I would let it pass if they exempted cattle and hogs. Thus, on December 30, 1971, after an all-night sitting, the National Farm Products Marketing Agencies Act passed third reading.

Part of the problem all along had been due to the Agriculture minister, Bud Olson. I remember once, after the 1968 election, being in an implement agency in Brooks getting parts. One of the farmers came up to me and asked, "What kind of a guy is Bud Olson anyway? What do you think about Olson?"

Well, I knew Bud had represented that area prior to 1968 and I had to be kind of careful. So I replied, "Well, I'll tell you. Bud's so busy trying to sell Trudeau and his ideas in this area that he's failing to sell the problems of this area to Trudeau and the cabinet."

The guy tapped me on the chest. "Maybe that's the problem," he agreed.

I knew I'd said enough, I said no more. Clearly, this had been Olson's problem in the debate over Bill C 176. Although he was Agriculture minister, he wasn't looking at the problems of agriculture in western Canada. Instead, he accepted the concept that Trudeau had announced in Winnipeg on June 2, 1968. Trudeau, like a lot of other people born off the farm, didn't really know much about agriculture, so I guess some civil servant had fed him this line. As I earlier observed, the *Federal Task Force Report on Agriculture* and Bill C 176 kind of flowed out of that thinking. The critical point is that Olson bought it. Thus, Olson had to sell it rather than sell the position of western Canada to the Liberal party. The fight over C 176 marked the demise of Bud Olson as a western member; he was defeated in 1972. In fairness, Bud was a good member of Parliament, both as a Social Crediter and as a Liberal. He worked hard, didn't play around with frivolous ideas, didn't get caught up too often on the Social Credit kick of funny money, and tried to represent his constituency well. When he became a minister, however, he failed to push western Canada's viewpoints strongly enough on the gang he had joined. I learned from his experience. When I became a minister, I was forever on guard that the same thing didn't happen to me, and I don't think it did.

There is a lesson in the stories of Bills C 175 and C 176. My holding up two pieces of legislation practically through two sessions, without the willing support of the party to which I belonged, exposes the fallacy in voting for the next prime minister without giving a hoot who is elected behind him. The minority regions particularly have to retain a deep interest in whom they send to Ottawa, because the leader, no matter who he is, will have to bow to the wishes of the central Canadian majority within the party. Thus, it is important to send stout-hearted individuals to defend the interests of their region.

6/Leadership

In the 1972 election, the Liberals were wiped out in Alberta. I was not surprised. Bud Olson went down to defeat in Medicine Hat mainly because of the fight the western Conservative members had put up over Bill C 176. Allen Sulatycky, who was the best member the Liberals had from Alberta at the time, lost to Joe Clark in Rocky Mountain because of the unpopularity of Trudeau. Although Allen himself was very popular, he just couldn't carry the image of his party. Nationally, the Liberals, reduced to a minority government, took their public rebuff badly. Donald Macdonald made some off-the-cuff remarks about the rednecks in society who wouldn't buy the French fact; and when the House opened in January 1973, Trudeau made the worst speech of his career, lamenting the fact that English Canada and the rednecks had moved en bloc against him in the election. When I told John Turner what I thought of the Prime Minister's speech he advised, "Well, don't reply to it." I said I had no intention of doing so. Even Stanfield — who rarely spoke to me these days, except through Mazankowski — came over to my desk before I spoke in the Throne Speech debate.

"Now, for heaven's sake, be careful and don't answer all the accusations."

I assured him I wouldn't, but I did have on my desk the necessary material in case any catcalls were directed at me. I was prepared to do battle if necessary. I had entitled my speech "How the West Was Lost". One of the main points of that speech of January 16 dealt with the capital gains tax the government had passed in the previous session. Here again Stanfield had refused to stand and fight. Surely, he argued, people who belonged to the jet set, inheriting huge amounts of wealth, should pay tax. I couldn't disagree with that. My problem was I didn't know many Canadians who belonged to the jet set. I had fought hard against the capital gains tax being applied to agricultural land. This legislation treated the land a farmer bequeathed to his family as if it had been sold at fair market value, thus creating a tax liability that often forced his heirs to sell their birthright. Land was part of the heritage of western Canada. Thousands and thousands of immigrants had come into western Canada to acquire land and to own it for the first time. With its capital gains tax, the government appeared to be reaching out to destroy an important part of western Canada's culture.

I said all this in my speech. I also dealt with the effect of tax reform on the oil and gas industries, and the LIFT program (Lower Inventory for Tomorrow) which had placed so many restrictions on the farmers that they had reduced production by 200 million bushels. This had cost western Canada $600 million. Bill Wilson, one of Canada's best columnists, wrote up my speech in the *Montreal Star* on January 19, observing:

> The Liberal disinclination to hear what Mr. Horner is saying is, however, a great pity.... It should be noted that in Mr. Horner's analysis there is no hint of anti-French backlash.... What does emerge from the Horner speech, strong and sincere, is the complaint of a region that feels slighted and misunderstood.

Contrary to Bill Wilson's observation, someone within the Liberal party was listening to me. When John Turner announced his 1973 budget later that year, he gave me credit for changing his mind when he brought in the provision that capital gains would not apply to a family farm that stayed in the family.

During that year and the next the government's legislative program was not seriously challenged by the Conservative party. Stanfield believed he was going to be the next prime minister and didn't want to appear negative-thinking. Thus, he quickly took public credit for being father to the government's plan to index pensions, which, next to the unemployment insurance revisions, contributed most to the escalation of government costs. What is more, once indexed pensions were introduced, the indexing of salaries had to follow, which meant the automatic rise of costs. I would contend that the root of our present rate of inflation lies not in energy prices, as so many believe, but in indexing.

During the period 1973-75, the cost of a barrel of oil in Canada was far below world prices. When oil was selling for nine dollars a barrel on the international market, Canadians were paying four dollars. The curse of the Canadian economy was indexing. I remember talking about this to Bruce Whitestone, the economist and writer who had been adviser to Diefenbaker.

"Indexing won't work," he said. "It's absolutely wrong because it perpetuates inflation."

"Well, will inflation ever stop?" I asked.

"The question isn't whether inflation will stop. The question is whether you believe it will. If you believe it won't, then for certain it will never stop."

Stanfield, oddly enough, was soon to advocate his ninety-day wage and price freeze to stop the expectations of inflation — ignoring, of course, his contribution to its cause. Still searching for the gimmick, the program with which he could rise to fame, Stanfield picked up the price-freeze idea from President Nixon's three-month freeze in the United States. By the end of 1972, Stanfield was doing a lot of talking about it. So was Marcel Lambert. Jim Gillies (Don Valley), Stanfield's main financial adviser, was also a strong advocate of it at the time. Without benefit of discussion in caucus, it became the policy of the Conservative party in February 1973.

During the summer of 1973, as I mulled it all over at the ranch, noting the drastic effect Nixon's freeze had had on the cattle market, I came to the conclusion that a price freeze was wrong for Canada. I remember listening to Joe Clark on CBC radio attempting to explain to the moderator the effect a ninety-day freeze would have and what the government would do thereafter. He failed to convince the moderator, and he certainly failed to convince me. Back in Ottawa in September, I told caucus we should rethink our position. Dr. Ritchie (Dauphin) was the only member to support me. Interestingly, Stanfield agreed that perhaps we should rethink it. However, a week or two later he announced that while he had given this second thought, he was wedded to the idea of wage and price controls whether we were or not. Jim Gillies supported him to the hilt.

Gillies subsequently changed his mind, but no one I know of in caucus was aware of this until the 1974 election had come and gone. We were all poorer because of the way in which caucus operated under Stanfield. I tried to explain this in a letter to Gillies on August 21, 1974:

In reviewing in my mind last week's caucus and the things that were said publicly and privately, I can't help but feel that you must have a completely different concept from my own on how a political party should work.

Naturally you joined the caucus being widely recognized as a financial critic and in a position in which you were looked up to by all caucus members; therefore in my estimation you owed caucus a debt in return for the respect in which many caucus members held you. Coupled with this, of course, you owed Mr. Stanfield loyalty and respect as Leader of the Party. When you came up to me at noon and said that of course I was right on the American devaluation and wage and price controls and attempted to convince me that you had struggled with Mr. Stanfield in an effort to convince him that it was wrong to hold steadfastly to wage and price controls, I suppose you thought this should have absolved you from any of the blame that I or any of my friends could attach to you for the Party's fatal error.

Actually a party must live far beyond any one leader. Caucus definitely looked to you for direction. Having dealt privately with Mr. Stanfield and failed, you must live and die with him. What you should have done was explained your true feelings to caucus, then maybe with the help of caucus, Mr. Stanfield could have been convinced to amend or modify his stand and the Party might well have won the last election.

Caucus members in any political party must work together, not run individually to the Leader in what might appear to some to be an attempt to vie for a better personal position. I can only regret that within the P.C. Party too many have gone the same route as you. They may have benefited personally but the Party has been harmed because of the lack of their overall wisdom. To me, caucus was a sham. There was not a free exchange of true feelings and the total benefit from all members of caucus will not be reaped until it becomes a more honest place in which to survive. . . .

In any case this letter is long enough and it will give you an idea of my thinking on the errors which you made if you truly were opposed to wage and price controls in the last election.

Lest the reader think I was just the disruptive force Stanfield believed me to be, I should point out that for the sake of the party I tried to help whenever possible. For whatever good it did, I kept on trying over the years. For example, in the fall of 1973, when we had a rail strike, the government brought in legislation putting the non-ops back to work at an increase of only 30 cents an hour (though the non-op unions had agreed to drop their demands from an initial 55-cent increase to the 38-cent increase recommended by the arbitration board).

"We've got a great chance here to get the labour vote," I told Stanfield in caucus. "Let's advocate a 38-cent-an-hour increase. Let's beat the NDP to it."

It was obvious the NDP were going to move an amendment increasing the settlement to 38 cents. But Stanfield wouldn't go for it. When the vote came on the NDP amendment, I voted for it. Well, this was a shock to a lot of people. Jack Horner voting with the NDP! What next? Stanfield sent Jim McGrath to see me. They were embarrassed. (Since Stanfield was going to be next prime minister, he wanted to show the world his party was united.) In an effort to smooth things over, McGrath said they were prepared to move an amendment for a 34-cent-an-hour increase. Would I support this? I agreed. When the amendment was brought up, it was carried, the NDP voting with the Conservatives against the government.

While I was instrumental in getting the railway non-ops an extra four cents an hour, because of inflation union workers were asking for increases of four dollars an hour about a year later. Thus, one can see how out of step this particular settlement was. In the months that followed, I saw — for the first time in my political career — a series of illegal strikes. Workers were striking before the end of their contracts, demanding wage adjustments to take into consideration the rapid rate of inflation. It was obvious, to me at least, that a party advocating wage and price controls when the workers were justifiably trying to catch up, was not going to succeed.

I did my very best to convince Stanfield to change his mind on wage and price controls. I started in September 1973 and worked at it in caucus repeatedly until the annual meeting in March 1974. Before the '74 election I had a long, long talk with Stanfield, urging him that until he became prime minister and had all the facts before him he should use the Mackenzie King tactic: "Wage and price controls if necessary, but not necessarily wage and price controls." If he had done this, he probably would have won the election. Stanfield did more than drop the football. He kicked it away.

The 1973-74 minority parliament was an important one for me because it gave me my first chance as a journeyman parliamentarian to show I could be something more than critic. The question came up as to whether Conservative members should accept the chairmanships of any committees. Stanfield seemed to rely on Erik Nielsen (Yukon) for Commons strategy. Nielsen, a member who rarely attended the House, was regaining some of the image he had had during the Rivard affair as the cold, cold hunter from the north. Now, he was the cold, cold strategist who was going to upset the government in its minority position. I didn't think Erik had spent enough time around Ottawa to develop as a strategist or in any way to take Gordon Churchill's place in this capacity. I remember expressing this view to Diefenbaker and he, of course, disagreed with me because of his fondness for Nielsen. In any case, it was Nielsen's concept that no Conservative should take the chairmanship of any committee.

The Liberals put up Gerry Duquet for chairman of the Transportation Committee. Gerry was MP from Quebec East. I had nothing against him personally, but I felt he didn't understand transportation problems and that we should get someone who was more interested. I suggested to Mazankowski that Art Portelance (Gamelin) or Jacques Trudel (Montreal-Bourassa) were better choices; both of them had been members of the Transportation Committee for a number of years and had taken an active interest. The Liberal party, however, made it clear that they had other roles to play and neither was scheduled to be suggested as chairman. It was obvious to us the government was using the chairman-ship as some kind of reward for Duquet. Maz and I wanted someone more suitable, and Maz suggested I take the job, despite our party's position on this question.

"You'd never get that by Stanfield and company," I told him.

Maz didn't think it impossible. By this time he had developed a great liaison with Stanfield. Maz told me everything that Stanfield was thinking and then went back to Stanfield with my thoughts. It was a crazy arrangement, hardly a way for grown men to run a political party, but this was the way Stanfield wanted it.

In order to win the vote in committee, however, we had to have the support of the NDP. I thought about it for a minute. I had worked well with Frank Howard after my fight with him early on in my political career. I'd worked very, very well indeed with Arnold Peters and Les Benjamin. I told Maz, "The trick would be to get the NDP to nominate me and the Conservatives to second it. If we had all our people there, I would win." Maz thought he could arrange that, and he set about doing so. Arnold Peters told me I was crazy, that as chairman, my ability as a critic would be severely hampered. I explained I had played the role of the critic for quite a while and I might even be interested in seeing what could happen as chairman.

When Maz was first in Ottawa, Ged Baldwin had told him, "If you want something accepted in caucus, raise it just as caucus is about to break up; no one will be paying attention and everyone will agree to anything." Maz used this tactic to get my nomination approved. When the vote came about in committee, first of all we rejected Duquet by a combined vote of the Conservatives and the NDP; then Frank Howard nominated me, seconded by a Conservative. I won.

I was more than pleased in my role as chairman. We called the witnesses we wanted, and I was able to allow the Conservatives quite a bit of latitude in their questioning. No one took exception to this. In fact, the committee functioned so effectively that columnist Charles Lynch reported in the Ottawa *Citizen*:

> Horner's chairmanship of this important committee has been one of the wonders of this Parliament in that it has brought out a hitherto hidden side of the Hon. Member for Crowfoot, once best known as a partisan, hot-tempered roughneck.
>
> There is a lot of respect for Horner on the Hill, but most of it stems from his penchant for speaking his mind, a quality all too rare among our parliamentarians. The idea that Horner might possess hidden depths of statesmanship had occurred to few, and when he

was elected to the chairmanship of the transport committee, it was widely anticipated that the committee's proceedings would be chaotic.

Yet, in the course of yesterday's debate on the committee's report, there was praise for Horner's chairmanship from all sides of the House.

Nevertheless, when the chairman had to be re-elected the next year, Stanfield — aware that we had finessed him — said, "No Conservative members will be accepting chairmanships." I argued with him that I thought I'd helped the Conservative party quite a bit, while not being overtly partisan in my rulings. I likened the chairmanship to the umpire in a ball game. If the umpire is too one-sided in his decisions, the ball game breaks up because there's no use in playing. But Stanfield didn't want me to take the job for a second term. I think he felt I was getting too much recognition and growing too much; he was deadly afraid of me and of what I might do in the years ahead.

Maz came to me, on Stanfield's instructions, to tell me that under no circumstance could any Conservative place or second my nomination. When the Liberals asked what I was going to do, I told them straight. I said, "The Conservative party thinks that I have been too generous to you fellows and not kind enough to them. Consequently, they're not going to nominate me." This had the effect I wanted, because if Stanfield didn't want me to be chairman, I wanted to be chairman. This was the state of our relationship. The Liberal members said, "If that's the case, Jack, we'll nominate you. You've been doing a good job. But we'd like a Liberal to be vice-chairman."

Well, when the Liberals nominated me, the Conservatives couldn't very well vote against me, and as the NDP had no qualms about my chairmanship I was chosen unanimously. Stanfield could like it or lump it! I was not a subservient child and didn't see why I should behave like one. Transportation is a mighty important thing to western Canada, and if in some small way I could help western Canada by being chairman, I wanted to be able to.

The most humorous incident connected with my chairmanship of the Transportation Committee resulted from a personal initiative to get through a potentially difficult sitting when the CNR was before the committee. One of the renowned characters around the Hill is Walter Smith, in essence the public relations man for the CNR in Ottawa. He came to me at six o'clock following an afternoon meeting to ask if I had seen Mr. Paul in the gallery. Paul was a contractor from Toronto who had built a CN overpass but hadn't been paid for it: the CNR had ruled that the cement used in the structure didn't conform with their requirements. As the CNR trains kept using the overpass, Paul believed he was entitled to compensation, and he had taken the CNR to court. He had lost.

Well, any individual in Ottawa can walk in to watch committee proceedings — though of course he can't take part in any way unless he's there on official business. I had seen Paul in the gallery that afternoon and had called him out to tell him that I didn't want any trouble. I told him that if he left matters in my hands, I felt I could get him something (the CNR was considering an out-of-court settlement) but that if he interrupted our proceedings in any way, his case was lost as far as I was concerned. Paul assured me he would do nothing untowards.

I told Walter Smith all this, but it wasn't good enough for him. He was a dutiful servant of the CNR and he was obviously worried. He said that if Paul was in the audience, then a plain clothes security officer should also be present that evening when the CNR officials came back before the committee. Although I didn't think it necessary, I agreed to phone Security and arrange it.

As it turned out, all the Security staff had been allocated their duties for the day. There was no one available to come to the committee meeting. I was still wondering what to do about it when at supper I met Bill Skoreyko and a mutual friend, Lawrence Bitusak. Lawrence was a big man, broad-shouldered, thick-necked; looked important. It occurred to me that he might provide the solution to Walter's problem.

"I need someone to pose as a security commissioner this evening," I told him. "If you're going to be around, how about coming to my committee? Come in about three minutes after I do, survey the room, then take a chair at the side and listen to the proceedings."

Lawrence thought this would be kind of interesting. He had never sat in on any of the committees.

Just before eight when the committee was due to start, Walter came running up to me: "Have you got your security man? Have you got a man to protect my officials?"

"Walter, rest assured."

"Who is he? Who is he?"

"You'll see him when he comes into the room. He's wearing a brown suitcoat and I think he has some yellow in his tie. He'll come in and take a seat at the side. You go over and tell him who you want him to watch."

When Lawrence came in a few minutes later, Walter thought all was well.

The committee went along smoothly. Mr. Paul didn't interrupt, didn't get up and shout or make any wild accusations at Bill Hunt (who was the main spokesman for the CNR). When we finished at ten o'clock, I said my normal thank-yous to the CNR officials and left. As I passed Lawrence, I said, "For your services, sir, I'll pour you a drink if you come up to my office. But don't leave the room at the same time I do." Meanwhile, the CNR officials — there was a whole host of them — were gathering up their books and papers. They were a few minutes after me in leaving.

Up in my room, I had just poured a drink for Lawrence and Bill Skoreyko when Walter Smith burst into my outer office. He was completely beside himself.

"Where was Security?" he shouted. "What happened to Security?"

"Walter, what's the matter?" I asked.

He proceeded to tell me. Mr. Paul had created an incident in the hallway. He had spit in the face of the CNR vice-president. It had been with the greatest control that Hunt hadn't hit him.

"Security should have been there!" shouted Walter. "Security should have prevented this and should have arrested Paul on the spot! Where was Security?"

Just then, Lawrence walked by the open door of my inner office with a drink in his hand. Walter looked over at him and saw Security. I couldn't hold a straight face any longer.

"I've been conned!" Walter roared at the top of his voice. "I've been conned. You S.O.B., Horner, you've conned me!" I'd never seen Walter so agitated. "There's going to be a lawsuit over this," he shouted, "and you're going to have to appear as a witness."

I tried to calm him. "Come on in. I'll pour you a drink. Let's get Mr. Hunt on the phone."

In a situation like this, there's no other course but to tell the exact truth, and I gave Bill Hunt the full story. He took it in his stride, said it was one of those unfortunate things one had to put up with. He found it very difficult, but the matter was closed.

Overall, there is no question that my experience as chairman of the Transportation Committee helped the Conservative party as well as helping to maintain an interest in western Canada's problems in the field of transportation and the moving of grain. Also, my experience as chairman substantially helped me as a parliamentarian. In later years, when Prime Minister Trudeau asked me to join the Liberal party, he referred to my role as chairman of the Transportation Committee, saying how smoothly that committee had functioned and how well I had handled my responsibilities.

Meanwhile, the press were recognizing that Horner was more than a rabble-rousing member of the Opposition. Some of them started to see me as a capable and serious-minded parliamentarian. On April 11, 1974. Bill Wilson wrote in the *Ottawa Journal*:

> In this sombre and depressing transport situation, one of the few bright spots is the chairmanship of the Commons Transport Committee, from which some good — or at least some common sense — may come. The chairman is the Conservative MP from Crowfoot. . . .
>
> His reputation as a maverick is suffering serious damage by his habit of making good speeches in the House which stand up well long afterwards.

I had always taken my work as an MP seriously, and no more so than during the early months of 1974 when it was obvious to all of us that we were heading into an election. On the day the government was defeated, Stanfield phoned me.

"Jack, I think you and I should have a talk."

"Yes," I said. "We should have had one two months ago." I had become so thoroughly fed up with the Conservative party's death wish to proceed into an election on wage and price controls that I hadn't attended caucus for nearly two months. Wage and price controls could only do us harm. It was obvious to me that if the unions were demanding a catch-up position, then thousands and thousands of non-organized workers would also be caught in the squeeze.

"When do you want to see me?" I asked Stanfield. "This afternoon?"

"No. The vote's coming at five o'clock, and I think the government will be defeated. So I'll be preparing my speech this afternoon. I'd like to see you first thing tomorrow."

About five after nine the next morning, Stanfield phoned me. Said he would come over and see me on his way to caucus. My office was close to the old caucus room in the West Block, but psychologically this was a bad move on Stanfield's part. He was the leader; I should have gone to see him.

"Well, Jack," he said when he arrived. "You and I got along fairly well for a while. I don't know just what happened."

I agreed that we had, and mentioned wage and price controls. Stanfield was looking very, very confident. He almost threw out his chest (but he had such a bad back he couldn't) and said he was going to win the election. What's more, he said he was going to win with wage and price controls. I told him I disagreed. We talked about the polls for a while (I didn't agree with him there either).

We then went down the list of his shadow cabinet. I pointed to some less than acceptable appointments. Flora MacDonald, for example, had been given Indian Affairs in complete disregard for traditional Native views on a woman's proper role. By definition, she lacked credibility in the eyes of the Native leaders with whom she had to deal. Linc Alexander was another. Stanfield had him as immigration critic. And David MacDonald, who as a minister had probably never had enough money to decide anything more important than whether or not to buy a second-hand car, had been given Regional Economic Expansion. Then Joe Clark's name came up.

"I understand you don't like him either," said Stanfield.

"With his experience, what would I hire him for? Clark might make it as a sheep herder. That's about all the good I can see in him."

Towards the end of our discussion I apologized for being a difficult member of the party. "If you want me to run as an Independent," I said, "I'll run as an Independent." Stanfield said he wanted me to run as a Conservative. So I said I would, and I assured him that during the next sixty days I'd be the best boy he had. "I won't touch wage and price controls. You'll never hear me mention the words. I won't campaign for them or against them. But I'll give you only sixty days. That'll take you two or three days past the election."

As I had predicted, the wage and price control program proved a disaster in the election, though I hadn't calculated that the Liberals would campaign so strongly against it. They worked on the popular fear, but that's the game of politics. About two weeks before the election, the people went away from Stanfield in droves. In many, many instances, instead of voting NDP, the labour force voted Liberal just to stop Stanfield. This gave Trudeau his majority. Dief, of course, was absolutely right to come out during the campaign to try and soften things a bit by calling publicly for the limitation of controls to prices until wages caught up. I'd been up to his nomination meeting in 1974 and had told him my views.

As an instructive sidelight on the election, when preparing my campaign, I met with a group of right-wing free-enterprise Calgary businessmen who believed the Conservative party had not fought the NDP-Liberal moves towards socialism in the last parliament. They wondered what could be done to prevent this after the 1974 election. I said that Stanfield might win. They didn't think so, but if he did, he too would be in a minority position and would go down the road with the NDP. They didn't see any prospect of there being a substantial difference between a Stanfield or Trudeau minority government. Either would go hand-in-hand with Lewis; socialism would creep more and more into society, and government costs would continue to crowd the free-market economy. I thought there was some foundation for their fears. Certainly, Stanfield, eager to stay in power, would acquiesce to the NDP.

These businessmen told me that they proposed to raise money which, under my guidance, they would contribute to the election of hard-nosed free-enterprisers who would owe a greater loyalty to a free-market economy than to Stanfield and the Conservative party. If twenty or so such members were elected, a number equal to the NDP, they would be able to go to Stanfield and say, "If you're going to buy NDP demands, you've lost our support, so you're no farther ahead." Thus, they could act as a severe check on any concessions Stanfield might be tempted to make to the socialist philosophy.

At the mention of campaign money, my ears perked up. I had an inner fear that Stanfield and company would severely hamper the money flow to those who had voted against the language legislation. This was always the threat and always the worry of an independently minded or hard-line member in the House. If he went against his party, the party would remember come election day and cut off his finances. This had the effect of making many members subservient to the wishes of the party hierarchy. I didn't mention this to my friends at the meeting, but it was in the back of my mind.

When they asked how much money it would take, I told them, "You're looking at about a group of twenty to twenty-two, and you've got to give each guy at least two thousand dollars to make certain he notices your campaign contribution. If you give him anything less, he'll hardly know it's arrived. Money disappears very quickly in a campaign."

They were startled at the amount involved, but they agreed.

I said, "I'll give you the names. You guys collect the money. I'll tell each candidate who gets it that he owes his first allegiance to private enterprise over and above anything else. If they have any hesitation, they won't get the money." It was just that simple.

They raised well over the necessary amount, in fact twice as much, and the twenty or so candidates we had talked about received healthy contributions. But word somehow got out. Peter Bawden sent these businessmen a list of names, requesting that five hundred dollars be sent to each person on his list. I looked over the list and suggested the principle they advocated was out the window if they sent five hundred dollars to candidates like Jim McGrath, a left-wing Conservative. It was, of course, their money; if they wanted to send it, I wasn't going to stop them. A contribution to George Hees and Duff Roblin, I didn't mind. Certainly, both fell within the category of believers in private enterprise. The one I

140

did put my foot down on was Paul Hellyer. I said the jig was up as far as I was concerned if Hellyer got any money. I would be through with them completely. Even though things tended to get a little out of hand with the party aware of what was going on, it was an interesting exercise to see people who were Conservatives in more than just name making an effort on behalf of sound philosophy in an election.

During the campaign in Crowfoot, I lived up to my promise to Stanfield. This allowed my Liberal opponent, Ernie Patterson, to get up at every public forum to say: "Where is this guy Jack Horner? He's afraid of being kicked out of the Conservative party. He's afraid of Mr. Stanfield. He's afraid to say what he used to say about bilingualism and wage and price controls." The bilingualism bit was thrown in because everyone knew Stanfield had disallowed the candidature of Leonard Jones in Moncton because of his stand against the language legislation. This gave Ernie his ammunition. But every time he made these charges, I just sat on the stage and laughed. My constituents knew I wasn't afraid of Stanfield or anybody else. I never once entered the debate on wage and price controls, and my seat was never in any danger.

On election day, July 8, the Trudeau Liberals emerged with a majority. The Conservatives lost twelve seats overall. Although we gained in the West, we dropped in Ontario and the Maritimes. I had been a good boy throughout the campaign — just as I'd promised Stanfield — but the sixty days I'd specified were now up. A few days after the election, on July 13 to be exact, I publicly called for Stanfield to step down as leader. He'd had three kicks at the car. And he'd lost the election because he wouldn't budge on wage and price controls. Although I was not the first — or the last — to call for his resignation, there were some who took exception. Doug Roche (Edmonton-Strathcona) wrote an article criticizing my stand against Stanfield. To this, I replied by writing him a letter on August 2:

> Rather than writing a newspaper article outlining the weaknesses of your case I decided to write directly to you.
>
> First of all, you suggest that Stanfield should stay on because as yet he has not trained anyone as a back-up man to take his place. Neither Mr. Stanfield nor any other leader of the P.C. Party has the right to pick his successor and, in fact, leadership conventions, where there is the obvious laying-on of hands, do not in any way help a political party. Manning picked Strom and the Party nearly died.
>
> Leadership conventions must awaken the Party at the grass roots and entice all people from all walks of life to take an interest in the Party. Therefore, candidates from all walks of life and all regions

should be encouraged. The laying-on of hands tends to discourage this process.

Secondly, you suggest Mr. Stanfield should stay on until the Party can develop a whole new set of policies. A new leader tends to implant his concepts and policies in the Party. During a leadership convention each prospective leader outlines the direction in which he believes his Party and the country should be going. Therefore each prospective leader naturally favours a certain set of policies and, therefore, the establishment of a whole new set of policies before a new leader is chosen would be a complete waste of time.

If Mr. Stanfield and his supporters intend to have him go through another Federal Election then by all means they should encourage him to stay on, but to encourage him to stay on for a couple of years will only lengthen the leadership contest, with the various prospective leaders offering different policies or different concepts and this will create greater divisions within the Party. Also, some bitterness tends to develop between the candidates. This is evident even today in the Liberal Party; for example, Judy LaMarsh is still mad at John Turner. If Mr. Stanfield delayed his resignation for two years, the leadership race within the P.C. Party would then last a full three years. This would tend to divide the Party even more than it is now.

I thought these things should be pointed out to you and I hope you don't mind my doing so. Of course, if you favour Mr. Stanfield for another election by all means support him. If you don't, then try to help the Party unite behind a new leader and give that new leader as much time as possible to become known and accepted in the various regions of Canada and give him a chance to outline the general theme of his policies to the voters in the various regions of the country.

At a meeting of the Conservative caucus in Ottawa on August 14, Stanfield announced that he would resign before the next election. But he refused to set a date, other than saying that it would be before our annual meeting in March the following year. I was condemned for stating publicly that he should step down immediately. Beyond Stan Schumacher and Doc Ritchie, I received very little support in pressing for an immediate resignation. Few members seemed to understand what I was getting at. But I stuck to my guns. Obviously, Stanfield would be treated as a lame-duck leader once he had announced his decision to resign. This proved to be true. He ceased to be news. The party was in limbo from August 1974 until February 1976. Meanwhile, the media watched the prospective leadership candidates to see which one was making a move and which one was playing wait-and-see.

One of the problems in criticizing Stanfield was that all the time he was leader there was about him the illusion of the nice guy, of poor old Stanfield who never meant anybody any harm. Therefore, anyone who criticized him was looked on with a great deal of scepticism, if not downright distaste. It was like kicking a crippled child. You just didn't do such a thing, and certainly not in plain view.

As I predicted, the leadership race was on from the moment Stanfield announced he would not run in another election. This was a fact, whether he liked it or not and whether the majority in caucus approved it or not. "Mr. Stanfield is in an impossible position," I had written in my letter to Jim Gillies on August 21. "He cannot help but favour someone as leader and being a normal person, that someone will more than likely have similar views to his own. If others who hold different views do not feel it is a fair contest, then the division within the P.C. Party will not heal, only widen and western Canada will look for another route to express itself. If the party puts any faith in Joe Clark, Harvie Andre and Doug Roche, and thinks they are representative of western Canada, it is very foolish indeed. These are three men eager and willing to serve some master who can give them the recognition and personal advancements they want, not necessarily a political party or philosophy."

Shortly after our August caucus, Bob Coates (Cumberland-Colchester North) paid me a visit and outlined at length his belief that the next leader had to come from caucus rather than from the non-elected advisers. Coates was dead right in his assertion that caucus would not tolerate a new leader who was not from its ranks. We began to go down the list of caucus members, ticking off all who were possible candidates. In Coates's mind, it boiled down to one person — me. I was genuinely surprised because, while we had always been on very good terms, Bob and I had never really been what you'd call close friends. With the reputation I had established opposing Stanfield, I knew that if I ever did go for the leadership I would definitely need support from Nova Scotia, that this would be a prime requirement. So I told Coates I appreciated his thoughts, but that I had to do a lot of thinking about it. I would consider it and let him know when I had made up my mind. I certainly was in no rush.

In considering whether I should be a candidate, of course I was fully aware of the position I'd carved out for myself within the party. I was a rebel. I had attacked Stanfield. I had done myself considerable harm with the party power-brokers. However, I certainly thought that someone had to attempt to polarize what I considered the aggressive builders in the Conservative party — the builders of Canada in the Conservative party. And I knew I was on the right track in much of my thinking on economic questions. In May 1974, Alberta's minister of Federal and Intergovernmental Affairs, Don Getty, had written me in response to some of my pretty long and thoughtful speeches on the oil and gas industry in Canada (which I didn't even know he was reading) to tell me how impressed he was and how correct I was.

I shied away from the terms right- and left-wing, because in this conceptual framework I would be pigeonholed the absolute conservative of the crowd, which would leave me a pretty small base of support. Anyway, I never saw myself as an extreme or rigid right-winger. Neither, I suspect, did those NDP members with whom I worked closely in Parliament. Nevertheless, there were things in which I steadfastly believed: that we were giving away too much money in unemployment insurance benefits and indexing, that we were wrong in our approach to bilingualism, and so on. There were a number of issues (most of which I have already described) on which I had staked out a position that no front-running Conservative had a right even to claim. I knew these positions were very popular across Canada. Still, I was far from satisfied that I should run for leader.

When I went to talk to Diefenbaker about the leadership, he immediately said, "I know why you're here."

"Why am I here?"

"You want my opinion. You're going into the leadership race."

"Oh no, I'm not."

"Yes you are."

"Well, let me make that decision."

"Now, you be careful," he said. "You watch yourself. You've got to go for it."

I turned to him. "Well, Mr. Diefenbaker, if I were to go for it, where would you be?"

"Oh, you don't have to worry about me, Jack. I'll be with you. You've been too trustworthy a friend to me; I could never do a thing against you. But I don't want you to announce it. I will do the announcing when it's time."

As the weeks passed, I began to look at the leadership more seriously, as the would-be candidates began to make their moves. When the new parliament opened on September 30, some of the hopefuls took the opportunity provided by the Throne Speech debate to make ringing declarations of their conceptions of Canada. When I saw Claude Wagner and Flora MacDonald on the list, I thought I'd better put together a solid speech on some of Canada's economic problems. I spoke the full forty minutes. I was just starting in on what I considered should be an industrial policy for Canada when I ran out of time. I had numerous reprints of that speech run off, so after that, when anyone wanted to know my views on Canada's economic problems, I sent him a copy. I include a few paragraphs here:

The fundamental requirement for attracting capital and people, and trusting the judgment and skills of these people, is to create the proper environment in which the capital and knowledge can be put to work. Environment, in this case, can be defined as the position our government takes toward business and the marketplace system. The government should state its position as clearly as possible and deviate as little as possible over the longest possible term.

It is becoming increasingly important for the federal government to state its priorities, one of which should include an industrial policy. A clear enunciation of priorities should be given the Canadian citizen so that he may determine where is the best place to concentrate his effort or whether he should bother making any effort at all. . . .

What should an industrial policy include? Any policy being considered by Canada should be, in the future, only a Canadian policy if it is to be truly beneficial to the country as a whole. Why should we devise an industrial policy any other way? Regional policies will increasingly have a divisive effect in Canada. Every one of us in this House can think of policies which have been devised in the past which have been regional in concept. An industrial policy should be truly Canadian. We had an industrial policy which applied to regions all across Canada, within certain boundary lines. Some provinces were included, some not at all. This tends to divide.

Bargaining away any of the resources produced in one part of Canada to confer a benefit on another part of Canada is a dangerous act and leads to obvious divisions in the country. All parts of Canada are sufficiently sophisticated to understand the results of this type of action and should recoil against such political manoeuvring. As I was saying, this is a most dangerous route. Primary industry, resource industry and manufacturing industry which have an advantage in world markets should be encouraged to reach their highest economic level and bring maximum value to Canada as a whole. . . .

I dealt earlier with the foreign takeover of a number of Canadian companies. In the past we have seen many takeovers of the Canadian economy by American corporations. Probably in the future the only change will be that the purchasers will be Japanese, German or nationals of OPEC countries moving into Canada. If anyone is to be blamed for the loss, it should be the Canadian financial community, the people who control the money, not Canadian businessmen. Many members of the House have condemned our businessmen. However, in many cases it is not their fault; it is the fault of the people who are supplying them with the money. Where does the money come from to make purchases of Canadian companies? Studies indicate, as I stated earlier, that the greatest portion of these funds come directly from Canadian banks. Canadian depositors have supplied the necessary funds for foreign takeovers. This was pointed out in the Gray report.

Businessmen are well aware of the fact that if a company can finance through relatively low-cost debt, then the value of the equity — that is, the share portion of the company — increases correspondingly. Generally, it is this lever which the company seeks for the investment of foreign money. In other words, we want to use foreign money for operating capital, but not necessarily equity capital. . . .

The only approach that will work is to provide the Canadian entrepreneur, executive or proprietor, who wishes to build a Canadian corporation with a better deal to sell to a Canadian rather than a foreigner. This keeps him motivated, and Canada keeps control of her industries. Unfortunately, one of the difficulties in developing Canadian industry is the staggering overhead of carrying the cost of Canadian government. This overhead shows up as one of the civilized world's highest tax burdens which falls increasingly upon Canada's productive middle class. How many times have I sat in the House in the past few years and heard it said that this or that budget is increasing the burden on the middle class! We cannot do that forever or we will kill the goose that laid the golden egg.

As I looked at those testing the leadership waters, I was not impressed by the possible contestants. The only one who worried me was Peter Lougheed. I asked Hugh, who was Alberta's deputy premier, whether Lougheed would run. Hugh reassured me he would not. However, I wanted Hugh to arrange an appointment for me with Lougheed because I felt it important to be absolutely sure of this. If he ran, there was no question in my mind that he would win. I wasn't going to enter the race for the sake of being an also-ran. I finally met with him on October 23, 1974. He was very gracious. First, we talked about the problems of Alberta; I brought up the plight of east-central Alberta and suggested that Lougheed should consider the need for more water in the drier parts of the province. I then sought out his opinion on the Ottawa scene — what he thought about the leadership race and what his ambitions were in this regard. He was evasive to some degree. He said that he would not turn down a call to serve his country but didn't relish the idea of changing chairs. He looked over at the chair behind his desk and said, "Jack, that may not be the most powerful seat in Canada, but, by far, it is the most interesting. We are going to have the major part to play in the future of this country because we're going to have the money." I came away believing he wouldn't enter the race and that only in the rarest of circumstances could he be drafted. In retrospect, I think Lougheed was afraid to take the chance. Had he done so, he would be prime minister today and Alberta would have no quarrel with Ottawa.

I had watched Peter Lougheed with interest from the beginnings of his political career. As I mentioned earlier, my brother Hugh had joined him prior to the provincial election in 1967.

When Manning had retired in December 1968, Hugh told Lougheed they could win the resultant by-election in Strathcona East if they ran a candidate of ethnic origin from Edmonton. Lougheed and company had a number of people in mind, but Hugh's man, Bill Yurko, won the nomination and the seat: a feather in Doc's cap. Lougheed was taking careful note of who he had around him and he was utterly amazed, or so he told me later, that Doc could call their margin of victory within forty votes. When another seat became vacant with the death of Bill Switzer, the Alberta Liberal leader, Lougheed turned to Hugh. The by-election was in Edson, part of Doc's old federal riding. The Conservatives, with the one by-election victory under their belts, needed to demonstrate they were truly on the march. This, however, was no easy contest. Social Credit, under their new leader, Harry Strom, had to win to prove they were not in serious trouble; the NDP, without representation in the legislature, were desperate to elect their new leader, Grant Notley; and it was vital to the Liberals, now reduced to one MLA, to show they weren't completely dead. This was one by-election with all the makings for a darned tight race.

Hugh phoned me at the ranch about two weeks before the vote. He talked and talked. I thought, "Why's he talking so long? He wants something from me." Sure enough, he was telling me how bad things were in the riding, just hopeless, how everyone was through with the Conservative party because of what it had done to Diefenbaker in 1966.

I said, "You've told them, of course, how hard you fought for Diefenbaker. You don't have anything to be ashamed of."

"I've told them, but it doesn't matter, they still aren't going to vote for us."

Then Hugh asked if I would approach Diefenbaker. He knew I had more nerve when it came to Dief then he did.

"There's no use me talking to Dief," I said. "You know very well he doesn't even participate in federal by-elections."

Hugh said he knew that, but he had to do something. We talked it over for a little longer, and I learned that the Conservative candidate, Bob Dowling, had ridden with Dief on the campaign train in 1965. Dief might remember him.

"Would a telegram from Dief help you?" I asked.

"Oh, a telegram would be just wonderful. Could you get it?"

I said I didn't know, but I'd try.

I phoned Dief and told him about this long, depressing conversation with Hugh, how everyone in the constituency was down on the Conservative party for what they'd done to him. This pleased Diefenbaker, I could just see him smiling at that one. I went on to say that if there was just some way he could come out . . . .

"Jack, you know very well I never . . . ."

"I didn't want you to come out in person, but could you send a wire to this fellow Bob Dowling? You remember Bob Dowling; he's the druggist from Jasper who rode on the train with you and Olive when you went through Hugh's constituency in '65."

"Oh sure." (Whether he did or not I don't know, but he professed to.)

"Could you send a wire to him, saying he's an old friend and you know he would serve the constituents well?"

Well, no, Dief couldn't. That would be participating.

I said, "Mr. Diefenbaker, I hope some day I get to be as high and mighty as you."

"Now you're getting mad."

"No, I'm not getting mad. I'm just telling you the facts of life. We people who stuck together and fought for you — Hugh and I and Bob Dowling and the like — we've got to stick together now. I just wish some day I'd get so high and mighty I could neglect my friends the way you are going to be neglecting them in this case."

"Well, you didn't have to say that! What do you want me to do?"

"I want you to send this wire."

"All right then, send it."

"Send what?"

"Send just what you said a while ago."

I hadn't written it out, but I said, "All right. If I send it and put it in your name, where do I say you are?"

"Jack, I'm catching a plane for Regina. I'll be at the Saskatchewan Hotel tonight. If anyone wants to verify it or check it, tell them to call me there. You go ahead and send it. You've got it all written out."

I had just hung up and was walking around in a bit of daze, trying to remember what I'd said should be in this telegram, when Dief called me back. "Jack, I forgot to tell you. Put at the start, 'While I normally never participate in a provincial by-election, because of my personal friendship with what's-his-name. . . .' Put this right at the beginning and then you can go on." I said that was easily done.

I got back to Hugh and we sent the wire to Dowling. It read:

Dear Bob.

While I normally never express my view in a provincial by-election, because of our personal friendship I feel inclined to do so and wish you kind regards and much success realizing you have much to offer your people in these difficult times.

Sincerely yours

John G. Diefenbaker

Saskatchewan Hotel Regina

(When I later received the bill for $2.11, I had the bad-boy urge to send it to Dief. But, of course, I just paid it.)

In the meantime, I phoned Dowling to tell him the wire was coming, and in no uncertain terms I let him know I had begged for it and that I didn't beg easy. I said that I wanted it used in every paper and over every radio station, because it was worth that much to have me do what I had done for him. If he didn't make full use of it, I'd never speak to him again!

Strom later said that the only reason Social Credit lost was because Diefenbaker intervened. Notley contended he had it in the bag until Diefenbaker interfered. I can't remember what the Liberals said, but the only remaining Liberal MLA, Bill Dickie, saw that the jig was up, and before the year's end he joined Lougheed. In winning Edson, the Conservatives therefore won two seats. The one Independent sitting in the legislature, Clarence Copithorne, also switched to the Conservatives before the next election. Moving from six to ten MLAs without a general election set the stage for Lougheed's victory in 1971.

Following the Edson by-election, I asked Hugh to write Dief a letter of thanks and to make certain that Lougheed did too. Dief stopped me one day in November 1969: "Say, that's a very smart up-and-coming young leader you have out there in Alberta. I think he's going places." I knew he had received the letter. I thanked him again for the wire, saying that it had won us the by-election. And so it had. Consequently, it now annoyed me immensely that Clark, in his leadership campaign across Canada, was portraying himself as the organizer who had been instrumental in making Lougheed the premier of Alberta. A series of phone calls and one telegram from Diefenbaker had done more for Lougheed than ten men's organizational ability.

The popular wisdom during the leadership convention, drawn from the experience of Roblin and Stanfield in 1967, was that the last major candidate to declare had the best chance of winning the leadership. I was working hard through caucus to change some of the ground rules to eliminate last-minute candidates and delegates. I also wanted to establish that the national director and the national office would work equally for all candidates and not just for the choice of the party establishment. The constitution read that each constituency had to publish notice of any meeting to elect delegates to the leadership convention. It had to be established firmly, however, that these meetings actually had to take place and that each constituency did elect its own delegates. This was particularly important in Quebec. The Conservative party under Stanfield kept promising to get organized in Quebec but all the while accepted a system where a few front boys in Montreal made up the list of delegates and packed our conventions. Abiding by the constitution would thoroughly help in the organization of the party in the hinterland of the province, since the constituency associations would have to function. When I insisted on this, of course everyone said, "Certainly, we wouldn't have it any other way." The important point was they knew I would be watching to make sure it did happen. As the six delegates and six alternate delegates from each riding were the ones to whom we had to get our message, I advocated they be chosen three months before the convention so that the candidates could zero in on them. I was satisfied when the party adopted the principle that this be done by December 31, 1975, which, in my opinion, was sufficiently in advance of the voting on February 22. These changes helped the candidate who declared early; the notion of the successful late entry was undermined and the eleventh-hour entry eliminated entirely. Also undermined was the power of the media. If the delegates were chosen in advance and if they accepted their responsibility to get out and meet the candidates, they had to think about what they had seen and heard. Consequently, they were less likely to be captured by any candidate coming in late with a lot of fanfare, hoopla, and press attention.

Once convinced that Lougheed was unlikely to run, I was mainly concerned with the prospect of Paul Hellyer's candidacy. I would have stopped him from running had I been able. His decision to get into the race split my support. (At the convention, we had 466 votes between us on the first ballot. Even with a hundred less than this, I would have been second to Claude Wagner and in a position to do something.) From caucus, Bob Coates went to Hellyer. So did Craig Stewart and Jake Epp (Provencher). I couldn't convince them not to. Jake Epp, for example, didn't have anything against me at the time, although in the past we had had some violent disagreements over the Hutterites. As a Mennonite, he didn't think the Hutterites should be taxed; while of course I didn't think one's religion should interfere with one's judgement about fair treatment for all Canadians. Jake now was caught up with the concept of Hellyer as a religious force in politics. Hellyer got a lot of support purely because he was on the side of the Lord. I tried to convince Jake, Craig Stewart, and a number of others that Hellyer's judgement was questionable, that his past record was not good, that his book *Agenda* showed his economic thinking was badly clouded — but I couldn't sway them. As the campaign unfolded, it became clear that the establishment (Camp, Meighen, Stanfield, Bill Davis, and the Ontario entourage) had six horses in the race: Flora MacDonald to gather the women's vote; John Fraser to gather the B.C. vote; Brian Mulroney to gather whatever he could in Quebec; Sinclair Stevens to get the right wing; Jim Gillies to work the other side of the financial street and the more liberally minded; and Joe Clark to shepherd the youth vote. I recall trying to point out to Jake Epp that they had divided their forces because they weren't certain which horse they were going to ride. Would it be Brian Mulroney? Would it be Flora MacDonald? Who? This stalking-horse tactic gave us the advantage, because their support would be dispersed on the first vote.

Then there was an occurrence which caused a long friendship to go pretty sour. An acquaintance phoned me one night in November 1975 — at about 11 o'clock from Dorval Airport's first class lounge — to ask what on earth was going on: Diefenbaker and Hellyer were sitting in one corner of the lounge discussing a number of things, while Keith Martin, the Chief's very capable executive assistant, was telling a group of people that Dief was going to support Hellyer.

"Are you certain?" I asked.

He replied, "It was obvious, it was clear. What do you think I am? Deaf? I was sitting right there."

I phoned Keith Martin when he arrived home sometime after midnight and bawled the heck out of him. The next day, when Charles Lynch's column stated that Dief would be supporting Hellyer, I walked over to Diefenbaker's office.

Dief did his usual trick. "Have you seen this? Have you seen that? Have you read this column from the Calgary paper?"

"Yes, I have. Have you read Charles Lynch's?"

He looked at me. "It's not true."

I insisted, "You've really read it?"

Well, no he hadn't.

"I have it here with me."

Dief looked at it. "Well, that's not so. I've talked to Keith about this. I am not committed to Hellyer. I have told you who I am going to support but that I will pick the time. Now you don't have to worry." I knew Dief was playing a game. He wasn't fooling me and I had to tell him so, though I didn't want to believe it.

Despite Hellyer, I received the backing of some sixteen of my fellow MPS. The party establishment had a better grasp of my chances of success than the media ever did, and they took such steps as they could to lessen the effect of my campaign. For example, the most popular person in caucus was Don Mazankowski, who was widely known as my friend and strong supporter. Maz had been a good caucus chairman; and this presumably gave the party president, Michael Meighen, the opportunity — in a smooth move — to have Maz named co-chairman of the convention. Why they needed two chairmen, heaven only could answer. Again, much as the establishment disliked Dan McKenzie, they felt he would probably go to me, so they gave him some job scrutinizing delegates. They did the same to Ray Hnatyshyn because of Dief's influence over him. A number of official jobs were given to key people in caucus who might well have come to me. It was a good strategy, as such people could have influenced the delegates had they been left in a position to campaign for me.

In some cases, however, the pressures brought to bear on those who wanted to support me were somewhat less subtle. On August 20, 1975, I wrote to a young supporter to whom it had been made abundantly clear that there was no future in the Conservative party for anyone who supported Jack Horner.

> I have been thinking over our conversation of last Sunday and I feel I must write to you.
>
> If the young, idealistic people in our society are so readily prepared to admit that we have not got a free and open Party then there is really not much hope for democracy. If the young admit they are serving and are prepared to serve tyrants, and that is what one must call them, if they in fact threatened you in the manner in which you explained to me, then our society is as corrupt as the U.S. and we have learned very little from Watergate.
>
> I do not for one moment hesitate to believe that you were threatened but I do believe they haven't got that much power and that they could not stop you from winning a nomination in . . . and that they could not stop you from winning the presidency of . . . and I certainly hope you will reconsider.
>
> No matter whom you decide to support in the end, I beg of you not to knuckle under. You are faced with a difficult decision, perhaps the most difficult you have had in your young political career. If you knuckle under on this occasion you will continue to do so for the rest of your life and you will never reach your potential.

The establishment, in this instance, solved my young friend's dilemma by appointing him to one of the convention committees.

In putting together my campaign organization, I considered myself fortunate to be able to hire a Toronto-based graphic artist by the name of Jim Mooney. To assist him there was a delightful, soft-spoken Japanese Canadian, Al Fujiwari, and Bernard O'Keefe — highly educated, a nice guy and a fine writer. They were so professional in their work, so capable, that our campaign publications were by far the best of all the candidates.

We had one rather strange incident, however, which for a time rather unnerved my crew. We had scheduled a major reception for delegates in Toronto at the Royal York Hotel on December 9. For the event, we shipped down five boxes of campaign literature, weighing 164 pounds, by bus from Ottawa. As we had to go to London on the Saturday, Jim Mooney's wife was to pick up this material on the Monday. Come Monday, it wasn't there. No one in our organization had made the pick up, so we called in the Toronto police. In checking it out, they found an elderly person who remembered helping a young woman load five boxes into the back of a Volvo station wagon, but he didn't remember the licence number. The boxes had been picked up about twenty minutes after they arrived. We thought it rather strange. How would anyone know the boxes were coming? Jim Mooney, who had called his wife about them, began to wonder if his phone was tapped. The police informed us that in that part of Toronto, if the phone was tapped, Jim would find a wire off the telephone line running more than likely through some trees into the gutter or into the road allowance. By jove, Jim went home that night and found the wire lazily wrapped around the telephone post with two little plugs at the end to attach a tape recorder. Detectives watched his house over that next weekend, but no one attempted to use the tap, so we were none the wiser. Jim's family were quite frightened. One can imagine their concern. Jim had it in the back of his mind that Claude Wagner's bunch were responsible, but this was just suspicion.

The detectives were amazed that this would happen in a leadership race. "What on earth would they want with your literature?" one of them asked.

"It could be a dirty-tricks tactic," I told him. "I would be a good candidate for it because of the suspicion that I'm a bigot and anti-French. They could pack my folders full of inflammatory statements and so on, the sort of thing Nixon was accused of doing in Florida."

The police officers looked at me in utter amazement. "Yes, but that's the United States. It would never happen in Canada."

"I hope you're right," I said. In fact, the 164 pounds of literature were never seen again in any form.

My financial agent was Dick Bonnycastle. Dick was a Westerner but had large eastern interests. At the time, he had just sold Harlequin Books to the *Toronto Star* for a combination of cash and shares, which is how he became a director of the *Star*. Dick had relatives who ranched in my area and we had been acquainted for at least ten years. He also had a ranch, so we could always relate to one another. He liked my straight approach to things. His one criticism was that I repeated myself. Dick did not like to repeat himself. If he said something, you were to have understood it. If he had to repeat it, he judged you rather dull. I explained that in the game of politics one has to repeat because the people out there don't hear the first time. The first time, one just preconditions them to listen. The second time, they think they hear. And the third time, they know they've heard. This was news to Dick.

I didn't mind advertising the fact Dick Bonnycastle was my financial agent. I wanted everybody to know who was behind me. There were no skeletons in my closet and none in his. But unfortunately he was not a very good collector, though I wouldn't blame him for that. As a young financial man, he felt a little embarrassed asking his superiors in the eastern financial world for contributions. On the positive side, he did get me in to meet a lot of very influential people in Toronto: Conrad Black, Bud McDougall, Fred Eaton, Bill McCutcheon. We had a delightful hour or more with McDougall. He and I hit if off well. He really didn't disagree with my philosophy, and I was quite impressed with his.

On another occasion, in an attempt to try to understand the newspapers, I went down to Toronto to meet with the editorial boards of the *Toronto Star*, the *Toronto Sun*, and the *Globe and Mail*. They were interesting meetings. The eastern press dominates the news in Canada, whether we in the West like it or not. The sun gets up in the east and moves westward, so of course their day starts earlier and the teletypes relay their messages.

The *Toronto Star* was mainly concerned about my economic views. I told them that our interest rates were too high and that our dollar should go down, that this would stimulate export sales and create jobs in Canada. I had no trouble defending my views. As we came away, Dick was walking on air. He thought I'd really handled myself admirably and had done a tremendous job.

At the *Toronto Sun*, they were strictly interested in politics. They wanted to hypothesize as to what would happen "if". Peter Worthington kept asking me, "Well, what will you do if. . . ?" I told him that I wasn't making any deals, that I was running to win: "I think I'm the best candidate, and that's it." There's no doubt in my mind to this day that I was the best candidate, but I couldn't get Worthington to consider this.

"What if it comes down to a choice between Brian Mulroney and Paul Hellyer?" he kept asking. "Just tell me what you would do so I can analyse your judgement of issues and people."

"Well, you've put me in a corner with this question," I finally said. "When man is boxed in, in jail, he lives on hope, and hope alone keeps him going. Do you agree with this? Do you understand it?"

Poor old Peter Worthington and Doug Creighton couldn't understand where I was going with all this.

I continued, "Well, this is the way I reason. You asked me. You wanted to understand my reasoning. We have to agree that when boxed or put in a corner or put in jail, when all else is lost, man survives on hope: hope that it will be better tomorrow, hope that he will get out, hope that he will see a way out. Hope is the thing that keeps us alive." I was trying their patience. Of course, Jim Mooney, who was with me this time, didn't know where I was going either.

Finally, I said, "Now, let's look at the box you've put me in: Hellyer or Mulroney? I've seen what Paul Hellyer has to offer. He's been Defence minister. He's been Transport minister. He's written a book which I've read. He has exposed everything he has. There isn't a hope in the man. Mulroney is young. He hasn't done much. He hasn't said much. I don't want to go to either of these men, but you put me in the box and I have to rely on hope. There's hope with Mulroney." Well, politically, this was the wrong answer. I didn't know Hellyer was a major shareholder in the *Toronto Sun*. But they had asked for my reasoning.

At the *Globe and Mail*, Mooney and I sat there for at least three-quarters of an hour while they quizzed me on matters related to the concept they had of me as a solid, rigid right-winger. What was my attitude to the less fortunate people in the world or in Canada, and how would I treat them? Of course, the true conservative believes that, wherever possible, you teach man to help himself. You don't give him food, you teach him how to grow it. You don't give him fish, you teach him how to catch them. Where it is impossible for a man to survive or fend for himself, then he must be looked after. In a nutshell, this was what I told the *Globe and Mail*. We didn't come away feeling as high as we had on leaving the *Sun* or the *Star*, but we had a kind of satisfied feeling we had done our best. I heard later that the *Globe and Mail* editorial writers had commented that Horner was the best defender of conservative philosophy they had interviewed. I never did hear the reaction of the *Sun* or the *Star*.

Once I decided to run, I knew another handicap I would face would be the claim that I had no support in Quebec. Much to my surprise and pleasure, I found considerable support there. Consequently, I wanted to publish early the list of MPs and delegates who were supporting me. I wanted the media to see where my support was. The party required that fifty voting delegates and fifty party members sign each candidate's nomination papers. While I was the first candidate to make public his list of delegates, it received little attention. In fact, after the initial kick off, we went through a period of a month or better with absolutely no mention of the Horner campaign in the papers. We were travelling extensively, getting big interested crowds at delegate meetings — and no coverage. I stopped Jonathan Manthorpe one day and faced him with this: "I read a long column of yours in the *Globe and Mail*, and the only mention you made of my campaign was in two lines at the end — 'And then there's Horner.' Are you aware we're going over very well, that I'm not being rejected by the delegates at all?" He told me that the column he sent in had had plenty about my campaign in it. "I have no control over what they decide to print," he explained. Manthorpe was and is a hard-hitting reporter and I had no reason not to believe him.

One January morning in Ottawa, we went in to see Mr. Diefenbaker. Dick Bonnycastle wanted to meet him, so Dick, Jim Mooney, and I went over. Dief, an avid consumer of newspapers, had been reading as usual.

"Where are you? What are you doing?" he asked. "I haven't read a thing about you. Where have you been?"

"I've been all over and I've been having some very good meetings with the delegates. They are really interested in what I have to say and I think we're going to get quite a bit of support."

"Well, I don't read it in the papers. They don't even mention you."

After a while, we got into a discussion of the candidates. I said, "I just can't imagine a Conservative voting for Claude Wagner with all this talk about the $300,000 given to him to assure his income if he gave up his judgeship to join the party. Nor can I imagine people supporting Sinclair Stevens with his financial record. Or who would support Hellyer's crazy economic theories? And Flora MacDonald, a person who assisted in dethroning you, who on earth is going to support her?"

"If you think these things," replied Dief, "get out and say them. Get out and say them."

As we walked back to the office, Bonnycastle said, "Dief's right. You know, the old guy, I never did think much of him, but he's right. We've got to do something, but I've got to go somewhere." (Dick was always going somewhere.) "You and Mooney get to work. You've got to issue a statement. You've got to hit these babies just as Dief suggests."

We sat up until the late hours — Jim Mooney (worried sick about it), Bernie O'Keefe, and me — trying to figure out what we should say. It was obvious we had to get my name back in the papers. We carefully worked out short statements on each of the candidates. I wanted to avoid any legal problems, but I also wanted these to be cutting blows. I issued the following release at a press conference on January 7, 1976:

> The next leader of the Progressive Conservative Party must come from caucus. The times are too critical, the issues too grave to entrust the Leadership of our Party to anyone who has never won an election. This is no time to entrust the Leadership to anyone who has ever been tried and found wanting in smaller arenas. Nor can we entrust it to anyone whose parliamentary experience as an elected representative is so recent and so limited that there has been no time to learn how to follow, let alone to lead. And of the dominoes lined up in front of the thrust from the left, nothing need be said. Like all dominoes they will fall and follow.
>
> But of some who dare to seek the Leadership of our great Party, something must be said. And so I will say it:
>
> PAUL HELLYER
> This "great Conservative" is hailed by some as a new messiah. But he is not new to the political scene and he is no Conservative messiah. In the defeat of the John Diefenbaker Government in 1963, Paul Hellyer stated, on February 4 and February 5, "John Diefenbaker deceived the Canadian people on the question of nuclear arms." He also said: "Mr. Diefenbaker has tried to mislead." Who is trying to mislead us now? While many of us can forgive, there are voters who cannot forget.
>
> BRIAN MULRONEY
> I have already said what I think are the chances of *any* candidate from Quebec and about anyone who has never stood for public office. I would only add that the Power Corporation couldn't buy Argus and I promise that it can't buy Canada either.
>
> FLORA MacDONALD
> Flora MacDonald would like to be seen as the Canadian Margaret Thatcher. She is as much like Margaret Thatcher as Jack Horner is like David Lewis.
>
> SINCLAIR STEVENS
> Is our Party so bankrupt in its ideology, talent and resources that it would entrust its Leadership to a man who has already led so many Canadians down a ruinous road?
>
> CLAUDE WAGNER
> Claude Wagner entered the Conservative Party, *and apparently*

was paid for, in order to bring Quebec into the Party. Now the Party is being asked to embrace him as its National Leader. Is it not ironic that all the while he is on record as steadfastly opposed to the formation of a provincial Conservative Party in Quebec? Who can really believe in any hope this "great Conservative" would bring to our national quest?

And now, finally, I must say where I stand. In the weeks to come I will be issuing policy statements on all the important issues confronting us in this election. In the meantime, do you have any doubt where I stand or where I have stood for the past seventeen years? I stand with the people, the people who have elected me in seven successive campaigns and who have given me the largest plurality of any Conservative Member of Parliament in the last three federal elections.

As the next Leader of the Conservative Party and of Canada I stand apart, because of my experience and my record. But I do not stand alone. I stand in the forefront of that great band of Canadians who will fight with everything that's in them to preserve the private enterprise system and bring us the greatness which has been so often promised and so long denied.

Many people told me later I shouldn't have done it, but it was a calculated risk. We really had no choice. As soon as I made that statement, I began to receive ink again, even if a lot of it was devoted to condemning me. The delegates came out to the meetings wanting to see "this fire-breathing demon". In live TV interviews where the experts and pundits tried to tear me apart — why I had said this and why I hadn't said that — I found it very easy to defend my decisions. I was hot. I was sought after. I was in no trouble. We took the risk. It paid off. It paid off by bringing the attention my campaign needed.

After I had commented caustically on my opponents and their abilities, it wasn't likely that I would get any of them to swing my way at the convention, but then we had taken this into consideration as well. I didn't think any of the other candidates would come my way in any circumstances, though in the case of Stevens and Hellyer at least, a lot of their followers might. Surprising as this might seem, throughout the campaign Flora MacDonald and I got along well. Our paths crossed often. She was always interested in my campaign and I in hers. Here again, I don't think Flora ever would have supported me, but possibly some of her supporters might have. Looking back, the interesting thing is that I didn't mention Joe Clark in my press release. When Charles Lynch or someone asked me about this, I brushed it aside as not worthy of consideration. Obviously, this was an error. But if one goes back to the period 1972 to '76, Clark is to be remembered, in terms of his participation in the House, as a young fellow with a loud voice and a file full of rude comments for the purpose of heckling the government.

As a matter of fact, I had observed Clark setting up his machinery as early as 1974. He had been youth co-ordinator in Stanfield's shadow cabinet, and at the '74 convention the party youth had voted *en bloc* to change the constitution to where two constituency delegates out of six to any national convention had to be under the age of thirty. They had wanted two people under the age of twenty-five, but I had protested, as had Marcel Lambert, and it was amended to two delegates under thirty. (The old constitution had provided one out of five delegates under thirty.) There also was a change in the delegate provisions for student associations in post-secondary institutions. These could now send three delegates each to national conventions, provided they had twenty-five or more members. I fully believe students in universities and colleges should be encouraged to participate in our democratic institutions, but to think that a college could sign up twenty-five new members just prior to a leadership convention and send three delegates (half the strength of a constituency organization) is something which requires re-examination.

Clark doesn't have much charisma, but he doesn't leave much to chance. He took a page out of Dalton Camp's dumping of Dief and used it very effectively. He had a group working for him at each of the colleges and universities, and was more effective here than any of the candidates. I knew what he was doing, strange as this might seem. At the time, I had two of my sons at college. Craig was fairly well known and fairly active in the Conservative club at the University of Calgary; but Brent, at the college at Olds, couldn't find the Conservative club. He was notified only after they had chosen their delegates. Clark had done his work. I suspect that I believed too much in the good judgement of our young people. For the love of me, I couldn't see anybody going out for Clark. I thought they would take a look at him and listen to him and say, "Well, he's good with words, but he doesn't mean what he says."

As I mentioned earlier, Stanfield, throughout much of his leadership, was considered by many a fill-in as leader; the party seemed to be marking time until the right man came along. Thus, at every convention, there was a jockeying for position. When Camp was re-elected president in the big fight of 1966, he put himself in the driver's seat to make Stanfield leader. So it was established that in order to make a move for the leadership, one had to have one's man in as president. Clark was Michael Meighen's campaign manager in 1972. In 1976, Meighen was where Clark needed him. I could see Clark making all his moves. Unfortunately, I thought that he was a front for someone else.

To my knowledge, many of the candidates have never been called upon to answer for their change of platform halfway through the campaign. Once these left-wing or Red Tories discovered they were out of step with the thinking of delegates across Canada, they changed their convictions as easily as a man might change his shirt. In Calgary, I was astounded to hear Clark at one point advocate a means test for all social benefits. Who could believe him? Of course, we have had now the proof of this pudding.

Nick Hills, writing in the Montreal *Gazette* on February 10, 1976, observed:

Jack Horner is a maverick whose time has come philosophically . . . . In some ways, Horner is the most interesting of the Conservative leadership candidates. He has often been dismissed as a jackass by the media and a lightweight by some of his parliamentary colleagues. In fact, Jack Horner has a better mind than most of his fellow MPs and his consistency on the major issues confronting the country suggests it is possible to be both a really honest man and a politician at the same time.

The record of Jack Horner, illuminated in the pages of Hansard, shows that he has stood to the right of his party since he entered Parliament. For years, his views were unacceptable even to many of his colleagues. Now, as the pendulum swings his way, Horner suddenly is in a crowd — and they are all articulating what he has been saying for years.

He believes in capital punishment as a deterrent against killing, he wants a less generous unemployment insurance scheme, he seeks an end to the right to strike in essential services, he is a devout defender of the private enterprise system.

If there is some sort of natural justice in Canadian politics, Jack Horner would be a winner today. Instead, he sits in a pack of Tory leadership candidates who are espousing the politics of the right.

As my campaign moved across the country, many delegates were coming out and committing their votes. Bill Skoreyko was doing a count. It was so high, I was disbelieving. Mind you, the meetings were excellent. In Thunder Bay, Saulte Ste. Marie, Timmins, Ottawa, Toronto, we put on tremendously good receptions and dinners for the delegates. I was really impressed by the expressions of support.

In Thunder Bay, a professor brought a group of his students to participate in the question period. He later commented that I was the best prepared candidate they had encountered. We had a bang-up meeting in Montreal. The CBC's Bill Boyd was there to tape a lot of it for TV, believing I was going to bomb out. We had a huge crowd. I think the reception cost about $2,400, but the people came out. I remember the Conservative bagman for Quebec telling me he was tired of hearing about all my relatives in Quebec. "Introduce me to one," he said. Bud Horner, a young guy from Shawville, was standing within six feet of us. He had red hair and a big, red bushy beard. I said, "There's one right here, and furthermore he's a delegate." We had a good meeting in Peterborough, and all down that line. I outdrew Paul Hellyer when our meetings coincided in Hamilton. I received delegate support in Windsor, in Sarnia. I guess if I wanted to register a disappointment, it was with the Alberta MLAS, most of whom did not attend the convention, but of those who did, I had far more than Clark. When Hugh first arrived in Ottawa for the convention, he told me how surprised he was that I had so much more support than he'd thought. Of course, the support he thought I had was what the papers were giving me credit for.

What annoyed me most about the press was that about two or three weeks before the convention, they began giving Clark quite a bit of attention and CTV interviewed him as a possible winner. No one interviewed me as a possible winner. What on earth led them to consider him one? There's no question this put him in third place. He would have been back behind Flora in fifth or sixth place without this extra attention. When Doug Fisher wrote a column suggesting Clark could win, I wasn't surprised. Ever since Fisher and Camp served together to study the salary levels for MLAS in Ontario, Fisher would occasionally echo Camp's thoughts. This was one of the rare times he turned out to be right.

I had moved into fourth place without an ounce of help from the media. Where would I have been with even a modicum of attention? When it was all over, of course, they all wanted to do interviews, but I was in no mood to put up with them. Had I received any fair coverage, I could have won it. I was the one most in tune with the mood of the country. And, unlike the others, I didn't have to lie about what I believed in.

It is my belief that two weeks or so before the convention, the establishment group decided they had to do something to head off Flora or she would be the top runner of their six and there would be no way to stop her. They had decided that Canada wasn't ready for a woman prime minister. Consequently, they delivered as many of Flora's votes as they could to Joe Clark. A lot of delegates-at-large were in the hands of the Toronto group. Forty delegates-at-large from Ontario, for example, had been hand-picked by Bill Davis and Alan Eagleson. They were manoeuvrable.

The establishment decided not to go with Mulroney because caucus had attempted to blacklist him. Caucus signatures were being gathered to state they wouldn't work with him, until Don Mazankowski, as chairman of caucus, nipped this in the bud. But nipping it in the bud didn't stop its expression. Mulroney would have had trouble getting caucus to work for him. Although he'd been a very influential member of the party, had worked hard, collected money, and so on, he had never run for elected office. I don't think he was particularly committed to the direction of the party from outside caucus, but the fact that he had been a Campite at the 1966 convention didn't exactly help him. Nevertheless, he seemed a very capable young man, fluent in both languages, with an easy personality which could have caught on making him very popular. The establishment, however, decided they might not be able to control him. This left Joe Clark to reap the benefit.

Looking at the votes, many people have said I should have stayed in one ballot longer, but I didn't think so. On the first ballot I was in fourth place, behind Wagner, Mulroney, and Clark; but, with 235 votes, I was ahead of Hellyer, ahead of Flora, and ahead of Stevens, Fraser, Gillies, Nowlan, and Grafftey. On the second ballot I gained 51 votes, but Clark picked up 255. The oddity here, of course, was that no one knew after the first ballot where Sinclair Stevens was going. One of his campaign managers, Don Blenkarn, told Jim Mooney they were going to deliver to us, but Sinc walked the other way. I never believed Stevens would come to me, his old enemy over the Bank of Western Canada. He knew I didn't hold him in very high esteem. Everyone, however, was surprised when he went to Clark. As soon as he did, Gillies and Grafftey followed. The establishment's directions were clear. Flora had a hard time going after the second ballot, but she went. I couldn't go to Clark. Bonnycastle and I called our people together. Dick said, "We've got to move now." I agreed. To head off Clark, we had to go to Wagner.

It was at this juncture, as those watching television became aware, that things got quite upsetting. I looked around at our people — Bill Skoreyko, Paul Borham our youth co-ordinator, Mike Southam, Jim Mooney, and a number of others — and said, "I guess we've got to move to Wagner."

Jim exclaimed, "For heaven's sake, not Wagner!"

"Why not?" I asked. Everyone else had agreed.

Jim said, "Horner, you've listened to me for two months. You've done everything I asked you to, but when the important decision comes along you won't listen at all." That really hurt, because Jim and I had been pretty close and I did listen to him.

"Well, why?" I asked him. "Why?"

"We can't talk here," Jim said. "Look at the microphones every-where."

Just then I looked up, and there was a microphone within six inches of my nose. I became pretty angry. Although Bill Boyd of CBC (who had been covering my section) was sitting politely to the side realizing there was an inner discussion going on, Alan Hustak was right beside me. He was working for CTV at the time and he had received instructions from on high: "Get in there and see what Horner is going to do with his gang." Dalton Camp, Claude Ryan, John Bassett, and the others in the CTV gondola above the convention floor assumed I wouldn't go to Wagner because I was supposed to be anti-French. Well, this never entered my mind nor Dick Bonnycastle's nor the minds of any of our group, though I still didn't know why Jim Mooney was against the move to Wagner.

Emotions were feverish. We didn't have much time if our move was going to have its desired effect: we only had fifteen minutes to get my name off the next ballot. I reached up with my left hand, and if I could have crushed that microphone. . . . I just squeezed it, envisioning it crumbling into little bits of plastic and metal as if I were the Six Million Dollar Man. To my surprise, it was as solid as a rock. There was no way I could damage it. What was left for me to do? I just pulled it down as hard as I could. Alan Hustak was tied to the other end of it. He fell down and knocked over a couple of people. Jim Mooney's glasses fell off. The media announced to the nation that Horner had hit a newspaper man. Well, I hadn't, but he should have been more polite.

Jim and his wife got up to leave.

I stopped Eleanor. "You can't leave. Jim and I are too good friends to let this separate us. You have to understand I have no choice. I have to go to Wagner." I still didn't know Jim's reason, but I let them go, thinking they'd gone back to one of our trailers outside the Coliseum and that as soon as I could, I would join them.

I went to Wagner. On the third vote it was Wagner 1003, Clark 969, Mulroney 369. The final vote came. Before the announcement a rumour circulated to my group that Clark had won. (There were apparently bugs in the counting room. On the other hand, this may have been just a good guess — but it certainly was correct.) I told Wagner the news.

As a person, Wagner will forever remain a mystery to me. He had presence. He was aloof and carried himself erect at all times. Very close to himself, very polite, very correct, always very friendly to me. Certainly, he was a person who made up his own mind, could not be swayed by the establishment. He did not speak often in the House and a reading of his speeches reveals no great pearls of wisdom. Was he clever?

Was he far-seeing? I don't think so. I don't think he was anything out of the ordinary at all. I think he may even have questioned his own abilities, but I don't know. Had he been a little more outgoing as a person, had he been a more active participant in the thrust, the give and take of Parliament, he would have won the leadership.

Following the final ballot, all the candidates were to proceed to the stage to endorse Clark's victory. I went up briefly. Stanfield came over. He was shaking hands with the losers as they arrived. I said I hoped he was happy now he had the party really divided. He didn't shake my hand. Clark came over. Everyone was enthusiastically congratulating him on what a great thing his victory was and so on and so forth. I couldn't do this. I didn't believe it was that great a thing, and I told him so.

"Joe there's no use in my congratulating you and telling you how great it is because I don't feel that. I hope you understand that when I do feel it I'll tell you, but I'll wait and see and measure whether it was a great thing or not."

Joe surprised me by saying, "Jack, I understand. I understand."

I immediately left the stage to find out where the Mooneys had gone. I tore out of the Coliseum to check the trailer. They weren't there. I discovered the next day, when Jim came back, that they had walked out on the street, caught a taxi to the airport, and flown to Toronto. Jim told me that he had been against going to Wagner because of the bugging of his phone early in the campaign. This had continued to haunt him. I tried to explain that even if Wagner's bunch had done it, and we had no proof, Claude himself was not necessarily involved and probably never knew it had taken place. But I couldn't convince him. His phone had been tapped, and his kids and his wife had been frightened. He claimed I should have gone out like Turner at the 1968 Liberal leadership convention. I explained that this was fine for Turner, but not for rough, tough, mean Jack Horner. Had I done this, it would have been interpreted as a final proof that I could get along with no one and was just a stubborn fool. Interestingly, I had a long talk with John Turner before the '76 convention about his decision to go to no one in 1968. He said he still believed it the right decision and had no regrets at all.

All the leadership candidates had been invited to appear on CTV's "Canada A.M." the morning following the convention, February 23, 1976. When I give a commitment, I try to live up to it. Lo and behold, I was the only one to appear. We were to be interviewed by Eric Malling, but Eric couldn't make it up the next morning either, so Frazier Kelly (ironically, because Frazier was a very good friend of mine) took his place. I was determined to take a crack at John Bassett, and poor Frazier got the brunt of it. I don't think he has ever forgiven me.

My disenchantment with Bassett goes back to the simple democratic belief that because radio and television stations are granted a licence by the government to use the air waves, they are obliged to attempt to be fair in their coverage of political matters. A newspaper, on the other hand, can print whatever it likes. It does not have the same public responsibility. I felt that John Bassett did not use CTV fairly.

Early in the campaign, he had written an article in *Maclean's* giving his views on the candidates. About Jack Horner, he had said in effect, "This man cannot possibly be allowed to win. His prehistoric views would do tremendous damage to Canada." I had known John Bassett for many years, and I couldn't understand why he would write this. So I phoned him and asked him what prehistoric views he had in mind. He couldn't come up with any. His only defence seemed to be that I didn't have a chance of winning the leadership.

"If I see many more articles like yours, I won't have a chance," I said. Horner with his prehistoric ideas damaging to the country! I resented that very much. It was one thing, however, for him to write the article. (If *Maclean's* wanted to print it, I could answer by cancelling my subscription.) It was quite another thing for Bassett's views to be translated into CTV network coverage of the leadership race.

When I went on "Canada A.M." I knew exactly what I was going to do. During the interview, I said to Frazier Kelly and Norm Perry, "If I had it to do over again, I'd like to be a writer, but the Lord didn't give me the ability to spell." They didn't know what all this was about. "This network is so biased," I said. Then, having made my accusation, I continued, "I'd go to write something about John Bassett and I'd want to call him a prince, but I'd spell it so that it would end with a 'k'."

I found out later that Bassett phoned Eddie Goodman, who was the CTV's lawyer and Bassett's personal lawyer as well, instructing him to sue CTV (Bassett's own network) for not putting in the seven seconds' delay on my calling him a prince. This created a dilemma for them. They toyed around with the idea for quite a while before Bassett dropped it. Interestingly, as the summer of '76 unfolded, there was much discussion on "Canada A.M." about Stan Schumacher and Joe Clark and High River. In this connection, I'd venture my name was mentioned on "Canada A.M." at least a hundred times, but never once was I invited back.

Choosing the leader of a political party is a strange business. We often get the poorest person, not the best. The British system where the elected choose their leader merits serious consideration because it tends to produce leaders of men, people who have done something, who stand for something. In our system we tend to get the Mr. Milquetoast. In the minds of many, Stanfield was a front man for Dalton Camp and the establishment. In the minds of many, Joe Clark is a copy of this. Did Stanfield turn out to be the perfect front man? Will Joe Clark turn out to be the perfect front man? Not likely, but to a degree this will be there. No one can be a perfect front man unless he's absolutely brainless and without conviction. The American system of choosing a leader through the primaries has some merit because the party rank and file make the choice. The cost of this kind of system, however, is nearly prohibitive. It takes a huge amount of money to go the distance in American politics. Carter was able to amass enough money in 1976. Those who weren't fell by the wayside. Jackson is a good example of this. One had first to match Carter's depth of money rather than his brains or understanding. So the American system has its failings as well. I don't suppose there is a perfect system, but ours could certainly stand some improvement.

In retrospect, if I were to run for the leadership of the Conservative party again, in the same historical situation, I would start planning earlier and attend to detail a little better and get the youth vote lined up better than I did. With respect to the latter, I relied on their judgement, but judgement, I discovered, doesn't enter into it. It's who pays the Student Federation and the YPC the most attention. Clark had been tending those fields for a number of years before the convention, and he reaped the harvest. Another problem was that I had painted myself into such a corner in the Conservative party that any candidate who publicly moved towards me had to be a pretty brave and independent person. I think this did me substantial damage. But when I was doing my fighting and trying to educate Stanfield, I wasn't thinking of my own benefit. I was thinking of the benefit of the Conservative party. Of course, had Stanfield taken my advice, he would have been prime minister in 1974. I suppose, to go about it in the proper way, if one disagrees with one's leader, the thing to do is to get out and let things cool off. But everyone has to play the game the way it fits his personality best. I couldn't drop out. I had become involved in politics to serve the people. I believed in democracy and I put the country ahead of myself. I suppose all of this did me some harm when I came to look for support in 1976.

Leadership races often tend to result in the victory of the person who has offended least, who has done least. If he's done something, he has offended someone, somewhere. Stanfield is an obvious example here. So is Clark: the young man who had done nothing but help organize, who had been everywhere and had his presence noted. His accomplishments weren't great, but he had offended no one. The establishment thought they could control him, so they went to him.

7/The Switch

I suspect that Joe Clark knew his credentials as a Westerner were weak. Probably this was what led him, shortly after his election as leader in 1976, into the unnecessary and politically embarrassing squabble with Stan Schumacher over which of them would represent the new Bow River riding. Because of redistribution, Bow River was to encompass much of Stan Schumacher's old Palliser riding and a substantial portion of my Crowfoot riding. Important to Joe Clark, though, was that it took in the town of High River, and for the first time in his life he wanted to be known as "the boy from High River".

Probably, this was Harvie Andre's idea. Andre, the member for Calgary South, lent a lot of his ideas to Clark. Apparently, they were out to copy Jimmy Carter. Carter came from Plains, Georgia. Carter's identification with Plains had captured the fancy of the American voters. Clark wanted to do this with himself and High River. There were, however, tremendous differences between the two situations. To begin with, Plains was a distinct community, whereas High River — although important in Alberta's history — had by the 1970s fallen under the shadow of Calgary. More important, the Carter clan were fully a part of the social and business life of Plains. It is true that Clark's dad, although long since retired, had run the local newspaper. But Clark's own connection with the community he now laid claim to had ended, except for visits, when he graduated from high school. From the time he was eighteen, Clark had tried to rid High River from his mind, his body, and his soul.

In my view, he should have run in the new riding of Calgary West. (Before redistribution, Alberta had nineteen seats. It was gaining two, one in Calgary and one in Edmonton.) The people of Calgary would have been very proud to have the leader of the Opposition and the next prime minister from their city. Also, Clark had already run provincially in the Calgary area. But he wouldn't hear of it, wouldn't hear of it at all. He told me on a number of occasions that he didn't want to run there federally because Calgary West took in part of Lougheed's provincial seat and he and Lougheed might well wind up at odds over one issue or another, which would make things difficult. I could see the logic in this, but I felt it was nevertheless possible for the people to understand that Lougheed was representing them provincially and Clark, nationally.

Clark was not a rural person. Not only had he lived all his adult life in the cities but he had never really participated, even as a boy, in rural life. He just seemed to fit better in a city. Even so, he wanted the security of a rural political base. "City seats tend to change quicker than rural ones," he said, which is very true. Urban populations shift a great deal, they tend to be overly swayed by the media and national trends.

The other fact which I thought he should consider was that a prime minister's time, or a leader of the Opposition's, is very, very limited in terms of his own riding. A rural constituency likes to see its MP. Each town or village, every district in a rural riding, has its own peculiarities that a member has to be aware of and to which he must devote some time. Rural constituents like to know their member first-hand, by name, to be able to stop him on the street and talk to him. In the cities, this degree of familiarity is never achieved. Clark would have been able to breeze into Calgary, and it wouldn't really have mattered which part of Calgary he was in; the media would make the entire city his constituency. This argument didn't carry any weight with Clark either. He was determined to be "the boy from High River". And this was the man who once admitted he was so fearful of horses that not even as a school kid would he pat one on the nose!

It is probably significant that two days after the leadership convention, Clark told me he was interested in running in the new Bow River riding and asked what my intentions were. My family, my home, and ranch were within the new boundaries of Crowfoot, so it seemed appropriate that that was where I should run. I told Clark he should talk to Schumacher, whose Palliser riding had been more critically affected by redistribution and who was certainly interested in the Bow River nomination.

In any event, the question uppermost in my mind when Clark and I met on February 26 was not where I was going to run come the next election, but "if". What future could I have in a party led by Joe Clark? In retrospect, I think Clark may well have had his mind made up about this too, save only the circumstances of my departure.

Jack Horner may be a poor loser, but he is no quitter. Clark's election as leader, however, made my position difficult. I didn't like him. More important, I didn't respect him. I thought about leaving politics altogether, but the prospect of being branded someone who could not take defeat was completely repugnant. I knew that I didn't have to like Clark to serve him. Finally, I decided to find out if I could help him, to work to give the guy a chance, if only out of fairness to the system.

Thus, I was pleasantly surprised when he phoned me that Monday morning following the leadership convention. Was I in? I said I was. He thought he'd like to stop by my office and talk. When he came in, I did what I hadn't done at the convention. I stepped forward to congratulate him on his victory. I explained that it had been difficult for me at the time but I had now faced the issue, decided to support him, and was at his service.

Clark responded by inviting me to join his shadow cabinet, saying that in his judgement there was no question of my ability, and so on. What department would I like to be responsible for?

"Transportation."

"All right, that's fine," he replied.

We then sat down and talked about the rest of his front bench. Of interest to me was his choice as Agriculture critic. He remarked that Bob McKinley wanted the position. I wasn't surprised. McKinley had been whip and Agriculture critic under Stanfield. Clark also remarked that he couldn't give Agriculture to McKinley. I said this was his decision, but as he had asked my opinion, I had always thought John Wise would do the job well if he wanted it and felt he could handle it. He'd have a new image and a fresh face. "I don't think he'll get you into any trouble," I said. "He knows a little bit about agriculture. He's a quiet, nice young fellow." Joe said he hadn't thought of Wise but would consider him, that it sounded like a pretty good idea.

A week or two rolled by. Joe hadn't named his shadow cabinet critic for Agriculture, so I had a continuing interest, and I asked John Wise if he had had a conversation with Clark. He said he hadn't. Lo and behold, the very day I spoke to Wise, so did Clark. John told me later that he was very thankful I had put in a plug for him because Clark surely would have missed him otherwise. To my satisfaction, when Clark formed his government, John became Agriculture minister.

Really, Clark and I got off to a very good start, much better than I expected. When he left my office after that initial meeting, I was sure he would win the next election. Trudeau was so far down, down in spirit, down in the polls, that during the Conservative leadership race everyone assumed the winner would be the next prime minister, just as sure as guns. So I thought Clark might hold things together, although I must admit I paid scant attention to his High River plans — it was not my problem.

Leola, and I then left for Hawaii. I had promised her a two-week holiday in the sun, but we only stayed the week because I simply had to get back to find out what was happening in Ottawa. Clark organized what he called a "strategy committee", of which I was a member. It was a select group of about fifteen (including people like Bill Neville from Clark's office) charged with the overall direction of the party. There was also a chairmen's group of about thirty people who met each Tuesday to assess our participation in the House of Commons and what was going to be happening the next day in caucus. Clark, in my impression, never seemed as apprehensive about caucus as Stanfield, although nearly so. The strategy committee was interesting because of the people Clark had on it and those he left off. People like Pat Nowlan found themselves left out in the cold. Me, I couldn't complain, I was in the inner sanctum.

As I look back, however, I suspect that Joe had two counts against our relationship from the beginning. He didn't feel at ease with me. I could sense he was afraid that my determination and strength would get him into trouble eventually. He certainly knew that I couldn't and wouldn't in any way kowtow to him. He could treat me as an equal, but he couldn't treat me as a superior too far up the line. This, I think, was unsettling for him. Also, when his problem with Schumacher flared up that summer, it made Clark look weak; and I think a few of Clark's close advisers kept telling him I could settle things for him, that Schumacher would move out if *I* asked him to.

As far as I'm concerned, Clark's was an unnecessary squabble with Stan Schumacher. Although Clark had told me in February he wanted to look into the possibility of running in the riding encompassing High River, he didn't talk to Schumacher until June. By this time, Stan was fully aware of Clark's ambition and not just a little annoyed at his leader's attempting to move in on him without even the courtesy of consultation. It became the talk of the country that first summer.

Everybody in Ottawa knew that Stan and I were the best of friends. Thus, I was not surprised when Clark asked me to try and tone Stan down, to get him to understand the situation. I did my best to mediate, but one can only ask a friend to do so much. Certainly, I was not going to lose my friendship with Stan, and getting mad at him was not going to get Clark the riding. All summer, Clark steadfastly held that Schumacher should step aside and run in Calgary West. I had many a frank discussion with Stan, but the longer the dispute went on and the more public statements there were, the more rigid Stan became. "I'm not moving for Clark," Stan told me, "but I'll move for you if it will help in your particular riding situation."

"I am not asking you to move for me," I said, "I'm asking you to consider the plight of the party. The media have had a heyday all summer long, and Clark looks pretty poor overall. If worse comes to worst, he or his agent will not sign your nomination papers and you will not be a Conservative candidate in the election. He has that power."

Of course Stan was fully aware of this. "If Clark does that," he said, "I'll run against him as an Independent."

"You'll lose."

Stan said he knew he'd lose, but he would still not move for Clark, given the way Clark had gone about trying to steal his riding. This was not an honourable action, he maintained. Clark should have called him in at the beginning. Eventually, I had to tell Clark. I told him in August when he was in Saskatoon on a speaking tour.

"I'm thinking of moving myself," Clark told me, "but we've got to get this out of the press and off the airwaves. For heaven's sake, if you can talk to Schumacher, tell him to shut up and let's let the thing lie quiet for a while. Then I will make a move. I'm not sure where I'll move, but I'll move."

It was with a sense of relief that I phoned Stan with this news. I suggested the best thing he could do would be to lie absolutely low on the question, as it looked to me that Bow River riding was going to come his way. Stan said he'd got the message and would handle it accordingly. As good as his word, he kept the issue out of the press.

In October, Clark publicly announced an Alberta caucus to thrash out constituency problems once and for all. All of the Alberta MPs except Eldon Woolliams were present. Eldon had an ability always to miss those meetings likely to cause any amount of tension or hard feelings. To my surprise, just before caucus, Clark phoned to ask that I come over to his Centre Block office. Joe, Steve Paproski who was party whip, and Harvie Andre were there. Andre had no official capacity within the Alberta caucus. Peter Elzinga was the secretary and Stan Schumacher the chairman. Joe stated his intention to announce to caucus that he was going to seek the Conservative nomination in the new riding of Yellowhead which took in much of the constituency that had elected him to Parliament, the old riding of Rocky Mountain. However, he didn't want it to look as if the Alberta caucus or anyone else had forced him to do this. He also intended to announce that he didn't want any two sitting members in Alberta contesting the same nomination. He was being generous in backing out of the fight with Stan Schumacher and he wanted to set the example.

This naturally brought to mind the new riding of Crowfoot and my probable fight for the nomination with Arnold Malone whose Battle River–Camrose riding was disappearing. I felt I had a good claim, as my old riding's name had been retained in the new riding, and I lived within its boundaries. When I raised the matter, Clark immediately said that he thought it should be my riding: "Arnold Malone hasn't got a family, hasn't got the same roots in the riding you have, Jack. He should be the one to move."

"Will this come up in caucus?" I asked.

He agreed that it should and could. First, however, he wanted me to make a motion asking Stan Schumacher to step down as chairman of the Alberta caucus. He was giving in to Stan, and Stan had to give something in return. As Harvie Andre put it, they wanted "their *quid pro quo*, their tit for tat". I had been summoned to do the dirty work.

That Stan was a friend of mine didn't bother Joe. In fact, he wanted to see whether I would serve him in this. It was a difficult task, and I very much would have liked three minutes privately with Stan to explain. But I realized I was not going to be afforded this privilege because the meeting in Clark's office was immediately prior to caucus.

I asked, "Do you really want this?" Chairman of the Alberta caucus is a nothing position. We only met once a month.

Andre made it abundantly clear that he felt Joe should get something, and Paproski vouched for it.

Reluctantly, I agreed. "But I'll handle it my way. I don't think a motion will be necessary. Stan and I are such good friends that if I merely suggest he should maybe step down, I think he will. If it becomes an absolute necessity, I'll put it as a motion, but I want to try it my way first." This seemed to satisfy them.

Because the caucus had been summoned to settle constituency questions once and for all, Stan Schumacher was obviously on guard as he called the meeting to order. Joe said he had a statement to make. In it, he dealt with his position in relation to High River and his decision to seek the nomination in the new riding of Yellowhead. He stated that he wanted to set an example for all Alberta members. He wanted to announce this at the beginning of the meeting so that it would not be perceived by the press that the Alberta caucus had forced him to move in any direction. He wanted it clearly understood before any discussion took place that he was making his move, not at the wishes of the meeting, but on his own (which was certainly the proper thing for him to do if those were his intentions). There was a general sigh of relief and many words of appreciation by the members. Most had come with the thought that this was going to be a stormy session in which friendships would be tried and emotions tested.

After a bit of discussion, I made my little speech on how well Stan had served his people and how well he had served the Alberta caucus as chairman and how, in this spirit of co-operation and the desire to get along, perhaps he could give in a little too and step down as chairman. How I wished I had had those three minutes with Stan privately! I could have done it so much better, made it so much easier. It was like hitting him in the face with a wet towel. To have his best friend suddenly suggest he give up his position — even though it looked as if he wasn't going to need it to protect his riding — came as a complete shock. Of course, this registered on his face, and I felt bad, very bad, even though I knew I would be able to explain my actions to Stan without any trouble (and of course I later did). Almost before I had finished, Peter Bawden jumped into the act to say some unflattering things about Stan and to suggest the least he could do was step down and that if he didn't, Bawden would make a motion to this effect and call for a vote. Stan quickly caught the mood of caucus and took my suggestion.

I then brought up my own situation. "All right, Mr. Leader, I want to bring up Crowfoot. Right after the leadership race, you announced your plans to spend your time meeting the people. You did this. Subsequently, you decided to devote your energies to the House of Commons. As far back as last June, you asked me to begin to travel on your behalf. Initially, you wanted me to get as much publicity as possible for the Conservative party during July and August when you were to be absent much of the time touring the European Common Market countries. In consequence of my efforts, central Canada, where most of the votes are, knew that the Conservative party was active on its behalf. We received tremendous press."

Joe agreed that I had been of great service. He was fully complimentary.

I went on: "I have continued to travel on behalf of the party at your request, but I can't do this any longer if I have to contest the nomination in Crowfoot against Arnold Malone. I don't mind running against a sitting member. I've done it before, I'll do it again. But if I have to run against Arnold, I have to be relieved of this other responsibility."

Joe responded immediately. This was the purpose of the meeting, he said. His own situation and Stan's had been resolved, and now similar questions affecting other members had to be settled. "Jack lives in Crowfoot, his family and his roots are there. Arnold, you're single. You've worked in Edmonton. It's far easier for you to take one of the new seats there or, for that matter, one in Calgary. I want you to understand clearly that you have to start looking. Further, I want every member in this room to assist Arnold in every way possible to get him established in the riding he chooses."

Arnold realized the position he was in and spoke up. But he didn't commit himself one way or the other. Much to my surprise, Marcel Lambert tried to pin him down. Malone dodged the question. He explained that with the new seats and the talk of some of the Alberta members not running again, the way he figured it, he had six options. He wanted to explore each one of them before he reached a decision. Joe then told him that he wanted the decision within a month.

I went out of that caucus feeling that while I had been forced to perform a difficult task and put my friendship with Stan Schumacher to the test (it survived), I had achieved what I wanted. My nomination in Crowfoot was secure, or so I thought, and I could continue to travel for the party.

Actually, I was quite happy speaking from one end of the country to the other. It was often exhausting physically, but I've always enjoyed making speeches and, more important, it kept me away from questions related to Clark's day-to-day strategy in the House of Commons. I knew that if I had to spend most of my time in Ottawa, eventually I was going to disagree with Clark and company over whether something should be held up, filibustered, whatever. So, if I kept away from them, I got along with them better. Party headquarters would phone up with meetings hither and yon. I fitted them into my schedule and away I went. If there were any undue expenses, the party covered them; if they were minor, as most were, I simply absorbed them. At least, for my job as Transportation critic, I was acquiring a detailed knowledge of the various public transportation facilities in the country!

On the first Saturday in March 1977, I had a speech to make in Kamloops, British Columbia. It seemed like an easy go, for a change; I didn't have another speech until Monday night in Vancouver. I asked Leola if she'd like to come along. We could spend the Sunday visiting with my cousin Ralph and his wife Audrey in Kamloops, and Leola could get a day's shopping in Vancouver before I returned to Ottawa. We arrived early. The local Conservative executive, knowing my professional interest in the cattle industry, had arranged to take me to a bull sale that afternoon, where I talked to all sorts of interesting people. I even met a fellow who wanted to buy some rodeo stock; sold him three horses. My speech was well received that evening, and we had a good time at the Conservative dance that followed. It was an unportentous beginning to what would turn into one of the more incredible weeks of my life.

On Sunday morning at Ralph and Audrey's, I received word that I had to get to Vancouver right away: I had been booked on television that night. Ralph had to go to Vancouver anyway, so he drove us down. We had barely arrived at the hotel when the Conservative party organizers whisked me off to this TV show. The next morning, I thought I could browse around Vancouver with Leola, but instead I was hustled off to radio programs, to meet the people, to meet the editors. They kept me going all day, with only a break for supper before my speech that night. Tuesday was much the same, only in another part of Vancouver. They just whistled me around. The president of the B.C. Conservatives, a nice fellow by the name of Tony Saunders, was with me at all times — at the press conference, on Jack Webster's program, and so on. The polls that day showed Clark coming down substantially and everyone wanted me to comment. I said a number of things, but the one which made headlines was "Clark can no longer take it as automatic he will win the next election. He's going to have to go out and work for it," or something to that effect. I made another speech that night in Benno Friesen's riding before going out to the airport.

I flew all night and, on arrival in Ottawa, went straight to caucus. So I was not exactly feeling bright-eyed and bushy-tailed when one of the caucus members got up to ask about a headline in the *Globe and Mail*. It was not complimentary of my relationship with Clark. I hadn't read the *Globe*, but I grabbed it to take a look. Joe was sitting right there.

"The president of the B.C. party was with me," I said, "and I thought the news conference went very well. If one reads this entire story, it's not damaging at all to the leader or to myself or to the party. As to the headline, I didn't say the headline, they printed it. The headline serves to capture your attention so you will read the article. I hope most people read the whole thing" — knowing, of course, that they wouldn't. "The leader can question my defence of him if he wants to. However, I understand he has already met with Tony Saunders who had the good fortune of being able to fly yesterday and sleep last night. Furthermore, I've got to speak tonight in Mount Royal. If anybody here wants to go make the speech in Trudeau's riding, I'll phone and tell them I broke my leg or have the flu or whatever. I haven't even decided what I'm going to say yet. All I know is I'm going to take a run at René Lévesque. If you don't like what I'm saying across the country, throw up your hand and you can take my place."

Joe stated that he had indeed met with Tony Saunders and that I had done an admirable job in defending the party and him in Vancouver, that in no way would he want to criticize me. Then he added that he hoped I wouldn't be too hard on Lévesque, that the only hope for the Conservative party was in capturing the anti-Liberal vote in Quebec, which was the PQ vote, and that I couldn't help the party much if I attacked Lévesque. I let this pass, never said a word. But later, when something else came up on which I wanted to comment, I took the opportunity to respond. By this time I had thought about Clark's admonition on Lévesque.

"Look, nobody held up his hand to go make this speech in Montreal for me. I'll try, Mr. Leader, I'll try to be easy on René Lévesque, but I view him as a traitor to my country, a person determined to destroy the country as I know it. I can't be too sympathetic to that kind of a person." I made a strong and emotional pitch. I might have added that Clark's ability to take Lévesque's victory in his stride, trying to turn it to a political advantage, didn't sit well with me at all.

As caucus broke up, CTV's Craig Oliver cornered me and asked what I had been saying. He had heard my voice and the applause. I said I'd been telling caucus about the speech I was going to make in Montreal. I went back to my office and found it full of reporters wanting to know what I thought about an article by Doug Fisher suggesting that the Liberal party was seeking Conservative members who might cross the floor, and might even be after Jack Horner. I hadn't read the article and didn't know where Doug Fisher had got the crazy idea, but I couldn't shake the reporters. I was dead tired. I was late for a television interview with, of all people, Doug Fisher. I'm a stickler for being on time, but I couldn't get out of my own office.

"Look," I exclaimed with some annoyance, "I haven't read the article. I'm going to see Doug Fisher right now. I'll ask him about it. But don't be stupid. How could I join the likes of Otto Lang?"

When I arrived at the TV studio, I asked Fisher where on earth he had got hold of the story. He just laughed and said he had his sources. "There's not an ounce of truth in it," I told him, and promptly dismissed it from my mind. At four o'clock, I had to rush down to the Conference Centre to make a speech on behalf of the Conservative party to some civil servants on how to improve relations between the public service and members of Parliament, not a bad idea. Then back up to my office, with I suppose enough time to change shirts, before catching a taxi to the airport for the plane to Montreal. Anyone who thinks a disgruntled servant of the leader of the Conservative party would keep this kind of schedule has got holes in his head! I was just thankful that I was as strong as I am physically and could stand it.

The Mount Royal Town Hall was packed and the TV crews were out in force. I was to speak in the anteroom, but the place was so jammed that we had to move into the big hall. In that it was Trudeau's riding, I felt I had to devote a few remarks to his faults, the most important of which was his failure to address himself sufficiently to René Lévesque's plan to destroy Canada. There was a wall directly behind the podium, and for some reason I began to use the expression, "That's one star I can't put on the wall for the prime minister of my country." At the end of each new point I said, "That's another star." I think I got to about seven stars minus. It was one of those speeches! I threw away the text. It was a rarity in the sense that I didn't know where the speech was going to go, but go it did, and it came off really well. I was just tickled pink with the response of the crowd.

Well, having flown all night Tuesday and then had a full day on

Wednesday with a late night in Montreal, I was up at six o'clock on Thursday to catch a plane for Calgary; I hoped to spend an hour or two relaxing with my family before speaking to a ladies' meeting in Hanna that evening. At about three o'clock in the afternoon, the phone rang. It was Jim Coutts wondering when I would be back in Ottawa. He said that Prime Minister Trudeau had asked him to talk to me about how I could serve my country in a more fulfilling way. This could mean only one thing.

"Oh, I'll be in Ottawa next week," I told him. I had more speaking engagements the following week and had planned on lying around at home on Monday because I was nearly exhausted. Jim wondered if we could have supper together in Ottawa on Monday. I said it had better be somewhere where we wouldn't be readily seen: "Anyone seeing the two of us together is going to reach conclusions that we wouldn't necessarily want." So we arranged to meet at his apartment hotel, the Inn of the Provinces.

I hung up the phone and I said to my wife and my son Craig, who were sitting in the living room, "Well, you'll never, never guess who that was."

Leola said that she would never try. "Who was it?"

"It was the Prime Minister's principal secretary, Jim Coutts. He wants to talk to me. The Prime Minister thinks he can figure out a way in which I can serve the country better. That only means one thing, and the fact that he wants to see me Monday means they are in a real hurry." I tucked all this away in the back of my mind and tried to get some rest before going out to speak to the ladies' meeting in Hanna.

I had Friday at home with my thoughts. I had travelled great distances, and not just in miles, since the Saturday before. The next day — this would be Saturday, March 12 — I phoned my brother Hugh to tell him about my conversation with Coutts. It was obvious, we agreed, they were going to ask me to join the Liberal party or the cabinet, and probably the latter. Doc advised me to go to the dinner and see what they had in mind, but he cautioned me not to make any concessions: I should try to join the cabinet as a Conservative rather than leave the party. Trudeau, he thought, might be reaching out for a group of people to form a government of all parties in the cause of national unity. Certainly, this was a possibility. Hugh asked me to call him first thing Tuesday morning. The only other person I told was Bill Skoreyko, with whom I was at the time sharing an apartment in Ottawa. His advice was the same as Doc's: "Go have your dinner with Coutts. Come back and we'll talk about it."

So on Monday evening I arrived at Coutts's apartment hotel. We ordered steaks from room service and had a scotch while we waited.

177

Coutts came straight to the point: "Jack, the Prime Minister has asked me to see whether you would consider joining the cabinet to serve western Canada. The Prime Minister thinks it's the wrong time in Canadian history, with the country so divided, for his cabinet to be without a strong western voice. In particular, he needs an Alberta voice because of the energy question. He would very much like you to join the cabinet and he would be prepared to give you a very important portfolio, possibly Transportation, if you would join the Liberal party."

Even though I had known more or less what he was going to say, when I heard it, I was frightened. I just was frightened! I said, "Jim, fine. I've got the message. My first reaction is to tell you to go plumb straight to hell, but this is from the prime minister of my country. Whether I like the guy or dislike the guy, his office is still pretty important to me. If my prime minister thinks I can serve Canada better, I owe it to the country to consider it."

Jim went on to explain further the need for a strong western voice in the cabinet. Poor old Otto Lang, member for Saskatoon East and Transportation minister, was really in the dumps; he had made some serious political errors.

Finally I said, "Jim, let's not talk about it any more. Let's talk about something else. I just. . . it's too upsetting." I was experiencing a violent response, right from my very boot-straps. I didn't want to talk about it. I'd heard it, okay!

So we changed the subject. Liberals now laugh about it, but I didn't know Jim was not a hockey fan. It's Senator Keith Davey who's the hockey fan, who knows all the hockey players and the ball players and so forth. Jim doesn't know a puck from a baseball, but as I didn't know this, I talked hockey the rest of the evening. I was very interested in Lannie McDonald. A local boy from around Hanna, Alberta, he was just starting out with the Toronto Maple Leafs. I wanted to go down and see one of his games, and I thought maybe Coutts might arrange it. Eventually the steaks came. We ate them and I got out of there. I told Jim we'd be in touch, that I just had to think about it. It was too shocking to reject right offhand.

I went back to my office. Bill Skoreyko was there waiting for me, anxious to know what was going on. I told him.

"What in the heck are you going to do?"

"I don't know. I've got to think about it."

On our way out, we passed Don Mazankowski's office. As Maz was such a good friend, I decided to pop in. I was thinking of maybe confiding in him, but he wasn't alone. Peter Bawden was there, holding forth. I just wasn't in the mood for light banter. It didn't take me long to insult Bawden and leave. The next morning I knew I had to apologize, and I phoned Peter: "Look, I was under great pressure and I'll tell you why some day." Peter, who is a pretty good sport, accepted the apology, but it's a night he'll remember.

I phoned Leola. She appreciated my dilemma. She had no liking for Trudeau, but she had always left the political decisions to me. She simply said, "Well, you're not going to do anything in a hurry." I assured her that I wouldn't.

As arranged, I phoned Hugh on Tuesday. He agreed that it was a big decision. "As Transportation minister, you might be able to do something. Let's think about it for twenty-four hours. I have always found it a good policy to sit on difficult decisions for a while. Don't tell anybody."

"I've got to tell Clark," I protested.

"Don't tell Clark for twenty-four hours. We'll talk again tomorrow morning." That was fine. I wanted more time to think about it myself.

When I phoned Hugh on Wednesday, he agreed that I would have to tell Clark and see what he had to say. So, towards the end of Question Period that afternoon, I went up to Clark and asked for a private word with him. We went to his office as soon as Question Period was over. Then, with the door closed behind us, I informed him that Trudeau, through Jim Coutts, had offered me a cabinet post if I would join their party. I said my immediate reaction was to tell them to go to hell, but I had restrained myself because the offer had come from the prime minister and because I had felt that western Canada, certainly on questions like energy and agriculture, was not being well understood. Maybe I'd be able to do something as a minister.

Much to my surprise, Clark showed no emotion: "I'm not surprised, although I thought they would have gone after Claude Wagner first."

I pointed out that Claude Wagner had nothing to offer. "They've got all the votes they can get out of Quebec. I never thought they'd go after Claude Wagner, but I didn't think they'd go after me. Apparently they look to me to deliver votes in western Canada."

I was utterly nonplussed that Joe wasn't surprised, that he was not in the least angry or frustrated. He was cool as a cucumber. As I wanted him to understand clearly my position, I said, "Before I can consider their proposition, there is one thing that has to be thrashed out. Last October you told Arnold Malone to decide inside of a month in which riding he was going to run. I was asked to continue travelling across Canada. I've done this. But Arnold still hasn't announced a decision. Instead of getting out, he's continued to work towards the nomination in Crowfoot. I'd like this matter settled. Before I reach any decision, I'd like the three of us to sit down: you and me and Arnold. I want to know where I sit in the Conservative party."

Clark agreed to that and said we'd have a meeting at the beginning of the following week. That was the earliest I could manage in view of my speaking engagements.

I spent the weekend looking forward to Monday when Joe and Arnold and I could sit down and thrash out once and for all what I thought had been thrashed out the previous October. On Monday morning I arrived in Ottawa and phoned Clark's office. Joe wouldn't be in today, I was told. What about tomorrow at eleven o'clock? The next day I was right there, right on time at eleven. I walked in, exchanged pleasantries with Clark, and looked around. I asked, "Where's Arnold?"

Clark explained, "I decided, Jack, that you and I should meet alone. I'll meet with Arnold separately." I knew immediately that there was a double cross in the wind.

I protested, "Joe, that isn't what I understood we were going to do. Last week I thought you said the three of us would sit down together. This isn't satisfactory at all."

He acted surprised, he didn't know I'd look at it that way, and so on and so forth.

I put it bluntly. "I want to know what you tell Malone. I clearly remember our October caucus when I did a job on Stan Schumacher for you. I wanted Crowfoot cleared up. You told those assembled that Crowfoot was mine. Arnold was to find another seat within a month. He hasn't even attempted to find it; he's going to run in Crowfoot. I want a showdown. I want to know what the Conservative party really thinks of me."

We then got into a long discussion on my contributions to the Conservative party, on whether or not I was John Diefenbaker's troubleshooter, whether or not I had been, on whose man I was. I clearly told Clark that I was my own man. It was true I had been a hard loser in the race for the party's leadership, but I had served Clark to the utmost of my ability and no man could do more. I said that I hadn't told Diefenbaker a thing and that Clark had to understand this. Clark claimed he understood. Said he had never thought I was Diefenbaker's joe boy or puppet — oh no, he knew that I was capable of making up my own mind.

I asked, "Can you understand the position I am in? I want to know. Are you going to make Malone live up to the obligation you set forth last October?"

Well, Clark's memory started to fade. He didn't quite remember it the way I did, but he was going to meet with Malone. . . . The whole

180

thing gave me a rotten feeling in the pit of my stomach. I thought, "Well fiddle!" I left his office with the clear impression that he would be happy, in fact, to get rid of me.

Diefenbaker's office was right across the hall. I wanted to find out what Dief had heard. Mrs. Eligh, his secretary, sent me right in. I thought surely to goodness the story must have got out somewhere. I asked the Chief, "Well, how is your grapevine today?"

Dief muttered a bit and said, "I've got no grapevine. What do you mean? I just read the papers. I've got no grapevine."

"You've got the best grapevine on Parliament Hill. You hear from everybody, you get letters from all over the country; you put everything together and reach your conclusions."

Dief said, "If you came in here to tell me something, tell me. I don't know what you're talking about."

"I just wondered if you had heard Trudeau has offered me a position in his cabinet?"

His reaction was one of genuine surprise. I knew then that the story wasn't out. He said, "No, I hadn't heard. You want to be a cabinet minister? You'd be a good cabinet minister. You want to be a cabinet minister; you've got no more chance of ever being in Clark's cabinet than I have of flying to the moon this afternoon." At which point, he walked over to his window and looked up as if to see the moon in the sky. He asked, "How's all this come about? Where did this all start?" So I gave him a brief rundown, told him about my meeting with Clark that morning, about how dissatisfied I was. He shook his head. "Well, you've got a big decision on your hands."

Just then, Bob Coates walked in. I turned to the Chief, "I've got to go. You can explain my problem to Bob Coates if you like."

Dief, ever careful through long legal practice, caught me up short. "No sir, no sir. You want Bob Coates to know what you told me, you tell him, because I'm not telling him. I'm not going to be party to the gossip that goes around the Hill."

That was a neat bit, just came right out of old Dief just like that! It more or less put me on the spot. Coates could not help but be curious. I was luke warm to Coates because he had let me down badly in the leadership race. Certainly, he wasn't of the stature of Diefenbaker. I didn't feel obliged to forgive him as I had John D. Nevertheless, I told him as briefly as I could and made him understand that I wanted it kept confidential until I reached a decision.

The rest of the day was uneventful. That night there was a vote in the House at nine forty-five. The bells had started when my phone rang. It was Bill McPherson of the Ottawa *Citizen*.

"Jack, I want to talk to you."

I told him the division bells were ringing and that I had to go in and vote.

He called back at about twenty past ten. "Jack, I've got a hot rumour from a very good source that Trudeau has offered you a cabinet post, possibly Transportation, and you're considering it."

Never before in my life had I used the expression "no comment", but I didn't want to talk about it. The next day, in big red headlines in the Ottawa *Citizen*, my "no comment" looked like "yes". It was the worst thing I could have said. Obviously, in looking back, it was Coates or Clark — and most probably Coates — who leaked the story to the press.

The next day at caucus Clark sent me a note about McPherson's scoop: "Jack, in today's Ottawa *Citizen*, there's a story suggesting that you've had an offer to join the Trudeau government. I think you should explain your intentions to caucus." So I got up and gave an account of the phone call and my use of the words "no comment" in an attempt to get rid of the guy as quickly as I could. I said I now realized that it was the wrong thing to say and that of course I had no intention of joining "that gang of thieves". I just marvelled at Clark, knowing all the facts he did, sitting there calmly watching me commit perjury. In fact, he seemed to relish it. Perhaps a satisfying position for him. But not for me!

Thursday came along. I had further phone discussions with Jim Coutts. I told him, and I guess Clark, that I would be going home for a week or so to give the whole problem some thought. And home I went. According to the press reports, I was at the ranch with my family and supporters, weighing all the factors in the major decision of my political life. In a way this was true, but I was also enjoying myself curling in the annual Pollockville bonspiel.

There is a bonspiel in Pollockville in the last week of every March. In recent years it's become pretty hard to get a team in because it's the wind-up bonspiel for the whole area and a lot of people like to come out. I had missed the previous year and had said to the drawmaster, way back at the beginning of January, that I would be in it this year for sure. Little did I know at the time how badly I would need that week away from the Ottawa scene.

Of course, all the people at home had heard about Trudeau's offer to me. I wanted to talk to my neighbours, close friends, and to those I thought interested in politics — people whose judgement I valued and sought out. Many of them shook their heads at my dilemma, and I guess were happy that it was my problem, not theirs. All those I talked to in the area said they were sure I would do the best thing: "If you accept Trudeau's offer, you'll want results, and you'll get them and we'll be with you." I phoned some key people in my organization, such as George Fawcett in Consort and Eugene Kush in Hanna, and got a very similar reaction. Later, when CBC was out interviewing everybody and anybody in the town of Hanna, Eugene was front and centre with his comments of support, which I appreciated very much. I got through the bonspiel all right, although I can't remember whether we won any prizes.

Immediately on my return to Ottawa, Clark phoned me. He wanted to know whether I had reached a decision. My decision was that I had to talk to Trudeau. Thus far, our communications had been through Coutts. Obviously, there was no way I could make a final decision without talking to the boss himself. Clark couldn't seem to understand this at all. To my utter amazement, he said, "I strictly forbid you talking to him."

"Joe, you can't prevent me from talking to him," I protested. "I can talk to anybody I like. It's a free country. Put yourself in my boots. I have to live first and foremost with myself. I don't want to look back fifteen years down the road and be bouncing some grandchild on my knee, telling him the story about having the offer to serve Canada in a more fulfilling way as a cabinet minister, which I turned down because I didn't like the then prime minister when I'd never even talked to him. I don't know how full the offer is, how I'd be able to serve, whether I'd be able to serve independent of the prime minister's direction or not. Joe, having heard it from the foreman of the ranch, I couldn't live with myself without hearing it from the boss. I firmly decided when I was home that this was the least I could do for my political career."

Clark got pretty huffy and puffy with me, but I was in no mood to entertain his wishes. I didn't think he had dealt me right at all — never at any time telling me of his conversation with Malone or anything else. From my point of view, he left a lot to be desired. All he could say was, "I forbid you." To which I again replied, "You can't forbid me. I'm going to see Trudeau, but if you like, Joe, I'll guarantee that I'll make no decisions during my talk with him and that I'll give you a full report. You must understand, however, that I have to see him." He didn't understand.

I phoned Coutts and asked him to arrange a meeting with Trudeau. It was set for six o'clock at 24 Sussex. Right on the nose (I wasn't a minute early, I wasn't a minute late) I got out of the taxi at the Prime Minister's residence. Two RCMP constables were standing at the door. I told them who I was. One carried a walkie-talkie and reported, "The Prime Minister is just leaving the west door of the Centre Block. He'll be here in three minutes." I went ahead in. The maid took my coat and ushered me into the library.

There was an awful roar in the house. From the sound of it, the

Trudeau children were just having a ball in one of the downstairs rooms. I couldn't for the life of me figure out how three kids could make so much noise. When the Prime Minister arrived, they came tumbling and rolling and shouting to greet him: three blond-haired boys and a little black one. They reminded me of a litter of pups. Trudeau picked up each one and gave him a big hug; you could see the love. Then they ran around the house shouting and hollering, came into the library. One said to me, "And who are you?" I told him, "I'm little Jack Horner. Haven't you heard of him?" Around the room he went, hollering "little Jack Horner" until he bumped into one of his brothers. There were a few tears until his dad picked him up. It was really quite a scene: the Prime Minister, with all the cares of the nation on his shoulders, and his three young sons and a fourth child, who I imagine was the maid's. Once the salutations were over, they went away quite quietly. Trudeau kind of shook his head and apologized.

I said, "Don't apologize to me. I grew up in a large family and I kind of enjoyed seeing the kids romp around."

"What will you have to drink?" he asked.

"Really, nothing is fine for me," I assured him. This wasn't a social call. I had come to get down to some serious discussion, and I knew that Trudeau rarely took a drink. But he stated that he was going to have his usual and that I might as well join him. Successful on his third attempt to find the maid — she was off somewhere with the kids — I got my scotch and water, and Trudeau got his pernod. Then he closed the library door and we got down to business.

Trudeau, rather naturally, had been worried about my position on the official languages legislation. He told me, however, that a number of his close colleagues had read my every word on the subject and had pointed out the pertinent parts to him and that he could live with my views. He was somewhat surprised that what I had said wasn't as bad as he had been led to believe by the press.

I observed, "There's no use you and I getting into it now, but I remember your saying in 1969 that as prime minister you had a mandate to make Canada bilingual. I didn't think you did. It was your prerogative, however, to feel that way; you could go ahead with your legislation if you wanted to, but in my view, you were doing it the wrong way. The correct way was through the schools not through retraining civil servants. Your way wouldn't work. You should take twenty years rather than two. Your answer was that you didn't have time. You had to do it in two years to ameliorate the growing feeling of alienation in Quebec. We're not here to rehash that debate, but that's the way I recall it and that was my view."

There was no quarrel. "Jack, there's no doubt about it, we weren't all that successful with the civil service. This year we are going to spend less on the civil service and more on the schools. I respect your criticism and I can live with your thoughts." I'm certain a lot of people in Crowfoot and across Canada wondered how we two could ever reconcile our views on the language question. It wasn't difficult.

I told Trudeau, "My reason in wanting to see you was the expression Coutts used when he conveyed your desire to have me join the cabinet so I could serve my country, and particularly my part of the country, 'in a more fulfilling way'. To do this, I would have to have a portfolio of vital interest to western Canada. If I took anything less, I would be seen as merely a pawn, able to deliver very little. Just what did you have in mind?"

"I assume you would like Transportation," he replied.

"Yes, I would. The West believes it has been short-changed in the field of transportation. While I don't think we are really as badly off as many believe, this is the popular view. I have studied the question for a long time, and yes, I'd like Transportation."

Trudeau then explained that no matter what had been written or said about him and the handling of his cabinet, there were some things one could do and some one couldn't. "I don't want a cabinet shuffle which will thoroughly disrupt the system. Sometimes you can get the changes you want without doing this. I'd really have to give the whole matter some thought. I may or may not be able to move Otto Lang. I have never, in all the years I have been prime minister, promised a particular portfolio to any person. I've tried generally to work within some parameters. Let's have a look at a couple more."

I said, "Agriculture is another which is perceived as very important to the West, but I don't know what on earth you would do with your present minister. Otto Lang can handle many other portfolios, but what do you give Eugene Whelan?"

Trudeau kind of laughed and rejoined, "Yes, that would be a problem, wouldn't it?"

I stated that as much as it might surprise him and many others, I wasn't keenly interested in Agriculture, because the federal agricultural portfolio is primarily concerned with the dairy end of things. I wouldn't take Agriculture without the responsibility for the Canadian Wheat Board; only then would it relate to western Canada. He understood, but his problem still would be what to do with Eugene, and he'd have to wrestle with that one.

"Well, there are two others that are of primary importance to western Canada," I added, "and I would like either one of them. One would be Energy. I'm not in any way connected with the oil companies and have no financial interest in any of them, but energy is vitally important to Alberta. I think our position has been badly understood in the East. I believe I could handle Energy to the satisfaction of all of Canada."

Trudeau agreed that this probably was true but felt there would be difficulty explaining an Energy minister from Alberta to the people of Ontario and Quebec. He would like to think on that one.

"The second," I said, "is Industry, Trade and Commerce. For years, western Canada has objected to the East being protected by high tariffs to our disadvantage. We in the West are the major exporting part of Canada, and we have always advocated freer and freer trade. We believe we could export even more if there was a greater effort to assist us. The West would appreciate having a western minister in that portfolio." I then stated that beyond those four, I wouldn't be interested, and that I would have grave doubts about Agriculture without the Wheat Board.

"Well, that gives me a good understanding, Jack," Trudeau responded. "How do you see the economy?"

By this time our dollar had started to drop below par. I expressed the view that interest rates had been too high in Canada for the period leading up to all of 1975 and '76, which kept our dollar at a premium, that our dollar should have come down sooner than it did. He wanted to know my views on wage and price controls, which were being eased back at this time. I didn't want to go into all the detail as to why I had been opposed to wage and price controls in 1974 or why I could live with them in 1975. I did observe, however, that being opposed to them at one time doesn't mean one is opposed to them forever. It's a question of when they're applied. Will they help the economy or not? I said, "Your staff can look up what I had to say in 1975 when you implemented them. You'll find very little. Nevertheless, I do believe in the market-place functioning." He didn't disagree.

Finally, Trudeau asked me what he could tell the press. He was holding a press conference next day before going on a trip to California. He really wanted me to cross the floor immediately. He added this rider: "I can put you in the cabinet right away, but I can't give you a major portfolio until September; at that time I will give you one of the four we discussed."

On that basis, I was in no hurry to decide. Besides, I wasn't satisfied I'd be able to live with myself. I said, "Prime Minister, I'm not prepared to make a decision today. I'm not prepared to join your party tomorrow."

"Well, what do I say at the press conference tomorrow? I guess I tell the press nothing. Does anybody know you're here?"

I looked him straight in the eye. "Yes, Joe Clark knows I'm here."

He registered disappointment, in fact he seemed quite annoyed.

I explained, "Prime Minister, he's the leader of the party I still belong to; I thought in fairness I would tell him I was coming to see you."

"What do I say to the press?" he asked again.

"I guess you could tell the press we have talked about the problems confronting Canada and we may or may not talk again about the problems confronting Canada. Something like that is all you have to say."

"That sounds all right. That's good."

I added, "I guess you should know that, no matter what, I'll never tell a direct lie. As a politician, I can equivocate with the best of them, but I have not, nor will I, ever resort to lying. And that's why I had to tell you that Clark knew I was here."

Our conversation had lasted about forty-five minutes. I came away convinced that Trudeau indeed wanted western Canada at his cabinet table, that he felt, as Coutts had told me, his cabinet should clearly represent all parts of Canada. He wanted me to join him. He considered me a very strong-minded man, typical of what he judged western Canadians to be, and he felt we could get along. We had been very frank with one another. To sit down and talk about the language legislation was something I could never have done with Stanfield. I was impressed at his openly admitting that maybe he had been in too big a hurry, that it hadn't worked, and that the slower approach through the schools and the educational system now seem advisable. He struck me as deeply concerned about Canada. I came away with a very good impression.

I knew the opportunity he was offering me was relatively rare. Many people have crossed the floor, but few have been asked to join the cabinet. It had happened with Crerar and Forke in 1926, but there were no recent examples. Bud Olson had joined the Liberal party from the Socreds, but he was neither asked to join nor given a cabinet post. Only after he had joined, run, and been elected as a Liberal was he made a minister. Yet here was I, receiving a direct request from the Prime Minister, and me a person who had been a thorn in his side in Parliament. I had held up two pieces of agricultural legislation so long that Trudeau had complained publicly over radio and television that Parliament wasn't working.

At one point in our discussion, Trudeau had suggested that my position was similar to his in 1965: "Jack, you are a politician. You want to do things, you want to do things to help the country and to help your particular part of the country. You are in the same boat as I was in when Pearson came to me. Neither one of us was a Liberal to begin with. I certainly wasn't. I could have gone on teaching law at universities for years. I didn't need the job. I faced a difficult decision. Should I continue to be a writer and a teacher, only participating on the edge of politics, or should I get right in and do the things that I felt should be done? I'm giving you a chance to do things you want to have done." I found this an interesting parallel.

I could see the Easter holidays coming up, a ten- to fifteen-day stretch in which I would have more time to talk to my constituents. So I told both Trudeau and Clark that I'd reach a decision right after Easter. I went back home saying little else.

I wanted to get back and talk some more to the people, and I did. I wanted to talk to the president of my riding association, Paul Marshall from Delia. He was a young, intelligent person, keenly interested in the country, the kind of guy you like to see take an interest in politics. Luckily for me, I ran into him in Hanna one day at a farm auction. We sat in my half-ton and I told him the story. He was utterly amazed that the rumours he had been hearing were correct.

"It's a difficult decision," he said, "but if you take Trudeau's offer, we'll know you've concluded you can achieve something worth while, and we'll be behind you."

I met a number of people. They all said they were behind me. The only negative vote was from Jim Proudfoot of Chinook. Jim's father, Lorne Proudfoot, had been a member in the old United Farmers of Alberta government. A very fine gentleman, he had worked for me, travelled with me at times, and was a person I keenly respected. I saw Jim at that same auction sale and called him over for a little talk.

"Jack," he said, "I have a hundred per cent confidence in you and your ability to represent this area, but if you join the Liberal party I won't be able to support you. I cannot support the Liberal party."

"You'll still be supporting the same man," I argued. "He'll be in a position to serve you better. I've never served the party. This is what got me into trouble with the Conservatives. I always put the people and the country ahead of the party, and I will treat the Liberal party the same way I treated the Conservative party." I didn't make a dent on him. In the elections that followed in 1979 and 1980, I don't think Jim did a thing to oppose me, but I'm willing to vouch he didn't vote for me.

As I considered my situation, it appeared obvious that Clark was not going to ask Malone to get out of Crowfoot, especially after all this. Malone would hang tough, and my political future as a Conservative would be a one-night stand at a nomination convention where Clark would have all his forces behind Malone. My alternative was to take Trudeau at his word and see whether I could serve the country, and particularly western Canada, more effectively than before. These were my thoughts when I returned to Ottawa.

Clark immediately wanted to know what I was going to do. I told him I hadn't made up my mind. "I think it's only right and only fair," he told me, "that until you have resolved your dilemma, I'm temporarily taking away your position as Transportation critic and asking you to stand aside on the strategy committee." This was fine. I could understand this. That afternoon, however, bingo, it hits the papers: HORNER STRIPPED PERMANENTLY. And I had thought I had a private agreement with Clark. The press were all over my office. What did I think of it?

"I'm damned annoyed, damned annoyed that he had to issue a press release."

Did I know it was coming?

"I knew that I was going to be relieved temporarily, but this looks pretty decisive on Clark's part. I think it's tantamount to pushing me out of the party."

In the meantime, Coutts was phoning me. He had read the story and considered I had practically joined the Liberals. I asked him to get Trudeau to confirm his offer. Certainly, I would no longer be able to serve in the Conservative party.

The next morning, Clark phoned to demand I sign a declaration of support to him and the Conservative party. He was insistent I do this in caucus. I was thunderstruck. I was born into the Conservative party. I had done nothing wrong. I had not accepted the government's offer. There was nothing I could do to stop the government from talking to me. True, I didn't have to go to 24 Sussex, but Trudeau could hardly have talked to me in the street. Every conversation I had reported to Clark. I was just a little angry.

I went into caucus to make my last appearance. I must have spoken for an hour. I gave them the full story — where it had started, where it was ending. In a way, I attempted to prove to caucus that I had not yet joined the Liberal party. I remember telling the story I had used in Black Diamond, Alberta, in 1972 when I spoke on Clark's behalf in his first election. I had said then that if I felt the Conservative party was the best vehicle to serve my constituents, and if they elected me, I accepted the responsibility to make certain the vehicle was kept in good repair: I would change the tire if it got a flat; I would change the motor if it needed a motor change.

I looked at Clark as I ended my remarks. "I suppose now I can go back and tell my constituents that the vehicle is a complete write-off and for that reason I have had to abandon it." Then I walked out.

That evening, Coutts confirmed that Prime Minister Trudeau wanted me to join the Liberal party and that I would be sworn in immediately as a minister of the crown.

8/Minister of the Crown

I was sworn in as minister without portfolio on the morning of April 21, 1977. Prior to the ceremony at Government House, I had breakfast with Trudeau at 24 Sussex. It was a magnificent spring morning. We decided to walk over to Rideau Hall. We talked of many things as we made our way, surrounded by newsmen and photographers, to the Governor General's official residence. Trudeau seemed to delight in the occasion.

After my swearing in, we went out to meet the press. I guess Trudeau was watching me very closely to see how I would handle the questions. He commented later, "The press don't bother you at all. You like to play with them." At cabinet later that morning, Trudeau introduced me as the cabinet minister from Alberta. He was absolutely fair and straight with me; he told cabinet that any appointments in or from Alberta were to be cleared through me. As Alberta's representative in cabinet, I could veto any appointment related to my province. This statement did much to reassure me that I would have a full part to play in cabinet and would not be merely a pawn to be used by Trudeau and the Liberal party. I greatly appreciated his introduction; it kind of set my mind and heart at ease that this whole thing was going to work, that Trudeau and I, maybe to a lot of people's surprise, were going to get along. And that's about the way it turned out.

I didn't physically cross the floor; I walked in on the government side of the House. I think my new colleagues were anxious to see how I would respond to the inevitable barbs I would receive from the Opposition side. I endeavoured to rise above them. I was hurt a little, however, by Pat Nowlan's attack: "Mr. Speaker, my question is directed to the Prime Minister. In view of the fact that the Prime Minister himself has been a convert to a party and in view of the conversion we have seen here today, in view of the fact that the Prime Minister has responsibility in establishing the political morality of the land, my question to him is whether it is part of his political philosophy that every man has his price."

I rose on a point of order, stating that it was not a question of price but of cost: "It is a cost I have been prepared to pay for the good of my country. In setting that kind of example for all Canadians, I hope that Canadians will make a rededication to spend a little time and energy trying to help this country. I hope I have demonstrated that. The honourable member called it a price. I call it a cost. It is a cost which I am prepared to shoulder."

Diefs subsequent remark, "Now that the sheriff has joined the rustlers," I expected and enjoyed. Dief was so obviously delighted with it that he burst out laughing. I laughed myself. The only occasion on which I lost my cool came several months later when, during a debate, Arnold Malone referred to me as a Judas who had picked up his thirty pieces of silver on joining the Liberal party. I got up and asked him to withdraw this. Of course, I never did have an ounce of respect for him. His remark irritated me, but I took it from where it came. To my amazement, Lincoln Alexander, who had been a friend of mine, defended Malone, more or less implying that I had been paid off. I became violently angry. As I left the House, I met Erik Nielsen, who had also been supporting Malone. I had cooled off, but I grabbed him by the tie and told him I didn't give a darn what he and Malone thought, but he could bloody well pass the message on to Linc that he need never speak to me again. Of my many good friends in the Conservative party, quite a number told me, at the time, that in similar circumstances they too would have joined the Trudeau government. Of course, I was a cabinet minister and they were looking for favours.

Lincoln Alexander was the only friend I lost over my move. The others whom I considered friends before I left the Conservative party are still friends to this day. People whom I considered enemies or less than friendly when I was a Conservative are the same as well. Mazankowski, Skoreyko, Bawden, the gang, all those who had supported me in the leadership race, I called into my office before I left the Conservative party to tell them that the rumours they had heard were true, that they could think what they wanted of me but I would always be prepared to help them in any way I could. If I became a Liberal cabinet minister, I would not campaign in their ridings or do anything to upset them politically. I lived up to this except on one occasion when I went into George Whittaker's riding. My youngest son had just become engaged to the daughter of a Kelowna rancher, and I thought it a good opportunity to go in to meet the prospective in-laws. I apologized to George, but I don't know that it made him particularly happy.

As to the allegation that I had been promised a Senate seat and everything else, Trudeau and I never discussed this. Could I win Crowfoot as a Liberal? I was prepared to take this gamble and that was what I told caucus. Overall, my gamble turned out to be far better than I ever dreamed because when I moved to the Liberals in the spring of 1977 I thought that, if I was lucky, I would have maybe a year before an election. As it turned out, I had two years.

The Liberals gave me a free hand. I found everyone within the party tremendously willing to work with me. No one ever attempted to handicap or hobble me in any way, and it was just a real pleasure to work with guys like Jim Coutts, Keith Davey, and the national party president Al Graham. Marc Lalonde hosted a reception for the Quebec members to welcome me into the party and I discovered quite a few friends. I'd been around Parliament so long, most knew of my ability as a fighter and a critic in committees. Generally, I was well received by the Liberal rank and file too. If there was resentment (and I recognized there was bound to be some among the younger MPs in the government back benches who were seeking cabinet posts), it never really surfaced in my presence. Of course, none of them were from Alberta, and the fact that Alberta needed a voice at the cabinet table more or less set me apart. I knew the acid test would be answering questions in the House when I was given responsibility for a department. Until then, most of the Liberal caucus were prepared to reserve judgement.

The Liberal party, in the sense of the particular responsibilities of Senator Al Graham, Senator Keith Davey, Jim Coutts, and the Prime Minister, seemed to have it together better than the Conservative party. The critical aspects of the party's power structure all seemed to be right there on the Hill in contrast to the way in which the Conservative party operated. I never saw the clear division between the elected and non-elected within the Liberal party and, as an elected member, I liked this.

I was the interesting new acquisition of the Liberal party. Consequently, I was asked to go hither and yon to make political speeches for various members of Parliament. To begin with, this was quite difficult because I couldn't take credit for much the Liberal party and the government had done, nor could I speak with any degree of confidence about those accomplishments. Nevertheless, we had some good crowds (I suppose it was the old zoo psychology at work) and the members were pretty happy with what I said. I recall a big Liberal fund-raising dinner in Toronto at which there was a guest speaker from every region of Canada. I was the one from western Canada. This was a completely different scene for me because I had never really been well received by the establishment of the Conservative party, certainly not from about 1964 on when Diefenbaker's authority started to wane. The Liberal party was altogether a pleasant change. Here, I was accepted with open arms.

Basically, my time as minister without portfolio was a learning period. I wasn't under any pressure, nor did I find the process very difficult. I learned how cabinet functioned, why things were done, and how they were done. Trudeau didn't have a two-tiered cabinet nor the political strategy committee Clark had. Instead, there was a committee of cabinet called Priorities and Planning, or P. and P. I was on it as spokesman for Alberta and western Canada. I found very interesting the detailed discussions on the direction of Parliament and, from the beginning, was able to lend advice on how to get legislation through the House. One got to look at the early stages of Trudeau's proposed constitutional changes, for which he was seeking wide acceptance by the provinces. I would recommend that any new cabinet minister, if the prime minister can afford to give him the time, should serve for three or four months without portfolio as a preconditioning. One learns how the Privy Council Office works, how Treasury Board works, how the whole system of appointments and patronage within your region functions. It's not a bad process.

When I joined the cabinet, I was told that each minister could have a staff for which he could pay a maximum of $90,000. I suppose some of the senior officers of the party had a right to be suspicious of what this ex-Conservative would drag into their fold. I immediately asked Peter Thompson (a long-time friend and confidant, and a reporter for the *Montreal Star*) to be my executive assistant. He thought about it for a while and then accepted. The Liberal party was very pleased with him. After a while, I hired Bill Morrison, who also handily won the party's approval. I never had a complaint.

I always said my people were the best on Parliament Hill! The interesting aspect is that after the 1979 defeat of the government and, of course, my own defeat, my staff was quickly gobbled up by the new Conservative administration. In every case, they received better jobs at higher pay, which suggests they were as good as I believed them to be and that I underpaid them. Indeed, following my defeat, I had a very nice letter from Keith Davey, who was not only complimentary of my participation in the Liberal party but very complimentary about my staff, whom he thought most capable. I thought this a handsome gesture on his part.

By September 1977, when Donald Macdonald left the cabinet, I was ready for the added work and responsibility of a portfolio. Macdonald's resignation seemed to be by prearrangement, although Trudeau often in my presence told him he wished he'd stay on. Macdonald, however, never wavered from his determination to resign. As a point of interest, he told me he had been violently opposed to my joining the cabinet but had come to change his mind. He thought my job of representing Alberta, my federalist views, and my general participation in cabinet admirable.

When the Prime Minister had his promised cabinet shuffle, I knew he would prefer me either in Transport or in Industry, Trade and Commerce. I wasn't at all surprised when it turned out to be the latter because he wanted Jean Chrétien to be the first French Canadian to hold the position of minister of Finance. This meant Otto Lang had to stay in Transport. Otto could have handled Finance. In fact, Otto probably would have been a very good Finance minister because Finance ministers never seem to be popular.

Dief was having his eighty-second birthday celebration in the Parliament Building's Commonwealth Room the day I received my portfolio. I dropped in. I guess I wanted to show that, no matter what, we were still friends. Of course, this was the way in which he received me. I might mention while I'm on the subject that I had written him a very strong letter some months after the leadership race telling him how much he had disappointed me. He had been quite upset by it, but Olive, who for some reason or other always took my side, told him, "Now John, that's just Jack." This was their last conversation on the morning of Olive's death.

I was pleased to become the minister of Industry, Trade and Commerce as it was a new area for me. I knew that most of Canada's export products — lumber, grain, oil and gas — were predominantly from western Canada, but I was quite ignorant as to what the department did to help our exports or to facilitate commerce within Canada. This required a great deal of study on my part. At weekends, I took home mounds of material. I think what did surprise me was the depth of the department, the broad field of its participation in the Canadian economy, and the many areas the minister must master to meet the large responsibility that is his.

On the industry side, I was the minister responsible for watching over the development of two planes — the Dash-7 and the Challenger — to make sure there was justification for the government's involvement in their production. The government had taken over DeHavilland, which was making the Dash-7, and when I became minister the plane wasn't selling well. Precisely one aircraft had been sold. We had to shake things up. I decided to push sales, a move which fortunately coincided with a United States decision to deregulate the American airlines. Suddenly there was a market for the Dash-7. By 1979, when I lost my portfolio along with my seat in Parliament, seventy-five of the planes had been sold. This had given a big boost to the DeHavilland plant in Toronto, which in consequence was able to subcontract work to companies across Canada, from British Columbia to Nova Scotia. Meanwhile, the Challenger (a wide-bodied executive jet, which was being produced by Canadair and General Dynamics, also with government backing) was promising to be a tremendous plane. As of the end of 1979, Canada had orders for some hundred and thirty-five Challengers.

The automobile industry also came under my portfolio, and this one industry caused me more headaches than any other. There were two reasons for this: first, I was under constant attack in the House over the deficit in the Auto Pact with the United States; second was the importance of the automobile industry to the province of Ontario. Many people don't realize that one-sixth of the labour force in Ontario is directly or indirectly employed in some portion of the automobile industry. It means as much to Ontario as the oil and gas industry means to Alberta.

The big question was how we were going to get more plants manufacturing parts or assembling cars in Canada. Ford was proposing to build a new engine plant, but unless the Canadian government came forward with strong financial backing, it looked as if this plant would be situated in the United States. I felt strongly that this plant should be in Canada, and eventually Ford's board of directors agreed that they might be interested in siting the new plant in Ontario — if Canada would put up $75 million.

In cabinet, I came forward with a strong argument that the federal government should guarantee half the money and that the Ontario government should guarantee the other half (even though Darcy Mc-Keough, Ontario's treasurer, was taking the position that he wouldn't give Ford a five-cent piece). Trudeau didn't like the word "half" but agreed to $37.5 million, which amounted to the same thing. Now the ball was in Ontario's court. Bill Davis eventually offered $25 million, proposing that the federal government should raise its commitment to $50 million. This wasn't good enough. I knew I couldn't go back to cabinet and ask for more. I'd barely escaped with my hide on the last round. So the deal was off.

It was at this juncture that the Calgary Stampede Board invited Trudeau to be the parade marshal for the opening of the Stampede in July 1978. Independently, Peter Lougheed had invited Bill Davis to the opening. And I would be there, of course. Seeing that there was going to be such a gathering of the clans, Roy Bennett, the president of Ford of Canada, phoned me to say he would come to Calgary too if I could arrange a meeting with Trudeau and Davis. Bennett was determined to get the new Ford plant built in Canada, and he still felt there was hope.

Trudeau arrived in Calgary at about 11 P.M. the evening before the opening of the Stampede. I had just gone to bed when his assistant phoned me, telling me the Prime Minister wanted to see me. When I went down to his room, I told him about the meeting Bennett wanted. Trudeau was noncommittal, but surprised to hear that Davis was in town. I explained that Lougheed had invited him, and added that I thought

Lougheed was attempting to steal some of Trudeau's limelight. It was a strategy play, I said.

Trudeau looked at me in mild amazement. "You think he thinks like that? What's he worried about? He hasn't got any political worries."

Then he got down to the reason he'd called for me: "What do I wear tomorrow in this parade?" Someone on the Stampede Board had a suit laid out for him in the room. He said, "What do you think? I've got my jeans and an old shirt here."

"Well, does that suit fit you?" I asked. "Put it on. Let me have a look." It was a very handsome suit, not overly western in cut, but sharp. I said, "This might surprise you, Prime Minister, but a rancher likes to dress well. When he dresses up, he's as nifty a dresser as there is around. You're not a cowboy, you're the head rancher, really, in this parade. You better wear that suit." He agreed.

Although I knew Trudeau could ride a horse, for some reason I'd simply assumed that, as parade marshal, he'd ride in a convertible. When I expressed my surprise that he would lead the parade on horseback, he asked, "Isn't that what you do in Calgary?"

"Oh yes, that's what you do all right."

"I hope they've got a good horse for me," he said. "I don't want any plug."

Atop a lively big horse the next day, Trudeau looked like a million dollars.

Following the parade, we were to proceed to Fort Calgary, which is a building on the Stampede grounds in which the directors host the Stampede dinner. Trudeau had to slip over to the hotel to attend to some business, so he was a little late in arriving, but Roy Bennett was there, as were Bill Davis and Peter Lougheed. It was a lovely day and we were standing outside, sipping a bit of refreshment before dinner, when Bennett broached the matter of the Ford plant: "If I've got the true picture, Jack, you're prepared to put up thirty-seven and a half million."

I confirmed that and added, "Bill Davis is standing there. He's prepared to go to twenty-five."

Bennett continued, "I'm not trying to get the money out of you for the sake of it. The truth of the matter is I've got to have at least seventy million to go to the board with it. Anything less, they're not going to consider."

I thought for a minute and replied, "Well then, we're about six or so million short. I'll split the difference with Ontario. I'll go back to cabinet to try for another three million."

We asked Bill Davis what he thought of this. He hummed and hawed. When Trudeau came along, I had a quiet word with him to explain that we were in negotiations about the Ford plant. "This is some place to be dealing over the Ford plant!" he commented. I told him what I'd offered. He said, "We'll give them forty million and that's it." Well, that was fine with me.

Trudeau then stepped into the circle and said to Davis, "Mr. Premier, if you'll go from twenty-five to twenty-eight, we'll go flat forty. That ought to be good enough for Ford. What do you say?"

Davis said he'd have to consult his minister of Industry, John Rhodes, and the provincial treasurer, Darcy McKeough.

It is important to note that the federal government's offer was made on condition that the plant be built, that the Ford company spend so many million dollars (the plant was expected to cost $535 million), *and* that they produce so many engines per year. This wasn't any handout of $40 million. This was an important investment in Ontario's future. (It was expected the plant would directly employ 2700 people and create 5000 jobs in related industries.) Darcy McKeough and his resignation to the contrary, the Ontario government knew this as well as we did and upped their ante the necessary $3 million. I went down to meet the board and have dinner with Henry Ford II; we clinched the deal in fine style. When I was at the sod-turning ceremony for the plant in Windsor, Roy Bennett said that in the plant's offices, prominently placed, would be a set of Texas longhorns he had purchased at the Calgary Stampede to commemorate our negotiations.

Although I went into the automobile and aircraft industries pretty cold, in the sense of not knowing just what they were doing or why they were doing it, as I look back on the short term I was minister I can say without doubt that I had considerable input into both industries. I adapted readily to the wheeling and dealing aspect of my portfolio. I had dealt with money all my life in the ranching business. If I forgot how many zeros were behind the figures, it was as if I was still involved in horse trading.

I also knew how to present a case strongly. At the departmental level, the senior officials judge their minister by his ability to sell the department's ideas in cabinet. Have we got a guy here who is a winner? Or have we got a guy that cabinet walks over and shoots full of holes? Those in the deputy minister's circle knew there was a heck of a lot of opposition to grants to industry and that normally one couldn't win arguments in favour of subsidies in cabinet. So my officials were pretty pleased when I got the money for the Ford plant. I had passed their acid test.

While the auto industry produced the largest headaches (and the Ford plant was just one example), the most frustrating single exercise concerned the dispute over patent rights to the Tilby sugar separation system. This system involved a new method for processing sugar cane; and, as its name implies, it had been invented by a man called Tilby: Ted Tilby. He was a Canadian who had visited the Barbados in the mid-1960s and had had occasion to witness traditional sugar-cane processing. He was dumbfounded by its inefficiency. The methods had not changed in two hundred years. The cane was still being crushed between giant rollers which pounded the juice from the inner pith, so mangling the husks that they could be used only as fuel for the sugar mill's boilers. More important than its inefficiency, however, was the fact that this method produced only one product, unrefined sugar, for which there was a limited world market.

On Tilby's return to Canada, he began work on what was to prove a technological breakthrough of world-wide magnitude. He invented a machine, requiring only one-fourth the expenditure of energy, that split the sugar cane vertically, separating the pith, the rind, and epidermis. The pith could then be employed for unrefined sugar, for animal fodder, or used with the rest of the cane for important by-products: alcohol, cane wax, fuel, paper, pulp, lumber, concrete blocks, fertilizers, chemicals.

Although I didn't know this until after I became involved in the issue, my brother Hugh, as Alberta's minister of Agriculture, had taken an early interest in the development of Tilby's process so far as it related to a new source of cattle feed. Hugh wanted to sell cattle in the cane-growing areas of the Caribbean and Central America. The problem was feed. With the pith removed intact by Tilby's process, a solution was apparent. Tests proved that ground-up sugar-cane pith made excellent feed. Consequently, Tilby received some of his early fundings from the Alberta government.

In 1974, Tilby's company had gone bankrupt trying to perfect his invention. It was at this point that Industry, Trade and Commerce (the department had provided Tilby's major funding) acquired most of the rights to Tilby's patents. In December 1975, these were turned over to Canadian Patents Development Limited (CPDL), an agency within the department. This was when the trouble began.

It was CPDL's job to market the Tilby patents. There was only one Canadian-owned company interested in acquiring these rights, a Windsor, Ontario, engineering and machine company called Arvid. Arvid, however, in the judgement of CPDL, did not have the financial base, the established reputation, or the international connections to penetrate the sugar industry. When, in June 1976, CPDL granted Arvid a licence to manufacture the sugar cane separator, it was therefore for cattle feed use only. As a condition of the licence, Arvid was to have a commercial machine ready by February 1977. Then, in October 1976, CPDL granted the British-controlled Hawker-Siddeley's West Coast Canadian Car operation, a company they thought fit to penetrate the international sugar industry, the rights to the sugar cane operation, except for cattle feed. Rind utilization (press board, lumber, blocks, etc.) was given to neither company. Hawker-Siddeley, as a condition of their licence, were to have a machine operational by October 1977. In effect, CPDL had given a licence to two companies to manufacture similar machines, producing the same primary products. Neither company was satisfied and a fight was inevitable.

This whole problem got dumped in my lap in April 1978 when Paul Martin Jr., the president of Canada Steamship Lines, came in to see me on behalf of Arvid. I didn't know a fat thing about what he was talking about. My deputy minister, Gordon Oswaldestin, had advised me in advance that the wisest course would be to have an independent study done to investigate the problem. Martin agreed to this, and we appointed Peat, Marwick and Partners to do the study.

I received Peat Marwick's report on September 18, 1978. Its conclusion made abundant sense:

> In our opinion, the current licensing position is not fair to either party. The present situation treats Arvid inequitably, leaves Hawker-Siddeley and Arvid with unenforceable and impractical licensing arrangements, and leaves Canada at a disadvantage in exploiting a promising export market. . . .
>
> In our opinion, the problem has arisen due to the fact that neither of the licenses granted is practical in relation to the market, and neither is enforceable in any real sense, and both fail to exploit the full potential of the underlying technology. Based on our analysis of the facts and underlying issues, it appears that both Arvid and Hawker-Siddeley have a right to the entire sugar cane technology, including the board application. The licenses must be renegotiated not only in order that the reasonable interests of Hawker-Siddeley and Arvid are realized, but also in order that the best interests of Canada are served.

It was obvious that CPDL had erred. The question was, how to change their decision. Within the Department of Industry, Trade and Commerce, CPDL felt (and this is a neat definition) that it was a crown corporation: the minister reported to Parliament for them, but he couldn't direct them. I said they were an agency which had to serve the minister. Unfortunately, I wasn't there long enough to get this problem straightened out.

The general manager of CPDL, W. Melville Hill, would not admit he'd made a mistake over the licensing, and he refused to accept the recommendations of the Peat Marwick report. So that left me acting as referee between three teams rather than two: CPDL as well as Arvid and Hawker-Siddeley. I must admit that I was rather doubtful of Arvid's capabilities at the time. Word had filtered up through the department that Arvid was a two-bit outfit run by a bunch of shysters. Nevertheless, I took the opportunity to watch a demonstration of their Tilby machine when I was in Windsor for the ceremonial sod-turning of the new Ford plant. The machine worked wonderfully well and I was very impressed. Next day, at the sod-turning, Roy Bennett volunteered the information that he respected Arvid's ability. "I don't know a thing about this machine they're manufacturing," he said, "but I can vouch for the quality of their work. They've had a lot of contracts from Ford over the years, and they're a good company."

Obviously, I didn't want to take a position on the question before I had also seen Hawker-Siddeley's machine, so I phoned Hawker-Siddeley's vice-president L. A. Mitten in Vancouver to ask where I could see one of his machines in operation. The only one they had operating was in Barbados with CIDA. Returning from a trip to Trinidad in November (where I'd signed an agreement for two airports and a prison) I stopped for a day in Barbados to see Hawker-Siddeley's machine in action. The amazing thing to me was the contrast. The fields of cane, no different than they were two hundred years ago. The Uplands Sugar Factory, antiquated and soon to be obsolete, I hoped. Huge boilers. Gear wheels twenty feet high. Heavy, heavy casts. One could picture the slow crushing of the cane. In the midst of all this, sitting outside among the factory's conveyor-belt system was the Tilby separator. The twentieth century was knocking on the door of the eighteenth. I knew that this patent was going to be as revolutionary as everyone claimed.

L. A. Mitten had come from Vancouver for the demonstration of the machine. Jack Cahill of the *Toronto Star* was there. The CIDA people were there. Everybody was there. We watched the separator run for twenty minutes. It was supposed to process up to twenty tons an hour, but it plugged up and broke down every three minutes; and it couldn't spit the stuff out the way the Arvid one had done. I was not impressed.

The Tilby separator sits about five feet wide, six feet high, and five feet long, with two big doors on it. At Arvid they had refused to open the doors for me when I asked to see how it ran. "No sir," they said. "What's inside that machine is patented to us. We're not letting anybody look in, not even you." Well, in Barbados the doors were open. I thought this was great, a real demonstration, but after it was over I came to the conclusion that they had to have the doors open or the machine wouldn't run at all.

It was an interesting situation because, whether the Hawker-Siddeley people realized it or not, I wasn't some green city kid. They had a farmer looking at their machine, someone who knew something about machines. When Mitten asked me what I thought of it, I told him straight: "If I brought that machine home to the ranch and told my boys to run it, they'd spend half a day with it and then they'd drop it in my lap and say, 'Dad, you bought it, you make it run. We can't.' There's no way its a marketable product. It never performed. If it was mine, I'd be out there with a cutting torch."

Mitten didn't like that too much. He had arranged for me to meet some of the Barbados government — the Prime Minister, the Minister of Agriculture, and the Minister of Social Services. When we were all gathered, he plugged in a video cassette and showed us a tape of a CBC "Fifth Estate" show, featuring Eric Malling as investigative reporter — a guy I like. Malling had done a report in which he showed Arvid connected with a salesman of rather questionable reputation in South America who didn't care whether or not he could deliver the product he was selling. The message was that Arvid was resorting to unscrupulous business practices because it was short of money. (In effect, Malling was confirming why Arvid hadn't got the full patent from CPDL in the first place.) Of course, Mitten and Hawker-Siddeley came out clean as a whistle, otherwise we wouldn't have been watching the program.

I was interested in the reaction of the Barbadian ministers. The Prime Minister couldn't stay. Their House was sitting and he had to go down to make a speech. I was all too familiar with that responsibility. The Social Services minister, a lady, regarded the machine as very, very promising. Instead of having the use of only 40 per cent of the crop, they could use it all. It would be a tremendous asset to the Barbados, she was quick to point out. All of their lumber has to be imported. With the new separating system, they could make fibreboard. Nor was she unaware of the cattle feed aspect. And the social benefits would be just tremendous for their small country, she asserted. I left with this firmly planted in my mind. I wasn't impressed, however, with Hawker-Siddeley's ability or their attempts to sell their product.

Back in Ottawa, I looked at their contract. In October 1976 they had been given the patent. What had happened? Here it was November 1978. They had not developed a machine that worked. Why not? There were two courses I could follow with Melville Hill of CPDL: bawl the daylights out of him, or try to appeal to his wisdom and understanding of the difficult position in which the department found itself. Over the years, I've always found there are all kinds of times to get tough but that the best approach is to use this as the last resort. So I thought I'd better try to persuade Hill to look at it through my eyes. Hill said, "Well, you as a minister have one recourse and that is to take the patent away from Hawker-Siddeley under the provision that they haven't shown due diligence.

Well, I checked out their contract, which had a clause saying that "if the company has not, before 1 October 1977, manufactured and tested to the satisfaction of an independent inspection agency, acceptable to both parties, specific apparatus used to separate pith and other components from the rind in sugar cane . . . the licence and the option granted herein shall be deemed terminated as of that date."

The next thing to look at was the "independent inspection agency" report of October 1977. It was a shabbily done piece of work. It was no real report at all:

> For the purpose of demonstration, the machine was fed by hand using "billets" of sugar cane imported from Louisiana. The billets were fed into the machine both singly and in multiple and the output observed in the form of pith, rind and epidermis which were collected in their respective bins.
>
> The machine performed satisfactorily throughout the demonstration of approximately fifteen minutes duration and the separation of the cane into its three components appeared to be satisfactory. It was not possible to test the machine at capacity throughout due to the lack of a feed system and a shortage of cane for this purpose. This latter aspect of the separator performance will be tested during the field trials of the two prototype machines in Barbados scheduled to take place from February to May 1978.

Armed with this, I then checked out CIDA's reports. They showed that the machine hadn't performed in May and June 1977. In the spring of 1978 it hadn't performed either. And I had just observed its poor operation in November. CIDA was now prepared to wait until February 1979. (There were all kinds of reasons to stall the minister, and I was getting them by the hundred.) Anyway, I waited until February and then sent D.R. Moffat, a departmental official, and W.O. Morrison, my special assistant, to the Barbados to report on the machine's operation. They presented a very thorough report which concluded "that Hawker-Siddeley has been unsuccessful in developing a machine which can be used commercially for separating pith from cane."

Hawker-Siddeley, of course, figured I was out to get them. Arvid figured I wasn't moving fast enough. CPDL figured the minister should keep his nose out of it. What I wanted to do was to say to Hawker-Siddeley, Arvid, and the whole bunch, as per the Peat Marwick recommendations: "The patents can't be split. So we'll give full patents to the two of you. As a farmer, I can buy a Massey tractor or a Versatile or a Case. I have lots of choice. They are similar machines, but there seems to be room for them to operate in the world. Why can't we have two sugar cane machines? One made by Hawker-Siddeley and one made by Arvid. If Hawker-Siddeley is so superior, then it doesn't have anything to worry about: Arvid will destroy its own credibility through the use of some phony salesman."

I wanted to settle the thing amicably — just send the senior civil servants down to talk to Hawker-Siddeley. But by February the civil service knew an election was coming up. It wasn't until March 1979 that it took action to renegotiate the licence, and when I left office in May 1979 nothing had been resolved. At this rate of progress, the patents will expire, freeing Tilby's invention to the world, before any resolution of the dispute is achieved. The losers: Tilby and Arvid of course. But, more important, Canada will have lost yet another opportunity to lead the world in the exploitation of high technology, creating jobs and export sales for Canadians.

Jobs and export sales are, of course, both affected by the Export Development Corporation, with which I had considerable dealings when I was minister. EDC isn't understood that well by the public generally. They think that it lends money at subsidized interest rates to foreign companies and foreign governments. They don't realize that it lends money for the purchase of Canadian-manufactured goods and that it doesn't lend the money at a subsidized rate of interest. As a matter of fact, the money doesn't leave Canada most of the time. It goes from the corporation to the Canadian manufacturer or the Canadian supplier in lieu of payment for the goods the supplier is shipping to Guatemala or Ghana or wherever.

The prime example of popular misunderstanding was the nickel mine issue. EDC was underwriting Canadian concerns assisting in the opening of nickel mines in other parts of the world. To the miner in Sudbury, the government was undermining his job. These mines, however, were going to be opened up in any event. There was a capital expenditure involved of $900 million. We had a chance to supply some of the required mining equipment in Canada. The Export Development Corporation, in agreeing to a loan, negotiated a larger purchase than originally planned. The outcome was Canadian sales amounting to some $80 million. Had we refused to underwrite this deal, we wouldn't have stopped the mine from going ahead. This equipment would have been purchased elsewhere. EDC neither directly hurt nor helped the miner in Sudbury. We increased the export of our manufacturers, which, to me, was the right thing to do. It was the same when we sold a pulp and paper mill in Czechoslovakia and one in the United States. The spin off or side benefit keeps our home industry modern because these sorts of sales create new technology. If we are manufacturing new machines for the pulp and paper industry, new machines for the mining industry, then our home industry retains a high technology. In this, EDC is indirectly helping the Canadian miner, paper maker, and others.

Among the many questions related to quotas and tariffs, with which I was concerned as minister, was our agreement with Australia and New Zealand on beef imports, which had been in effect since 1977. As a rancher, I was already fully aware of this because in 1976 Canada had let in 185 million pounds of beef from Australia and New Zealand, far more than the market could absorb, which severely depressed cattle prices on the Canadian market. Consequently, some of our cheap beef started to move into the United States market, depressing their prices. The Americans reacted by embargoing our cattle, resulting in a real seesaw battle with the Americans in the beef trade. This was rectified, to a degree, in 1977 when Australia and New Zealand were allowed to bring in only 122.5 million pounds.

In the fall of 1977, I increased this by 1.5 per cent to allow them to bring in 124 million pounds in 1978. In considering the quota for 1979, we had a long cabinet discussion and we decided in March 1978 to base our quota allotments on cattle coming in from Australia and New Zealand on Canada's requirements. We agreed to take as a base period the years 1971 to 1975 and adjust quotas according to the increase or decrease in the consumption of beef from this average and the rate of increase of beef prices relative to the rate of food prices generally. During the base period, the average total imports of dressed beef from all countries, including the U.S., was 127 million pounds. In the same period, consumption of beef was 2,177 million pounds. Taking into consideration the subsequent rate of consumption brought about by a larger population and slight per capita increase in consumption, it was estimated the average consumption during the period of 1977, 1978, and 1979 would be 2,422 million. If one placed the consumption during the base period under the estimated consumption and multiplied that by 127, this gave a figure related to domestic consumption of 141.3 million pounds. Taking the increase in the price of beef in relation to the increase in general food prices during the base period, the average index for beef was 124.9. The average index for food during the base period was 116.2. This resulted in an index factor of 1.075. The price ratio for 1978 in the Consumer Price Index put beef prices at 200 and general food prices at 1.163. When the index factor of the base period was subtracted from 1.163, the result was an increased ratio of 0.088. If one multiplied 0.088

by 141.3, this gave 12.4 million pounds. Consequently, for 1979, we added an additional 12.4 million pounds onto the 141.3 million pounds arriving, for a total adjusted import level of 153.7 million pounds. Because it was customary to allow an additional 1 per cent for prospective new customers in any given year, we actually allowed 154.7 million pounds of beef into Canada for 1979. The quota allocation to Australia and New Zealand was expected to be 130.7 million pounds.

Personally, I was satisfied that this carefully worked out formula would have a beneficial effect on producers, that knowing exactly how much was coming in would give them renewed confidence that the government was mindful of the importance of the cattle industry to Canada. At the time, the cattlemen accepted my formula for beef import quotas. I had what I called, the "tight lid" policy. I wanted to set the quotas in December for the following year and under no circumstances change this quota, so that a farmer or a rancher could go into the new year with his investments in cattle relatively secure. All he had to fight was the weather and the known market forces.

Australia and New Zealand had been on a voluntary agreement and we kept them on a voluntary agreement. Under GATT (General Agreement on Tariffs and Trade), we gave them a minimum guarantee which did not affect our trade with them at all. I thought the whole question really amusing when the cattlemen in Canada responded by asking for a beef import law similar to what was in effect in the United States. They ignored the fact that in the U.S. the president has the prerogative, if at any time he judges the price of beef too high, of opening the floodgates to allow substantial importation of cheap beef. The Cattlemen's Association are whistling in the wind if they believe they can get a meat import law which will not contain provision for the protection of the consumer. The formula of the Cattlemen's Association doesn't consider the consumer at all. They want to regulate the import of Australian and New Zealand beef in relation to the number of cows in a given year. Nineteen seventy-nine was a very difficult year in the cattle industry. Thousands of farmers and feeders lost money, buying too high in the spring and selling too low because there was a surplus of meat in Canada, a surplus of pork, a surplus of chicken which forced the price of beef down. The Conservative government, in setting the formula for 1980, took the advice of the Canadian Cattlemen's Association and it was poor advice. Their formula apparently worked out to where imports from Australia and New Zealand could be increased by 12 million pounds, nearly twice as much as I let in in two years. This telegraphed to Australia and New Zealand that they could increase production, that there would be more room for more beef in Canada. This was a mistake.

I had to do quite a bit of travelling in my role as minister. I went to Europe and Asia as well as countries nearer home. After the House reassembled in October 1978, Trudeau said he didn't want too much travelling. He wanted most ministers close at hand because of our tight situation in the House. The October 10 by-elections were a disaster, and our majority was too slim to take any chances. Nonetheless, he approved my decision to take a trade delegation to China early in the new year.

I particularly wanted to take a look at China's demand for technical know-how so that I could put Canadian businessmen in a position to take advantage of this. Eighteen businessmen accompanied me. Interestingly, none of them represented the grain trade, because I didn't believe there were any stones unturned in grain sales to China. It was quite a surprise, therefore, when Premier Hua told me: "We're going to make a wheat deal." We signed a three-year agreement, calling for them to take 380 million bushels of Canadian grain a year. Another surprise was that the Chinese were fully aware of everything that was going on in Canada. They had been up to see the James Bay hydro-electric project, they had been to the tar sands project, they had been to the Arctic. They'd set up what they called the Yangtze River Authority to do what we were doing with the James Bay project. They said to the Quebec Hydro representative who was with me, "When you're finished, load your equipment on ships and send it here. We can use it all."

The other area of real interest was oil and gas. China has discovered large quantities of each, but it has no distribution system. Not only do they not have pipelines to distribute the gas and oil; they haven't even got power lines to distribute electricity. They were very interested in how we had developed our North; and they were utterly amazed to see us doing so much on the prairies and in the Peace River country. I invited them to send a hundred and fifty students to Alberta to work on our farms and find out how we do things. They found this proposal very interesting; this seemed to me the only way one could get them to realize the advantages of our grass seed and of our livestock industry. Their cows were poor. Their hogs were even poorer. They wanted to know what could be done to teach them how to improve their agricultural methods; they wanted to buy big Versatile four-wheel-drive tractors for their northern plains, where they planned to extend cultivation; they wanted Massey-Ferguson to set up a model farm over there. Unfortunately, it was not a good time to do this, given Massey-Ferguson's financial picture.

I think, even though they knew a great deal about Canada, my trip was worthwhile in that it created a greater awareness in their minds of what Canada can offer them in their drive towards modernization. Anything the Americans can do, we can do just as well and sometimes better because our northern climate has added a dimension to our know-how that would be of value to them. I didn't hesitate to point this out time and again. On the other side, for many years to come, whether in the mining field, in hydro-electric and theremal-electric development, in railways, in pipelines, in oil exploration. . . all of our industries will benefit tremendously from awakening the interest of Canadian business-men in China.

The old Trade minister of China was a delightful fellow. I remember at our last dinner in Peking, he asked what my impressions of China were. I thought I'd better come out with something pretty good, so I replied, "I've been surprised by three things." This gave me a little more time to think. "First of all, I was told not to attempt to use humour, that I might end up insulting people because the Chinese don't have a very good sense of humour." Well, the Trade minister laughed at everything I said. I continued, "But I found you understand my humour and we get along pretty well." He laughed and agreed.

The popular view of the Chinese in Canada is that they're very quiet, very reserved, not at all boastful. I guess I expected everyone in China to be this, maybe even more so. The mainland Chinese, however, are quite boastful. They are referred to as the Texans of Asia. If one sees them as the owners of a huge country, with so many people that nothing can destroy them, and really quite ignorant of the world around them, well, you've got a Texan. However, I didn't want to say all this to the Chinese Trade minister. So I said, "The second thing is you're quite frank. You're quite open. You don't mind telling me your strengths and your weaknesses. I thought I'd find the Chinese more reserved." I just had one more to go. "Finally, I've been to Korea and I've been to Japan. I'm fairly tall. I've got to say that the people in Peking are taller than I thought they'd be."

He laughed again and said, "You're going to Canton tomorrow. You'll find the Chinese people down there are shorter than they are in the north because they eat too much rice. We eat more wheat up here."

I said, "All right, I'll take that. I'm a wheat salesman. I'll remember that." I had wanted to flatter him, but I was able to state my feelings pretty truthfully, albeit in a flattering kind of way.

I spoke at a college in Peking called the Institute of International Trade. On arrival, I went to the cloakroom and took off my coat — a technical error. This was in January, but there was no heat in the building. The students wore parkas to class. I spoke about Canada and Canadian-Chinese relations, and then I answered questions (all in English: they wanted practice at speaking the language). One of the teachers asked me, "How do you bring foreign technology into your country without foreign dominance?" It was a good question. I told them about FIRA, our Foreign Investment Review Agency, how it worked within my department and how its job was to make certain that any foreign investment coming into our country provided Canada "significant benefit". I went on to explain what we would consider significant benefit: employment; capital investment which enlarged production and contributed to export sales without any influence from a foreign parent company; investment in research and development which would enhance our technology; Canadian management and whether 51 per cent of the ownership of the company would be open to purchase by Canadian shareholders.

By the time I returned to Canada, it was obvious that an election wasn't far off. Trudeau could have waited until the fall of 1979 but he decided that spring was the better choice and called the election for May 22. I was anxious to get back home to test the political waters in Crowfoot and prove to my constituents that I had made the right decision in joining the government. My contest was bound to be a little bit different from the national one — not so much as to whether the voters of Crowfoot were tired of Trudeau but whether they would go along with my decision to cross the floor. Had I been able to prove, in the two years I was a cabinet minister, that I was able to do things for them, for the province of Alberta, and for western Canada, that I wouldn't have been able to do had I stayed a Conservative?

Much to my disappointment, the press never at any time wrote up any of my accomplishments in Industry, Trade and Commerce or my accomplishments as the minister responsible for Alberta in the field of patronage — getting the right people appointed to boards, and getting more Westerners and more Albertans appointed to the CRTC or the National Energy Board, to name two out of an entire host. The press was more interested in the political or personal difficulty that I might be in. Would Alberta accept a Liberal? Would Crowfoot accept a turncoat? There were daily stories throughout the '79 campaign on this aspect of my participation in politics. The *Calgary Herald* took a poll. Somehow everyone was obsessed with the idea that Horner had changed drastically, that in changing parties he was thinking altogether differently than he had when he was a Conservative.

I tried to tell the people of Crowfoot I was the same Jack Horner, only working in a better position to serve them. I attempted to sell those things I had done for them and could do for them, but, oddly, they seemed to be preoccupied with the concept that Trudeau had brought in bilingualism; Trudeau had brought in metric; Trudeau had done away with capital punishment; Trudeau had brought in gun control. And I had switched to

Trudeau. Therefore I didn't deserve their support. No matter how well I documented the case of Conservative party support for bilingualism, of me being the only one to question it, of me calling the recorded vote, I received no credit. My record was explainable and understandable. I had taken their side. If they condemned the Liberal party, they must also condemn the Conservative party. On metric, I pointed out time and again that I was the one in the Conservative party who had questioned metric, that I had been branded a right-wing reactionary for not accepting it. Here again, if they were going to condemn Trudeau, they should condemn the Conservatives as well. Gun control: I was opposed to Bill C 83 and had convinced the government, after becoming a cabinet minister, to bring in a modified piece of legislation, which the Conservative party had accepted. I quoted from Eldon Woolliams's speech in Hansard taking credit on behalf of the Conservative Opposition for the changes. The voters somehow linked gun control with their concept of Trudeau as a Communist. The first thing a Communist wanted to do, they believed, was take away all the guns. Gun control legislation was thus the first step to totalitarianism. I pointed out repeatedly that my sons and I had a house full of guns, that in no way would the gun control legislation affect us. We would not have to license those guns. We had to get a licence only to purchase new guns.

The sad fact is, no one was listening.

When they blamed Trudeau for doing away with capital punishment, I pointed out repeatedly that in the twenty-one years I had served in Ottawa there had been five debates on capital punishment and the last vote had only carried by eight members. Without doubt, the question would come up again in a different parliament and those eight members might well not be there. I further pointed out that if just five Conservatives had refrained from voting for abolition, we would still have some form of capital punishment. And further, that of the seventeen Conservatives who voted for abolition, eleven of them sat in the front benches, including Joe Clark and most of the people from whom he would form a cabinet if given the opportunity. All of them were believers in the abolition of capital punishment. I might as well have been talking to the wall. The voters were fed up with Trudeau and wanted — or felt they needed — a change. They thought they had a very good reason to vote against me. Although, I must say, throughout the campaign I was well received by my constituents. No one at any time said I hadn't been a good member. No one at any time said I hadn't served Crowfoot well. They simply were not interested in how much better I had been able to serve them as a cabinet minister.

It was an interesting election because all of my former Conservative

Executive, except one, supported me. Until then, I firmly believed that we had representative government and that the people of east-central Alberta appreciated me because I gave them representative government. I hadn't always bought the Conservative party line. I hadn't bought the party line on wage and price controls in 1974, and they had elected me. In this election, I had the support of community leaders in each town. The leaders in the Cattlemen's Association in the area supported me; the leading grain farmers supported me. One would have thought with the community leaders and the economic leaders within your constituency supporting you that this was the first step to winning the election. In this case, it didn't work at all. I'd switched parties and that was too much for my electors. Ironically, in the next riding, Gordon Taylor had switched from Social Credit to the Conservatives. No one seemed bothered by this. In my riding, the local member of the legislature, Henry Kroeger, had run once as a Liberal. This didn't bother the voters either. And, nationally, the biggest switcher around was John Crosbie — though in May 1979 the voters in Alberta weren't too aware of John Crosbie's existence.

There was a great deal of pressure on me, pressure to win for the government and pressure on me personally to convince the voters I had not let them down. I lost. And so, of course, did the Liberal party. I don't ever want to become a good loser, but I guess in losing under that much pressure I was just a little annoyed. For the first election ever, I had decided, because of the great number of people I had working for me, to throw a party on the election night, rent a hall and thank all the people who had worked so hard for me. It was a disappointment because we were invaded by television cameras and newspapermen. I couldn't really mix with our volunteers to thank them individually. Finally, I said to my assistants, Peter Thompson and Bill Morrison, that I was going off to congratulate Arnold Malone (Leola insisted I must) and that by the time I came back I wanted all the press out of the hall: "*I* have rented the hall. It should be my party."

Much to my irritation, when I returned the media were still there, wanting, it would seem, to provoke me. Apparently, there was a lot of money bet (as much as a thousand dollars) that they could provoke me to the point of taking a swing at one of them. Well, they were disappointed. Having stopped to talk to Roger Millbrandt, the NDP candidate, and cracked a number of jokes with him, I was in a fairly mellow mood when I came back and found the press still hanging about. The best I could do was call them parasites — and, being a rancher, I well know what a nuisance they can be.

Following the 1979 campaign, I was looking forward to getting back to the ranch. During a hectic political career, it had become a sanctuary.

Here, people wouldn't bother me, certainly the media wouldn't, and the cows couldn't talk back. There were things to occupy me that I enjoyed. What surprised me between the '79 and '80 elections, was that the press never left me alone. I'd be called out of the workshop, out of the machine shed to the phone and it would be some newspaperman asking me what I thought of this or what I thought of that. I said to several of them, "Why call me? Call somebody else. I'm out of politics. I'm retired." They all said, "But we've got to have an opinion and we can't get one from anybody else." They even called me about seat belts! They called me about trade with Russia. I said, "Call the provincial government. They've got a minister of International Trade now." They responded that they couldn't get any answers from either government. The press just couldn't seem to leave me out of it. I began to realize that no matter what I said about them, they found me good copy because I had opinions and expressed them. I always did my own thinking, which sometimes was different from what they had heard elsewhere.

I didn't know after the 1979 election that I'd have to run again. I thought Joe Clark would be smart. He had 136 seats. He only needed 142 for a majority. I thought he'd last a couple of years.

I started to worry about Clark's longevity when he would not change on Petrocan. Hnatyshyn had stated when Clark was in Africa that the whole energy scene had changed considerably since the election. In addressing themselves to the change, he expected that Petrocan would have to stay in some form or another. Clark came back from Africa and said in effect, "No, no. Mr. Hnatyshyn was just blowing smoke rings. Petrocan goes." The vote on Petrocan was Clark's first major test, and it was close. Clark, however, never tried to lower the level of confrontation building in the House of Commons. I knew then Clark wouldn't last long. He was ashamed of being labelled a "flip-flopper". Consequently, by trying to appear strong and decisive, he picked the wrong issues on which to stand. When he eventually had to back down or reverse himself, it looked all the worse. On the day of his defeat, December 13, 1979, I was in conversation with Ottawa and knew he was going down. A mood builds up around the House before the vote and you know what's going to happen. Even Clark knew: he had his speech all prepared. He felt it was better to go down with Trudeau still the Liberal leader, that the anti-Trudeau vote would hold.

I believed Clark would lose the next election. He had failed to mature and develop, although the press had sometimes attempted to make a statesman out of him. The Clark jokes were too strong. No one is proud of a prime minister who can be ridiculed. What did the Joe Clark jokes tell? First, that he was weak: "Why did Joe Clark cross the road? He was scotch-taped to the chicken." Second, that he didn't think: "What did Clark do when Maureen bought him a pair of cuff links? He went out and got his wrists pierced." Clark, of course, is far stronger than he looks, but that doesn't matter. He looks weak. There isn't a strong thing about his appearance, not the way he walks, not the set of his jaw, certainly not his hands, and hardly his physique. Thus, he is perceived as weak. Consequently, during all of Joe Clark's political career he's attempted to prove, he's bent over backwards to prove, that he's strong. And, in doing so, he makes terrible mistakes, foolish mistakes: sabre rattling at Breshnev as if Canada was going to frighten Russia. Couldn't hardly fight Switzerland.

I realized I was going to run again when I read Crosbie's budget. I didn't want to run. Certainly my wife didn't want me to. We had just bought some land for my second son, Craig, and a fair number of cows, and it was time to tend to the ranching business. But when I read the budget, my biggest fear was that it would pit Ontario against Alberta in the election. I didn't want this to happen. I didn't want the Liberal party using Alberta as a sacrificial lamb, and Trudeau didn't do this. I was very proud of him. Many, many members from eastern Canada must have been urging him to do just that. When I read the budget, I realized it wasn't good for Alberta and could be attacked on that basis. I sat down and wrote an article on its effect on our energy situation and circulated this to a number of leading papers across Canada. It received wide publication. Then, as other former cabinet ministers decided not to run — Barney Danson, Alastair Gillespie, Tony Abbott, Bob Andras — and as the media started to tick them off, I realized that if Jack Horner didn't run then it might well be perceived that the Liberal party's position could not be defended in the province of Alberta. I thought, "Well, all right, if I can clear away my personal problems and run, I will set this fear aside. I can easily attack the budget. I can run and have lots of fun." And this is what I did.

I campaigned strictly on the budget, using it to point out that Clark wasn't getting at a debt problem, that the budget didn't help us become energy self-sufficient, that, in fact, it set self-sufficiency back by imposing a transportation tax on a country which depended so much on transportation. Transportation costs are extremely high in Canada because of its very nature, a few people spread over 4,500 miles. It was more out of a sense of duty to my country and a sense of duty to the Liberal party that I felt I had to run. To protect the "One Canada" concept I cherish and to make certain everyone realized that this budget was bad for Alberta, bad for Ontario, bad for Canada.

I realized that I had to get outside my constituency and into Calgary and Edmonton to let the major cities of this province know how bad the budget was. I did this. I spoke three times in Edmonton, including taking part in two debates with Conservative candidates, the best the Conservatives could put up in Edmonton. On one occasion, I was scheduled to speak against Don Mazankowski and on the other against Marcel Lambert. As it turned out, they were both replaced by Bill Yurko, who is a man of considerable experience in the provincial House and a tremendously capable speaker. But I had no trouble in tearing the budget apart in those debates with him. I spoke in Wetaskiwin. I spoke in the Peace River constituency. And I spoke at the University of Calgary. I made my points clear and strong, and I certainly thought people were listening.

Finally, I tried to pound home to my constituents some political home truths. For instance, at a luncheon meeting in Castor on February 14, I drew attention to the polls. There was no doubt that the Liberals were going to win the election. This being the case, Alberta should make sure that it had good representation in Parliament — and in the cabinet.

"What does Alberta do?" I asked. "What does Alberta do? Do we shut the door on ourselves? This is an important part of Canada. If we shut the door, it reminds me of the old picture of the pony pawing at the granary door, trying to get a little oats out. The trouble with this is nowadays the granaries are steel and they don't leak very much oats. It is up to us to get in there, to get somebody inside around that cabinet table so that we won't be forgotten about, so we won't be walked over, but mainly so we won't be forgotten."

I may have been my own brand of politician, but all my life this has been my aim — to work for the people of Canada, and especially for the people of Alberta. When I was first in Parliament in 1958, I got the Farm Credit Corporation regulations changed on the tax recovery land. It was a little thing nationally, but it mattered a lot to the farmers in my constituency. It gave them the freedom to develop their farms. I have worked all my life for the things I believe in and for the people who believe that I will fight for them. As a cabinet minister, I had more power to fight than ever before. I told the voters this. My record was there for anyone to see.

But, again, nobody was listening.

Appendix 1 — Correspondence with the Government of Alberta

An article in the *Edmonton Journal* on August 23, 1977, quoted Premier Lougheed as saying to Albertans:

> Start to worry with me about the future of this province and the precarious state of its economy.
>
> Without the renewable resource of food production to replace the non-renewable petrochemical resource, the economy will flounder.

This inspired me to write on August 25 to the Hon. Marvin Moore, Alberta's Minister of Agriculture, with a copy to Lougheed:

> I was particularly pleased to read in the *Edmonton Journal* of August 23rd, Premier Lougheed's support of Alberta's need for greater food production. Sometime before the last provincial election I had a long talk with the Premier about Alberta's needs and during the last provincial election the Premier campaigned on the slogan of $200 million to be invested over a ten-year period to update the irrigation systems within the province. This in my mind is simply not good enough because it really means that ten years from now we will be exactly where we are today — maybe with a slightly improved irrigation system, but not a system any larger than it is today.
>
> The reason for my writing this letter is because of my concern over the animosity the province seems to have engendered over a small dam on the Red Deer River — a dam which is going to flood out three entire farms and portions of another nineteen. It is logical to assume that those three farms will be amply compensated. In my particular part of Alberta thousands of farmers had to move out because of dry weather and poor moisture conditions beginning in the early twenties and continuing on to the late forties, with practically no compensation. There are five dams on the Bow River and none at all on the Red Deer and my feeling is that the environmentalists have been allowed to kick up such a storm over this small dam on the Red Deer that the government might be reluctant to proceed with any further dam construction.
>
> From time to time we all talk of decentralization and further industrialization of some of the smaller communities; practically all of the smaller communities North of the Red Deer River are short of water. A dam at Ardley on the Red Deer River would greatly enhance the possibilities of rural development in East Central Alberta and would also provide much needed water to the agriculture industry over a tremendous area which would quadruple the productive capacity of over 200,000 acres.
>
> This project has been talked about for sixty years and should have gone ahead before the South Saskatchewan River Dam but money in those days was

scarce and Diefenbaker wanted to do something for Saskatchewan. Premier Lougheed, I hope, is of similar mind and would like to do something for Alberta. It is a building of a renewable resource, it would be immensely popular with the people, improve the quality of life in the smaller communities and with today's modern methods of irrigating it would not put rubber boots on every farmer or a shovel in their hands.

I note in particular in the *Edmonton Journal* the Premier's remarks urging the people of Alberta to start to worry with him "about the future of this province and the precarious state of its economy," and he says also that without the renewable resource of food production to replace the non-renewable petrochemical resource, the economy will flounder.

In closing I would like to point out that any study of the irrigation industry clearly states that it takes ten to twenty years to fully develop the economic potential and in the past, as the case in the Brooks area, it took even longer. So, time is of the essence and one way out of the dilemma in which the Alberta government finds itself with the agriculture industry West of the Red Deer is to announce major benefits to the agriculture community East of the Red Deer with the proposal of a second dam on the Red Deer at Ardley.

Moore, without reply, referred my letter to Alberta's Minister of the Environment. One of Lougheed's minions replied for him:

On behalf of Premier Lougheed, I wish to acknowledge receipt of a copy of your letter to Hon. Marvin Moore dated August 25th, 1977, with respect to the dam on the Red Deer River.

Please be assured that your letter will be brought to the Premier's attention, as soon as possible.

I was not deterred. On September 1, I wrote to the Premier:

Further to my letter of August 25th to the Hon. Marvin Moore, M.L.A. in which I urged his department to become actively interested in damming the Red Deer River at Ardley so that water could be provided to East Central Alberta, I would like to take this opportunity to draw some comparisons between the area which I will call East Central Alberta — namely Census Divisons 4, 5, 7 and 10, with Census Divisions 6, 8 and 11 — basically the Calgary-Edmonton corridor.

In land area one can readily see that East Central Alberta is more than twice as large as the Calgary-Edmonton corridor but contains about one tenth of the population and only 6.7% of the labour force; while the Calgary-Edmonton corridor contains 76.5% of all the manufacturing carried out in Alberta, East Central Alberta contains 1.9%.

The percentage of the labour force engaged in agriculture in the Calgary-Edmonton corridor is 5%, in East Central Alberta it is 61%.

The average income in the Calgary-Edmonton corridor is $11,000; in East Central Alberta it is slightly over $9,000. In fact East Central Alberta lags behind Western Saskatchewan in total income.

There has been a great deal of talk lately about renewable resources.

Water is a priceless renewable resource on the Prairies. Its supply is subject to extreme variation in terms of its month-to-month and year-to-year availability.

The drought on the Southern Prairies during this past Spring and Summer re-emphasized the critical role of water in the economy and social life of Western Canada. Future growth of many communities depends on the supply of water. This is necessary to attract new and expand existing economic activities since an assured supply of good quality water is a major requirement in the manufacturing and processing of most products.

Federal activity in water resource planning and development has been present since settlement. At one time, because of federal natural resource ownership, the urgent needs of the thirties, the limited fiscal capacity of the Prairie provinces and the lack of provincial technical expertise, there was an atmosphere which allowed and welcomed unilateral federal action.

This set of circumstances no longer exists. As a result, there has been a reduction in federal leadership in water resource planning. At the same time the federal government has attempted to forge new partnership arrangements for consultation, planning, implementation and financing water development with the provinces and has continued with small water development where the federal government traditionally had been involved.

Realizing that the small water developments in which the federal government traditionally has been involved are more often limited to one year's capacity and to meet major drought conditions in some of the drier regions on the Prairies requires major water development, I urge your government to seriously interest itself in providing adequate room for expansion in a large part of the province which finds many farms desperately in need of more water. Many towns and communities rationed water this Summer and there is a definite feeling in the people in the area that somehow or another the prosperity in Alberta is not bringing any major benefits to them. They see your government pumping water to towns along the Calgary-Edmonton corridor while many villages and towns in other areas put up with extremely bad water and a limited supply of the same.

I am certain you and many of your Ministers have noticed the vast difference in the irrigated areas of Southern Alberta — towns such as Taber and Brooks, which have grown far more rapidly than towns like Hanna and Coronation — and one can readily see the tremendous part water has played.

Thank you for your consideration and hoping for a favourable reply.

I was not encouraged by the reply:

Your letter of September 1st, 1977, outlining further your views with regard to the damming of the Red Deer River has been received in this office and will be brought to Premier Lougheed's attention at the earliest opportunity.

The next year, on January 31, 1978, I wrote the Hon. D. J. Russell, Alberta's Minister of the Environment, who, ultimately, had replied to my above letters to both the Premier and Minister of Agriculture:

Recently, Mr. John Lijdsman, Municipal Administrator of the Town of Oyen, handed me a letter dated January 9th (your file SA3-107) concerning your department's proposal to conduct a study of the basins near Hanna — namely the Bullpond, Blood Indian and Berry Creeks. I find this process rather amusing — from intelligent and well-educated people.

The federal government has built one dam on the Berry Creek, it has spent $600,000 on the Bullpond Creek trying to improve the water supply to the Town of Hanna. It has built a dam on the Blood Indian Creek and Ducks Unlimited has built a number of smaller dams on the tributaries of all three.

Anyone with an ounce of brain, who has lived on the Prairies for more than a year, can readily see that in a Winter with a heavy snow fall, the waters that these creeks collect could fill ten reservoirs, but in a Winter with no snow fall — such as the Winter of 1976-77 — there is barely enough water to half fill the existing reservoirs. I am absolutely certain, after a long and exhaustive study and the expenditure of the taxpayers' money, your study will come to the same conclusion.

All three basins need, as do a number of other basins in East Central Alberta, a larger reservoir which will hold water for two or three years and keep a steady flow in these basins. When your department has the will and your government has the strength, rest assured East Central Alberta will welcome your interest. Until then, please keep your studies a secret because the entire area has been surveyed at least three times since 1919 and the present residents are thoroughly tired of hearing of further studies being contemplated in this regard.

I received a reply in fine bureaucratise, to which I rejoined:

I received your long drawn-out letter which told me absolutely nothing new.

I would like to inform you that the interest alone on the Heritage Fund runs at $2 million a day. Your government can continue to study the water problem in East Central Alberta until you and I are both in our graves and the Heritage Fund can continue to earn interest, but only for so long, because the people of Alberta will rise up and demand the government have the gumption to do something with their money.

You suggest that additional storage may alleviate some of the problem but it is unlikely to be a panacea. I agree with you. You suggest I should agree that efficient and orderly water resource development is essential to realizing the best use of the limited water supply available to Special Areas. The whole point of my letter was to assure you that efficient and orderly water resource development has been studied for the past fifty years. If a government does not know what to do now, your efficient and orderly study will be of no assistance tomorrow.

Water development in the province of Alberta should be taken out of the Department of the Environment. It is a renewable resource which should be used every year. If it is not used every year it is merely wasted and East Central

218

Alberta and the Special Areas are crying out for some help from the wealthy province of Alberta in which they find themselves situated.

Recently I had discussions with Westinghouse Limited. They are developing turbines for a giant irrigation project which will cost $280 million for the Arabs in the Middle East. I was tempted to send them out to the blue-eyed Arabs in Canada so that the desert in Canada might receive the benefit of their expertise along with the deserts in Saudi Arabia and Egypt.

In any case do not let my letter deter your studies because your civil servants want something to do. May they study until they find six feet of dry ground in which to bury themselves.

Appendix 2 — Excerpt from House of Commons Speech on the Hutterite Question

Mr. Speaker, my grievance is that the Hutterite farms in Western Canada are not subject to income tax in the same manner as are all other farmers in Western Canada. I raise this question very seriously because the Hutterite problem is becoming more pronounced in Western Canada. No Member in this House from Western Canada will question my saying this. In the past dozen years there have been at least half a dozen commissions set up to study this question in the three prairie provinces. I want to make myself abundantly clear by saying that I have no grudge whatsoever against these people. I feel that they are in a sense receiving a subsidy from all the rest of the taxpayers in Canada and that is my only grievance.

I should point out, Mr. Speaker, that the Hutterites as individuals are subject to income tax, but that the colony in which all the property is held is not. The individuals do not receive high enough salaries, they do not receive any dividends from the colony, and therefore it is very doubtful whether they have ever been in receipt of a taxable income.

I should like to point out that these people are very good farmers. I have nothing against their mode of farming. They have excelled and are considered authorities on the question of farming. My main objection is that they are receiving a definite advantage over all other farmers in Western Canada. . . .

As I pointed out, the Hutterites are exempt from income tax under section 62 (1) (e) of the Income Tax Act which reads as follows:

A charitable organization, whether or not incorporated, all the resources of which were devoted to charitable activities carried on by the organization itself and no part of the income of which was payable to, or was otherwise available for the personal benefit of, any proprietor, member or shareholder thereof.

Certainly I have no objection whatsoever to their religious beliefs. I feel strongly that anybody should be able to worship according to his beliefs, but certainly their farming should not be considered as part of their religion. The neighbouring colony in my constituency operates a farm of approximately 22,000 acres. I am certain that all members will fully realize the size of some of these enterprises. . . .

I should like to quote what the English law dictionary in the library says concerning charitable organizations. It is one which has no capital stocks, no provision for making dividends and profits but derives its funds mainly from public and private charity. I looked up the word "charity" in the same law dictionary and I find that the word "charity" comprises four principal divisions; the relief of poverty, the advancement of religion, the advancement of education and other purposes beneficial to the community.

In considering these four things it can be said that these people are only trying to relieve the poverty of their children and certainly every Member of the House is doing the same thing. But these people contribute very little, if anything, to the general relief of poverty and to the well-being of the community as a whole. As for the advancement of religion, certainly they do not go out and try to impose their religion upon others but they do carry on religious worship in their own community and I have no objection whatsoever to that.

As for the advancement of education, the Alberta royal commission set up to study the Hutterite question found that they were actually retarding education. Of 923 pupils studying in Hutterite schools in Alberta, 699 were considered to be behind in their grades and to be retarded pupils. Out of 923, over two thirds were behind in their grades and were considered retarded pupils. The Alberta commission considered that 216 out of the 923 were average students and only 8 out of the 923 were considered to be accelerated pupils. When we compare this with pupils in the other schools of Alberta we find that in those schools 35 per cent are to be considered to be behind in their grades, 45 per cent are average and 19.61 per cent are considered to be accelerated pupils. This latter figure compares with only 8 of 923 Hutterite pupils. Therefore I think it is abundantly clear that they are not advancing education.

As for the question of other purposes beneficial to the community, they carry on their own business, buy all their goods wholesale and contribute very little to the community. As I said before, I have not got all the time I should like to have in order to go into how these people actually live. It is hard to describe. It would take a great deal of time to do it well because it is hard for a person who has never seen a Hutterite farm to visualize how they live and what their standard of living is. I say that in all sincerity. I am certain that other Western Members who are familiar with the Hutterite farms know exactly what I mean. . . .

I should like to deal for a minute with the question of the Hutterite farms in its entirety and whether or not the sect and their farms come within the definition of a religious organization. The citation I should like to read to the House is from the case of The King v. Assessors of the Town of Sunny Brae. This case arose in the province of New Brunswick and I quote from the Maritime Provinces Reports, 1951. This is the decision of the court of appeal and the court held that the religious organization, the English name of which was the Home of the Good Shepherd, was taxable because it was considered they were carrying on a business. The town, therefore, had every right to assess them to the value of the business, the value of the property they used in that business. Mr. Justice Richards had this to say:

> If this laundry and dry cleaning business were operated merely to do washing and cleaning for the inmates of the institution, then the equipment would be used as part of the charitable undertaking of the society. The equipment in the case before us is used in the operation of a laundry and dry cleaning business which gets customers who would otherwise have their work done by taxpayers. To exempt such a business from taxation would be contrary to the intention of the act as it would be an unjust discrimination against others carrying on laundry and dry cleaning business and paying taxes upon all

property and equipment used in such business. To exempt a competitor such as this society would, in effect, be a forced levy on the other taxpayers. It would amount to a subsidy to one competitor in the laundry and dry cleaning business which would have to be paid by other taxpayers.

I hold that the Hutterite case bears a great deal of similarity to this case. We farmers of Western Canada are, in effect, subsidizing one of our largest competitors. These Hutterite farmers go to the auction sales, the cattle sales and compete against other farmers. They have the same freedom as any other farmer. They buy machinery and repairs in the same manner and they put their produce on the market in the same manner as any other farmer does. . . .

I say to you, Mr. Speaker and to all other Hon. Members that this problem should be seriously considered. Hon. Members should try to envision the picture in the prairie provinces 100 years from now if these people are allowed to go on earning money untaxed and purchasing more and more land. For those in the colony this is their main purpose. The main revenue they receive from the sale of their produce is directed into the purchase of more land. As soon as a colony reaches a total of about 100 persons they immediately look for new land and swarm like a flock of bees to settle in another spot. Just try to picture the prairies 100 years from now if these people are allowed to go untaxed.

I hope that this government can cover all the problems that may have to be faced and that stand in the way, so that these farmers can be treated in the same manner as are all the other farmers in Western Canada and be subject to a net worth statement in the same manner as are other Western farmers in Western Canada today.

Appendix 3 — Excerpt from House of Commons Speech on the National Transportation Act

In considering a transportation policy for Canada we must do so with caution because today Canada is at the crossroads in many aspects. In recent years we have seen many policies which have done good but which have divided Canada. In looking back over the transportation history of this country we must realize that it was our transportation and railroad policies which brought Canada together in the very beginning. Those policies must remain sound and must remain fair and just to all parts of Canada. . . .

For those who are concerned, I might also add that the statutory rates, which are the Crowsnest Pass rates, account for 13 percent of railway revenue, competitive rates account for 27.3 percent and agreed charge rates account for 25.2 percent. Mind you, there has been no freeze on competitive and agreed charge rates. They have agreed to increase these and have increased them right along. . . .

The increased revenue which the railways must have and which hopefully will result from the passage of this bill will be derived from the movement of goods under the class and non-competitive rates. These account for 33 percent of their present revenue. Now we come to the crux of the problem.

Where are most commodities shipped under class and non-competitive rates? I want every member of this house to take note of this situation, particularly those members from Western Canada and the Maritimes because those are the areas from which this increased revenue will be derived. What did Canada's transportation policy mean to the unification of Canada? The transportation policy was the Magna Carta of the West and a basic reason for confederation in the Maritimes. This policy has a great deal to do with the uniting of Canada. What does this present bill do? It puts aside those historic facts and, to use a common expression, throws the Maritimes and the Western part of Canada to the wolves. It does not continue to help unite Canada but rather divides Canada in no uncertain terms. It will have the same effect in some parts of northern Quebec and Ontario. . . .

At page 37 this bill sets out that in not later than three years the commission shall make a study of the Crowsnest Pass rates. What will the commission attempt to determine and why is the government suggesting that a study should be made? Surely the answer to that question is that the government hopes a deficiency area can be found in order that the railways can be compensated for their losses and thereby gain increased revenue.

I look at this particular clause of the bill and consider how it will affect me or any other Member of the House in running an industry when we realize that within the next three years the government is going to have the commission make a study of that industry and ascertain how large a subsidy, if any, is to be paid after the three-year period has expired. I know what I would do. I would try to minimize my efficiency in the next three years. I would try to paint a picture of dire need of a subsidy as huge as I could logically expect to be paid. This clause is suggesting to the railways that they should be inefficient for the next three years and they will be compensated forever from that time onward.

This clause should be taken out of the bill completely. It is not necessary that it be there. If the government wants to have the commission to be set up make such a study, it can have it do so, but this is what I should like to know from the Minister. Does the government feel that the Crowsnest Pass rates, with the volume of grain that is being moved today, was moved last year and will be moved next year and in the future, are causing the railways to lose money? If this is what the government feels, let it say so. If it believes that railways will be losing money in the next three years, then it does not have too much confidence in the world wheat situation. I should like an answer to this question. . . .

I am not going to deal with all the aspects of this bill. The whole rationalization question could be dealt with. The whole passenger question should be dealt with and perhaps will be before the passage of the bill. In summarizing what I have tried to put before the House, Mr. Speaker, I would say this. We are told by the government and the Minister that the passage of this bill is important and he urges us to pass it quickly so the railways may begin increasing their revenues to offset the minimum increase in labour costs which they will have to face. I ask Hon. Members before they vote in favour of the bill to consider who is going to pay for it. Eighty percent of the increased revenue will come from Western Canada and the Maritimes from freight movement either to or from or within those areas. . . .

The Minister says "read the bill." I think I have read it backwards and forwards. Perhaps my interest mainly lies in the increased cost to Western Canada. I do not deny this. However, I am fully convinced, and I would like to convince more Hon. Members, that this bill takes the wraps off the railroads by allowing them to increase class and non-competitive rates. This puts the burden mainly on those regions which were brought into confederation by a transportation policy involving subsidies. It is those areas which will be thrown to the wolves so far as increased rates are concerned.

Appendix 4 — Excerpt from Unifarm Summary of the Federal Task Force Report on Agriculture

Major world-wide forces affecting the Canadian agricultural system are:
1. Technological development has dramatically increased the productivity of land and labor. This trend promises not only to continue but also to accelerate.
2. Commodity surpluses, overproduction and excess capacity depress commodity prices.
3. Agricultural development and economic planning in less developed countries is being pushed to achieve high and rising levels of self-sufficiency. Many previous importing countries now have their own surplus problems to contend with.
4. Political intervention in the form of subsidies, tariffs and trade agreements prevent the free market interplay of supply, demand and competitive advantage in many markets.
5. Slow growth in food demand cannot be expanded to absorb surpluses.

Major domestic influences include:
1. Declining political power of farmers.
2. Poverty, urban social disintegration, housing, regional disparities and pollution will require increasing attention and allocation of resources.
3. All levels of Canadian governments are experiencing shortages of funds, indicating that allocation of public funds to agricultural subsidies will have to compete with expenditures on other public needs such as health, education and elimination of poverty.
4. Wheat surpluses, excess carry-over stocks, diminishing exports and falling prices and incomes are reaching crisis levels.
5. The wheat problem may be shifted to feed grains, oilseeds, and livestock.
6. One-third of farm families are below the poverty line.
7. Both government and private sectors of agriculture are marked by the negative forces of disorganization, poor management, jurisdictional disputes and individualism.

The Task Force contends that most of these problems confronting agriculture today have as their cause the lack of effective formulation and implementation of policies and programs and its twin lack of an adequate organization structure to serve as a vehicle for integrated, co-operative action to improve the performance of agriculture. It is the purpose of effective government action to assist the transition from what agriculture is today to what it should be in the future.

Projection of present trends leads to the following model of agriculture in 1990.
1. There will be a substantial reduction in the number of farms, with those remaining being rationally managed, profit orientated businesses.
2. Farm organizations, marketing boards, co-operatives and similar organizations will be much larger and more professionally managed.
3. Government will become less involved in agriculture with the entire private sector of the agricultural system accepting a much greater degree of independence.
4. Management, survival, and cost-price realities will force a more effective rationalization of the relationships between production and sales; sales, costs and profits; and return on investment in agriculture.
5. A clear-cut separation of welfare and commercial farm policy programs will emerge. Some form of guaranteed annual income will be taken for granted.
6. As the necessity for planning increases, the drive for security will be manifest in increasing formal and informal integration.
7. Ease of entry into commercial farming will be drastically cut due to multiplying financial requirements and complexity of operations.
8. Farm employee unions may emerge and become a factor in the bargaining process.

The obvious keynote that permeates all recommendations is that the government should intelligently assist an orderly and planned transition that will encourage agricultural adjustment to achieve the largest possible gains at the lowest possible tangible and intangible costs. Another theme running through all recommendations is that governments should reduce their direct involvement in agriculture, thereby encouraging farmers, farm organizations and agribusiness to improve their management and leadership functions and stand more self-sufficiently on their own. The Task Force assumes that agriculture should be operated much as any other industry. If this is not feasible, the agricultural industry invites a degree of government paternalism that agriculture may not want. It is important to note that this in no way implies a reversion to anything approaching a simplistic laissez-faire system. The system proposed in this Report includes institutions such as national marketing boards, stabilization programs etc., and is compatible with a contemporary, complex industrial society.

The main principles of our recommendations, spelled out in detail in later chapters are as follows:
1. The surpluses must be controlled and reduced to manageable proportions by reducing production drastically, if necessary. Where alternatives exist, production resources must be shifted to more promising market opportunities. Where such alternatives cannot be found, land and other resources must be retired.
2. Governments should provide temporary, limited programs of assistance for the crop switching and land retirement necessary to cut surplus production. At the same time, this report emphasizes programs to expand demand, particularly on the international scene.

226

3. Agricultural subsidies and price supports that are not effective and efficient in achieving worthwhile, high priority objectives should be phased out.
4. Younger non-viable farmers should be moved out of farming through temporary programs of welfare, education and provision of jobs in other sectors of the economy. Older farmers should be given assistance to ensure that they have at least a "livable" standard of living.
5. Improvement of management must be encouraged by providing seed money for management training, provision of information processing systems, market and price forecasts and other management tools.
6. The organizational structure of agriculture both in the government and private sectors should be rationalized. Management by objectives, program planning and budgeting, cost-benefit analysis and other modern management techniques should be adopted. Every public policy should embrace these principles and procedures.

Index

232

Picture Credits

René Pierre Allain, XIV *lower*
Andrews-Newton Photographers, Ottawa, IV *lower*
Calgary Herald, XIII *lower*
Andy Donato, *Toronto Sun*, XII
Rusins Kaufmanis, Ottawa *Citizen*, VI *upper*
Boris Spremo, Toronto, VI *lower,* VII, IX, X, XI,
    XIII *upper*
Reprinted with permission of the *Toronto Star*, VIII
Van's Studio, Ottawa, V *upper*

While every attempt has been made to credit sources accurately, the author and publisher will welcome any information that will allow them to correct any errors or omissions.